DICTIONARY OF SOCIOLOGY

DICTIONARY OF SOCIOLOGY

Jagmohan Diwan

CYBER TECH PUBLICATIONS
4264/3, Ansari Road, Daryaganj, New Delhi-110002
Ph.: 011-23244078. Fax: 011-23280028
E-Mail: cyberpublicationsdelhi@yahoo.com

Dictionary of Sociology

First Edition 2009

Published by G.S. Rawat
For Cyber Tech Publications
4264/3, Ansari Road, Daryaganj, New Delhi-110002
Ph.: 011-23244078. Fax: 011-23280028
E-Mail: cyberpublicationsdelhi@yahoo.com

Printed at
Amit Enterprises, Moujpur, Delhi, Ph. -9810878184

Preface

Today the techniques of empirical investigation and their quantification meets most claims of strict rigour. Comparative and theoretical sociology are as rigorous as the data and the state of the advancing discipline allow. On the whole the methods of the subject do not permit of experiment but only of observation and comparison. In comparison the canons of Mill's Logic are still dominant, in particular the method of concomitant variation. Sociological theories have often, perhaps usually, been elaborated beyond the facts available. They are to be judged by the tests of their fruitfulness in yielding hypotheses, their power to explain and coordinate diverse and recalcitrant data, their economy in so doing, and their degree of internal logical coherence. Today there exists no dominant body of sociological theory, but most sociologists are discriminatingly eclectic. It is certainly true that there is a theoretical convergence of ideas in sociology, and that even theories very differently expressed in the past are being found to be complementary in practice.

The dictionary is a wordbook rather than a glossary, and certain terms are given fairly lengthy treatment. These are terms which cannot be dealt with adequately in brief and more space has been allocated for their explication. The treatment of a term generally follows the rule that after a short description there is an historical reference to its uses, and whenever possible one or two books or articles are mentioned to which the reader may turn. For further discussion. A number of short biographical sketches are also included.

Cross reference further aid understanding and the A-Z format makes the book exceptionally easy to use.

—Editor

A

Abortion Abortion was regulated by criminal law in Canada until January 1988 when the Supreme Court ruled the law unconstitutional on the grounds that it was applied in an arbitrary and discriminatory manner. No new law has been enacted so abortion continues to be legal. The trouble some law was an amendment to the Criminal Code made in 1969 allowing a therapeutic committee to authorize an abortion if it was deemed the life or health of the mother was at considerable risk.

Abstraction It is difficult to give a satisfactory definition of *abstraction* since its use often presupposes an oversimple conception of how both thinking and theory construction proceed. Abstraction can be said to take place when we select from the phenomena we study, and whose character we wish to describe, such traits as would form a basis for their classification. The term *abstraction* has two main meanings.

1. It refers to the fact that to describe or explain anything selection is necessary. Every theory, whether in the social or the natural sciences, omits some variables because they are less relevant, or apparently so, to the phenomena to be explained or predicted by the theory. To the extent that knowledge is possessed of the conditions under which the neglected variables are or are not significant, the more powerful is the theory.

2. In the natural sciences abstraction refers to concepts such as a perfect gas or an instantaneous velocity, and in the social sciences to such con-cepts as a perfectly rational act or a perfectly integrated group. These serve as logical devices

or constructs for the analysis and clarification of complex occurrences, and the making of predictions.

Accommodation The state or process of adjustment to a conflict situation in which overt expressions of hostility are avoided and certain compensatory advantages, economic, social or psychological, are gained by a minority or subordinate group.

Acculturation The process whereby an individual or a group acquires the cultural characteristics of another through direct contact and inter-action. From an individual point of view this is a process of social learning similar to that of adult socialization in which linguistic communication plays an essential role. From a social point of view *acculturation* implies the diffusion of particular values, techniques and institutions and their modification under different conditions.

Acephalous Society Literally 'headless', meaning that the society is without any formalized or institutionalised system of power and authority. Collective decisions are made in a variety of ways, including informal community gaterings.

Action; social action Action, or behaviour, is a psychological category and has been regarded as the basic unit by many psychologists. In this connection it is usual to speak of the Behaviourists, i.e. those who subscribe to the fundamental propositions of J. B. Watson. Yet a more useful term is that of *social action,* which is used both by social psychologists and sociologists. This is regarded by many as the proper unit of observation in the social sciences. Action is social when the actor behaves in such a manner that his action is intended to influence the actions of one or more other persons. Thus interaction is the context in which the personality develops.

In sociology it was Max Weber who first explicitly used and emphasized social action as -the basis for theory. His typology of social action: *Wertrationalitiit, Zweckrationalitiit, Traditional* and *Affektuell* was, he held, fundamental for his work, but it was the second category of action, i.e. purposively rational action, that he was mainly concerned with in his analysis of socio-economic systems, for this kind of action, he said, is oriented to a system of discrete individual ends, such that the end, the means and the secondary results are all rationally taken into account and weighed; this was the type of social action associated with Capitalism.

Action Research Much social science springs from the desire to alter and improve a social situation, or to help people in need. *Action research* is investigation of a kind oriented to these ends, where the aim is not only to collect information and arrive at a better understanding, but to do some-thing practical as well. Sometimes, the exponents of action research are dubious about the possibility of making detached and scientific studies of human affairs. They may argue, for example, that an investigator cannot but influence the behaviour of the people he is studying, that experimentation is extremely difficult, if not impossible, in the social sciences, that there is the intermediary of the human instrument in measurement, and that all these vitiate the scientific status of social research.

Usually, action research is concerned with social change, with therapy to individuals or a small social group, or has as its object to improve the efficiency of an organization. The theoretical basis of this practice has been set out by Adam Curle in an article in *Human Relations,* Vol. II, No.3, 1949. Action Research has been trenchantly criticized by Michael Argyle in *The Scientific Study of Social Behaviour,* 1957, where he argues that the discovery of scientific results is always secondary in action research. He further argues that action research should seek to obtain objective results of two kinds: (1) it should prove that the activity is genuinely effective in increasing output, or in reducing hostility in a group, or in achieving therapy, and (2) it should show the precise con-ditions under which successful results can be obtained, so that others can do the same.

Adapt; adaptation Originally, the term is biological in nature and refers to the processes whereby an organism accommodates to its environment. In sociology *adaptation* is used loosely to refer to the manner in which a social system, be it a small group such as the family, or a larger collec-tivity such as an organization or even a total society, like a tribal society, fits into the physical or social environment. In structural-functionalist theory it has been held that the adaptive system is one of the structural pre-requisites designed to meet a functional problem posed by survival. In any total social system the problem is met by the economic and techno-logical arrangements.

Adjust; adjustment A term that is psychological rather than sociological, used by some social psychologists to refer to the process whereby an indi-vidual enters into a harmonious or healthy relationship with his environ-ment, physical or social, but occasionally used by some sociologists to refer to a social unit, like a group or organization, accomplishing the same end. The difficulty posed by most discussions, where the term is used, is in coping with the value implications of what is harmonious or healthy, but sometimes in the literature this problem is blandly ignored.

Age-grades; age-sets The expression 'age-society' in the sense of *age-grade* was used by Heinrich Schurtz in *Alterklassen und Mannerbunde* 1902, when he suggested that there was a tripartite division in society which reflected the conflict of proximate age groups or generations. He considered the grades of 'the uninitiated', 'the initiated single men' and 'the elders' as potentially universal in human society.

In general, *age-grade* is used to refer to the division of society into a number of sections based upon 'sociological' age. Age-grades form the structural framework through which specific age-sets pass. Different clusters of rights, duties, obligations and privileges are associated with the different statuses in the age-grade divisions of society. Often particular ceremonial or military functions are performed by sets in different grades.

The *age-grade system* is a type of stratification which cuts across the division of societies into tribes, clans and lineages and permits of a high degree of central control within the society.

An *age-set* is a formally organized group of men or women recruited on the basis of 'sociological' age. There are usually public ceremonies when the sets are formed and when the different sets advance through the age-grade structure. Probably the most important of these stages is the initiation ceremony when youths and maidens acquire mature status. In several societies circumcision and clitoridectomy are associated with this *rite de passage.*

Agelecism A term coined by E. Benoit-Smullyan from the Greek word for group in order to characterize the 'synthesis of a positivistic method-ology with a particular set of substantive theories'. Chief of these are the sociologistic theories of Emile Durkheim. The origins of agelecism are to be found in the writings of Louis de Bonald and Joseph de Maistre who advanced the notion that the social group precedes the individual and indeed constitutes him, that the group is the source of values and culture, and that social events and changes are not, and cannot be, the effects of purely individual volitions and desires.

Agnate; agnation In Roman law *agnati* were kinsfolk, men and women, related to each other by descent from a common male ancestor and who were under a single authority in the family. In modern usage the term is restricted to men only without reference to a common familial authority, so that an agnate is one related by descent through males only.

AIDS (*Acquired Immune Deficiency*), A disease that attacks the immune sysem of the body that is often passed on through sexual contact.

Alienation Broadly speaking, *alienation* denotes a socio-psychological condition of the individual which involves his estrangement from certain aspects of his social existence.

'In one form or another, the concept of alienation dominates both the contemporary literature and the history of sociological thought.' So Melvin Seeman estimates the importance of this concept in sociological analysis.

Part of the difficulty in providing an adequate analysis of this concept, an analysis that is consistent with the need to provide a rigorous and clear conceptual apparatus for sociological investigation, is that the term occurs in such a wide variety of disciplines, including sociology, social and political philosophy, psychoanalysis, and existentialist philosophy. Furthermore there is the added difficulty that *alienation* is one of those concepts, which have tended to abound in sociology, used to explain almost every kind of social behaviour and usually succeed in explaining nothing. Among other things it has been used to explain ethnic prejudice, mental illness, class consciousness, industrial conflict, political apathy and extremism.

Contemporary emphasis on alienation began with Seeman's germinal work noted above. Faced with the general vagueness and unclarity of the literature, Seeman attempted to isolate the various uses of the term and, at the same time, to recast these in a way which would allow them to be used in more precise empirical work, while retaining as much of the original meaning as possible. The first meaning so isolated, 'powerless-ness', was that of alienation as a feeling on the part of the individual that he cannot influence the social situation(s) in which he interacts. The second variant, 'meaninglessness', is a feeling on the part of the individual that he has no guides for conduct or belief.'Normlessness' is the individual's feeling that illegitimate means are required to achieve goals. 'Isolation' is a feeling of estrangement from the cultural goals of society, and the final variant, 'self-estrangement' an inability to find self-rewarding activities. Each of these Seeman postulates as being independent from each other. Each has been measured by means of various attitude scales and allowed the further exploration of the social context of alienation.

Ambilateral A term used in respect of those kinship systems where a person is able to choose to which parental kin group he or she will become attached.

Animism; animatism The formulation of the theory of *animism* is the work of Sir E. B. Tylor and may be found in his *Primitive Culture, 1871.* The notion was part of a theory of primitive religion which endeavoured to account for the attribution by some peoples of a spiritual existence to animals, plants, and even on occasion to inanimate objects. Tylor argued that early man had a need to explain dreams, hallucinations, sleep and death, and that the need to understand such phenomena led to the belief in the existence of the soul or an indw.elling personality. When a man dreamed and saw in his dream a person who was dead, then this was the man's spirit or soul visiting him. Similarly, to dream of oneself in another place was one's own soul parted from the body in sleep.

Anomie: anomy The term *anomie* was first used by the French sociologist, Emile Durkheim, to refer to several aspects of social participation where the conditions necessary for man to fulfil himself and to attain happiness were not present. These conditions were that conduct should be governed by norms, that these norms should form an integrated and non-conflicting system, that the individual should be morally involved with other people so that 'the image of the one who completes me becomes inseparable from mine' and so that clear limits were set to the pleasures attainable in life. Any state where there are unclear, conflicting or unin-tegrated norms, in which the individual had no morally significant relations with others or in which there were no limits set to the attainment of pleasure was a state of *anomie.*

R. K. Merton uses the term to refer to a state in which socially pre-scribed goals and the norms governing their attainment are incompatible. Leo Srole has attempted to construct an index of *anomie.* In most attempts to make *Q1wmie* measurable, emphasis is placed on lack of clarity in goals and norms or upon the absence of social ties. All such attempts involve a more restricted use of the concept than Durkheim's which was related to a philosophical conception of human nature.

Antisocial Personality Disorder A personality disorder that involves disregard for the rights or others, as well as impulsive, irresponsible and aggressive behaviour.

Anthropology *Anthropology* is an inclusive term comprising disciplines studying: (a) the biological and cultural development of man; (b) biological relationships between contemporary communities; and (c) the principles guiding human relations in all living societies but particularly in those on the fringe of the industrial world. These biological and sociological disciplines are united by their common focus on man, the principal culture-using animal, but are often separated by the centrifugal forces driving specialists towards the preoccupations of the social sciences on the one hand or to those of the natmal sciences on the other.

The earliest English usage of the term (1593, NED) meant 'the science of man' in the widest sense. This accords with current usage. Intervening applications restricted the sense first to a study of the physiological and psychological nature of man, then, later, of his zoological nature alone.

The broad divisions of anthropological study are: *Physical anthropology,* which is the study of man's biological record.

It begins with the zoological view of man's status; attempts to trace his origin and development through comparative studies of fossil, recent and living primates; engages in an examination of the nature of racial diversity; examines the effects of various ecological factors on human adaptability and variability, on the growth and decline of populations, etc. The physical anthropologist, although using techniques of his own, is reliant on other disciplines, notably anatomy, archaeology, biochemistry, botany, genetics, geology and paleontology.

Archaeology, which is the classification of the material remains of human societies on the bases of function, chronology and cultural context as a preliminary to the formulation of explanatory generalizations re-garding the development of societies. *Social anthropology,* which is the sociological study of human values, rules and conduct in different types of society. In theory anthropological interest ranges over all human societies but 'in practice it has tended to restrict itself to those societies or parts of society which could be examined as small units, by direct observation .. .' (R. Firth, 'The Future of Social Anthropology', in *Man,* January-February 1944). This sociological anthropology has been castigated by G. Murdock as not anthropology at all. (See his article 'British Social Anthropology', *American Anthro-pologist,* LIII, 3, 1951.) American anthropologists taking this extreme position contrast social anthropology with their *cultural anthropology* (also termed *culturology* and *ethnology).* Culture is deemed to be the proper focus of study rather than social conduct. 'It is *culture,* not society, that is the distinctive feature of man.' (L. White, *The Science of Culture* (Grove Press edition), 1949, p. 116.) Here Nadel's corrective is a salutary reminder that our subject matter 'is essentially two-dimensional, being always both "cultural" and "social".'

Philosophical anthropology, or the philosophy of anthropology, a subdiscipline of epistemology, which is concerned with methodology. This is not concerned with technique, but with the logic of theory construction and validation. E. R. Leach has well observed that 'among social anthropologists the game of building new theories on the ruins of old ones is almost an occupational disease' (p. v of his *Rethinking Anthropology,* 1961). The bibliography is extensive. The reader may usefully consult:

Association of Social Anthropologists Monograph I, *The Relevance of Models for Social Anthropology,* 1965; F. Barth, *Models of Social Organ-isation,* 1966; D. Bidney, *op. cit.;* R. Firth, *Essays on Social Organisation and Values,* 1964; E. Gellner, 'Concepts and Society', *Transactions of the Fifth World Congress of Sociology,* 1962, vol. I; E. R. Leach, 'The Epistemological Background to Malinowski's Empiricism', in R. Firth, *Man and Culture,* 1960; C. Levi-Strauss, *Structural Anthropology,* 1963; S. Nadel, *The Theory of Social Structure,* 1957; R. Needham, *Structure and Sentiment,* 1960; A. R. Radcliffe-Brown, *Structure and Function in Primitive Society,* 1952; and R. S. Rudner, *Philosophy of Social Science,* 1966. *The study of material culture,* generally called technology, serves both archaeology and social and cultural anthropology, for here the elements of man's handiwork and the processes which produced them are examined ecologically with regard to their history, design, effectiveness, social impact and distribution.

Assimilation A term usually applied to an immigrant or ethnic minority n process of being absorbed socially into a receiving society. It should be distinguished from biological absorption or miscegenation. It implies a dispersion of the minority ecologically, their increasing participation in the social systems of the majority group and a measure of acculturation sufficient eventually for the minority group to cease to be identifiable. At one time it was assumed that this process involved changes in the immigrant group only and that intermediate stages would be characterized by instability and conflict. However, S. N. Eisenstadt in *The Absorption of Immigrants,* 1954, has pointed out that changes in the receiving society may be induced through contact with immigrants and that a state of cultural pluralism may be one of stable equilibrium.

Association The term describes either a process or an entity. The process is of a number of individuals interacting for a specific end or set of pur-poses. The entity is an organization of individuals who are held together by a recognized set of rules governing their behaviour to one another for a specific end or set of purposes. Although some associations are large and comprehensive they cannot express the totality of relations which constitute the total life of a com-munity, and thus *association* may be distinguished from *community.* The specificity of aim of an association is seen in F. Tonnies' use of the term *Gesel/schaft,* which he contrasts with

Gemeinschaft. Usually associations are classified according to function, e.g. occupational, religious, recreational, cultural, etc.

Arranged Marriage Marriage based on the family ties rather than the couple's personal preferences.

Attitude *Attitude* is normally used to refer to a learned predisposition, evidenced by the behaviour of an individual or group of individuals, to evaluate an object or class of objects in a consistent and characteristic way. Historically the origin of the term can be traced to two sources. The fIrst of these is its derivation from the Latin *aptus,* fro}1l which it derived the connotation of fitness or suitability, similar to that of the word *aptitude* which is derived from the same root. One of the earliest usages in this sense of the term may be found in the writings of Herbert Spencer who speaks of the attitude of mind necessary to arrive at correct judge-ments on disputed issues. This connotation still survives in common usage and is evidenced in expressions like 'the inquiring attitude', 'the scientific attitude', and 'the critical attitude'. This use differs from the current theoretical and research use since the term here refers to a narrowly defined range of behaviour directed towards a wide variety of different objects. In its more technical use the term refers to a wider range of behaviour all of which is directed towards the same social object.

The second source may be traced back to its use to describe a posture of the body in painting or sculpture. From this the term gradually became used to refer to postures of the body suitable for certain actions, and it was finally taken up by the early experimental psychologists to describe the various forms of muscular preparedness or *set,* which were becoming increasingly important in their experiments. Since these early workers saw mental states in terms of states of muscular readiness, the old distinc-tion between mental and motor attitudes, derived from these two sources, began to break down. The coupling of this distinction with the abhorrent doctrine of body-mind dualism has led to a virtual abandonment of the distinction between motor and mental attitudes.

One important connotation which the term has acquired is that of a predisposition to *respond* in a particular way to an external stimulus. This connotation derives largely from the use of the term by the Behaviourist School of Psychology, which they in turn probably inherited from the early experimental psychologists. The original Behaviourist insistence on the observation of single acts as they were related to single stimuli left little scope to explain the complexities of social behaviour. *Attitude* thus became used as an intervening variable to mediate between stimulus and response in order to cope with the extreme complexity of social behaviour. Thus J. B. Watson, the founder of this school, described social psychology as the study of social attitudes. The term was used extensively in this context by F. H. Allport in his book *Social Psychology,* 1924. While the Behaviourist's use of the term was similar to that of the earlier experi-mental psychologists, the behaviourists broadened its use by allowing an additional use of the term to refer to 'verbal sets to respond'. With time, however, attitudes became defined in increasingly more subjective terms, until Behaviourists, for example, began to speak less of attitudes to respond to social stimulation and more of radical-conservative attitudes.

Attitude Research The earliest concern of workers in this field was the establishment of unidimensional scales from which they could estimate the *extremity* or *strength* of attitudes. The earliest scales constructed for this purpose were those of L. L. Thurstone and his co-workers The method which they used involved drawing up a list of a large number of statements which they considered were relevant to the attitude in question. These were presented to about 200 judges who were asked to sort them into eleven categories, on a scale ranging from extreme favourability to extreme unfavourability, such that the distances between each category on the scale were seen to be equal. From this sorting statements were selected for the final scale on a number of different criteria such that the range of the full scale was covered. Subjects who were presented with the final scale were asked to check those statements with which they agreed, and the score for each subject was given by the median scale-value of the statements he checked.

Audience Studies Audience is defined as an individual's or a group of persons' cerebral and/or sensory and/or tactile intake/reception and/or perception of a culture product and/or products of communicative actions. Culture is defined as a system of communicative actions with several sub-systems of such communication in all media. Media is defined as the tools and venues of communicaton via which a culture product or products is/are assembled, processed, disseminated, and consumed (e.g., printed matter, television,film, radio, theater, etc.).

Authoritarian; authoritarianism Words in common use, they were brought into the limelight with the publication of *The Authoritarian Personality* (1950), where the concept was decomposed into nine over-lapping and loosely related variables: *conventionalism* (rigid adherence to conventional, middle-class values); *authoritarian submission* (submissive, uncritical attitude towards idealised moral authority of the ingroup); *authoritarian aggression* (tendency to be on the lookout for, and to condemn, reject, and punish people who violate conventional values); *anti-intraception* (opposition to the subjective, the imaginative, the tender-minded); *superstition and stereotypy* (the belief in mystical determinants of the individual's fate; the disposition to think in rigid categories); *power and 'toughness'* (preoccupation with the dominance-submission, strong-weak, leader-follower dimension; identification with power figures; overemphasis upon the conventionalized attributes of the ego; exaggerated assertion of strength and toughness); *destructiveness and cynicism* (general-ized hostility, vilification of the human); *projectivity* (the disposition to believe that wild and dangerous things go on in the world; the projection outwards of unconscious emotional impulses); *sex* (exaggerated concern with sexual 'goings-on').

It must not be assumed that the concept has the same meaning for different writers, and the merit of each test of *authoritarianism* has to be carefully assessed. See T. W. Adorno *et al., The Authoritarian Personality,* 1950, R. Christie and M. Jahoda (eds.), *Studies in the Scope and Method*

Authority: Legitimation of authority The performance of authoritative actions, i.e. the exercise of authority, is one of the major forms of power through which the actions of a plurality of individual human actors are placed or maintained in a condition of order or are concerted for the collaborative attainment of a particular goal or general goals.

Authority is that form of power which orders or articulates the actions of other actors through commands which are effective because those who are commanded regard the commands as *legitimate.* Authority differs from coercive control, since the latter elicits conformity with its com-mands and prescriptions through its capacity to reward or punish. The distinction is an analytical one, since empirically authority and coercive control exist together in many combinations.

Authority is therefore by definition legitimate authority. Its effectiveness in controlling the actions of those towards whom it is directed is affected by the concurrent operation of other mechanisms. Thus (legitimate) authority might be reinforced by the concurrent operation of mechanisms of exchange between the exerciser of authority and the person (or persons) commanded, e.g. the latter might receive a specific payment (wages or salary) in return for the performance of specific actions. The exerciser of authority and the person who is its object might also have *common interests* (although not equally shared) in the attainment of a collective goal such as the winning of a battle or the fulfilment of an economic programme. The exerciser and the object of authority might be linked through *solidarity* which will be served by their collaboration such as the winning of a game or the improvement in the quality of performance of a university; they might also have ties of *personal affection* or of *ethnic identity,* etc. In all these instances, the concurrent operation of the mech-anism in question with the exercise of (legitimate) authority might either strengthen or weaken the motivation for conformity with the commands issued by the exerciser of authority and therewith will strengthen or weaken the motivation for the performance of the particular action. It should be emphasized that the different mechanisms might not operate harmoniously. Thus, there might not be common interests between the exerciser and the object of legitimate authority.

The exerciser and the object might have no ties or solidarity; they might indeed dislike each other personally or be alien ethnically, etc. They might also be involved in an exchange relationship which is unsatisfactory to the subordinated person in the sense that the reward which he receives is, in accordance with his beliefs, incommensurate with the action which he is expected to perform.

Autocracy The concentration c´ power and authority in the hands of one person. Usually, autocracy refers to a situationwhere state poer is controlled by a monarch, religious leader or political dictator. The term can also be applied to particular social institutions where one individual has dominant power and authority.

Automation (1) Methods of productionthat rely on mechanical or electronic technologies as a replacement for human labour. See: Deskilling/Fordism. (2) The replacement of many workers by machines, as well as the monitoring an coordinationof workers by machines with only minimal supervisionfrom human beings.

Avoidance In many societies persons or groups who stand in particular 16 relationships avoid each other. As a mode of behaviour, avoidance always expresses respect.

Although avoidance involves two parties, and although the prohibitions are binding on both, it is usually the duty of one party specifically to avoid the other, e.g. as when it is the duty of a man to avoid his wife's mother. The extent of avoidance varies from society to society and may include such prohibitions as not eating from the same dish, to not entering the other's village.

B

Baby Boom The baby boom was most apparent in Canada, United States of America, Australia and New Zealand. In 1996 the baby boom generation were 33 per cent of the Canadian population. This large 'bulge' may partially explain the labour market problems and high unemployment Canada has had for the past decade or more.

Balance of Power The theory that military conflict can be avoidedif both sides have roughly equivalent military power.

Barbarian; Barbarism A term used colloquially to describe a rude or uncivilized person, but originally used to describe a non-Hellene or a non-Roman. The sociological connotation gained currency as a result of the famous book by Lewis H. Morgan entitled *Ancient Society,* 1877, the sub-title of which is *Researches in the Lines of Human Progress from Savagery through Barbarism to Civilization.* The word *barbarism,* therefore has been used in a context of social development of the human race as a middle stage. Morgan held that there was convincing evidence that, as he put it, 'savagery preceded barbarism in all the tribes of mankind, as barbarism is known to have preceded civilization'. And he added: 'The history of the human race is one in source, one in experience, one in progress.' Few modern sociol-ogists would be as confident as this.

Moreover, the stages of social develop-ment were equally clear to him, less so to contemporary sociologists. *Savagery* describes the long formative period of human existence from the earliest times up until the advent of those inventions which ushered in the *barbaric* stage. The latter is marked by four features: the domestication of animals, the discovery of cereals, the use of stone in architecture, and the invention of the method of smelting iron ore. Hunters and gatherers characterize the stage of savagery; the growth of agriculture together with the sedentary manner of life associated with it are features of the barbaric state. Morgan, however, discerned three stages within barbarism. The first of these stages, and the one marking the end of the upper stage of savagery was notable for the invention of pottery; middle barbarism was the period when the domestication of animals took place in the Eastern hemisphere and the cultivation of land with the help of irrigation in the Western hemisphere. The invention of iron and its use characterized upper barbarism, a period which closed with the growth of the phonetic alphabet. This and the use of writing and the making of metal tools marked the beginnings of civilization.

Various writers made use of Morgan's scheme, altered or improved upon it. Notable among them was Gordon Childe, who in his' book *Social Evolution,* 1951, emphasized the technology of food-production as the mark of the change from *savagery* to *barbarism.* Childe questioned Morgan's criterion of writing, as the invention which distinguished *barbarism* from *civilization,* arguing that this would mean the inclusion of the Maya Indians among the civilized even though they had not in-vented the wheel and relied for cultivation on the primitive slash-and-bum technique.

Bilateral A term used to describe the transmission of descent or of property rights through both male and female parents, without emphasiz-ing either one or the other lines. The term *bilateral* is used in contradistinction to the term *unil ineal.*

Booth, Charles (1840-1916) British shipowner, manufacturer, and statistician; his ultimate aim was the improvement of the lot of the common people, but he realized the need for accurate and relevant evi-dence. Results of his scientific enquiries into statistical aspects of pressing social questions were published in *Life and Labour of the People (1889*-1891), and the more elaborate *Life and Labour of the People in London* (1891-1903). This work aimed to show the 'numerical relations which poverty, misery and depravity bear to regular earnings and comparative comfort, and to describe the general conditions under which each class lives'. Instrumental in the passage of the Old Age Pensions Act, 1908, he wrote several works on the aged poor.

Bilineal Descent A system of family descent where blood links and rights of inheritance through both male and female ancestors are of equal importance.

Bioethics Ethical questions relating to life and the biological well-being of the planet.

Biosphere The total inhabitable are of land, air and water. Within the biosphere the basic unit of analysis or studyis the ecosystem.

Birth Rate Calculated as the number of births in a given populaiton durign a particular year divided by the actual poulaiton and then multiplied by 1000 to give a birth rate per 1,000 of the poulaiton. Teh resulting figure is known as the 'crude birthrate'. Generlaly, to observe trends and predict poulation growth, demographers (statistical analysts of population) use 'fertility rates' which relate the number of births not to total population butto the population of women in their child-bearing years defined as from 15 to 49 years of age.

Bourgeoisie *Bourgeoisie* and *Bourgeois* (from the Latin *burgensis)* are late Medieval terms of French origin which refer to the middle class of French citizens, more specifically to the freemen of a burgh. Such people were distinguishable from peasants, on the one hand, and gentlemen, on the other. The terms were used by Karl Marx, who contrasted the Bourgeoisie with the Proletariat. Between these two great classes there was an in-creasingly antagonistic relationship, which in the last analysis would lead to the destruction of the Bourgeoisie and the establishment of the Dictatorship of the Proletariat. Marx's use has coloured the subsequent use of the term, but there are some variations, for it was not used precisely by him or 'by those who owe allegiance to his ideas. It may thus refer in a general way to the middle-classes, but more usually to non-Proletarian classes of all kinds, sometimes to non-Socialistic political parties, and commonly to Capitalist society, thus described as Bourgeois society.

Bride-price A marriage payment by the kin of a bridegroom to the bride's kin. It is a solemn token of obligation although the exact jural implications may vary from one society to another. Because it was in earlier times thought by Europeans that a wife was being bought, the practice was severely criticized, but today with better understanding of the ritual nature, and often of complexity of marriage payments, the older term has tended to give way to another and it is now customary to call the practice *bride-wealth.* It should be pointed out that where bride-wealth is given as part of the marriage ceremonies there is usually a gift made by the bride's kin to the bridegroom's, although this may be smaller in value. Usually the practice is associated with a patrilineal descent system.

Brown Vs. Topeka Board of Education A case before the Supreme Curt of the United States which resulted in a 1954 ruling that set aside a Kansas statute that permitted cities of over 15,000 to maintain separate school for blacks and whites. The court ruled that all segregation in public schools was inherently unequal. This ruling began the desegregaton of schooling and eventually of other public placesand programmes. In the early decades of the twentieth century the Supreme Court had foudn that segregation was constitutonal and America became increasingly racially divided.

Bureaucracy The term is used both to designate the tasks and procedures of administration as a collective word for a body of administrative officials. Frequently it also indicates inefficiency and an improper exercise of power on the part of officials, and thus has become a term of abuse. First use of the term *(Bureacratie)* has been attributed to the economist Vincent de Gournay (1712-1759). In the nineteenth century, under con-ditions of increasing state intervention, it came into regular use among European writers, especially in German as *Biirokratie,* to describe govern-ment by officials. In England the term became current in the 1830s during resistance to the centralization of poor relief and public health measures. To Thomas Carlyle it was 'the continental nuisance' *(Latter Day Pam-phlets,* iv, 1850). John Stuart Mill wrote in 1860, 'the work of government has been in the hands of governors by profession, which is the essence and meaning of bureaucracy'.

C

Calvinism A Christian doctrine associated with John Calvin (1509-1564). Calvinism is important for sociologists as a component of the Protecstant ethic, a set of social and religious ideas considered favorable to the development of capitalism.

Capitalism The term refers to a form of industrial society in which the greater proportion of economic life has the following characteristics: the concentration of the means of economic production (capital) and the control of capital is in the hands of private (i.e. non-governmental) owners; resources and wealth are acquired through the operation of the free market; labour is performed by formally free workers who sell their services on the market; and, the maximization of profit is the goal and stimulus of economic activity.

In what might be termed *classical capitalism* the economic functions of society are served by numerous, highly differentiated and relatively small producers. Each producer, either wholly or in part, owns and controls his enterprise and bears the full risk and benefits of his activity. Control and co-ordination of the many activities and decisions of both producers and consumers are achieved through the operations of the free market in which what is supplied, in what quantities and at what price are largely determined by demand on the part of consumers and by competition between producers. Essential to such a system is a monetary unit which acts both as a source of wealth and as an accounting medium measuring the profit and loss of the enterprise. The role of government in such an economy, when compared with a socialist type of economy, is secondary and is generally confined to the removal of restrictions upon the full, unimpeded operation of the system. It is the 'invisible hand' of the free market which ensures that production is adapted to meet human desires.

The nineteenth century saw societies which came closest to this *ideal-type* of classical capitalism, especially in parts of Western Europe, notably England, and the United States. It was in this period, also, that the term itself came into general use through the writings of the early socialists. A number of writers, however, have suggested that elements of capitalism are to be found before the nineteenth century. Henri Pirenne, for example, suggests that 'all the essential features of capitalism-individual enter-prises, the advancement on credit, commercial profits, speculation, etc.-are to be found from the twelfth century on'. (Stages in the Social History of Capitalism, *American Historical Review,* 1914.) Henri See, Max Weber, Werner Sombart and others all suggest that capitalistic elements are to be found in most historical societies. However, they concede that it was only in Western Europe during and after the Industrial Revolution that there is to be found on a societal scale the whole complex of features known as capitalism.

The last fifty years have seen an increased participation by governments in the functioning of the economies of capitalist societies, encouraged partly by a desire to alleviate the worst consequences of periodic depres-sions to which capitalism has been subject. Along with this increased governmental responsibility there has also been the tendency for capitalist enterprises to increase in scale until the small, individually owned and controlled enterprise is secondary to the large corporations controlled by a group of managers who exercise their control on behalf of the legal owners, the shareholders.

Sociological concern with capitalism has been mainly directed towards its origins and its development. Weber, in the *Protestant Ethic and the Spirit of Capitalism,* translated 1930, saw the origins of capitalism to be, at least in part, due to the rise of ascetic Protestantism in Europe, especially England. He suggested that the Calvinist 'ethic' of asceticism and increasing activity in the world for the glory of God, gave rise to a secular variant which formed the 'spirit of capitalism', the idea that hard work carried its own intrinsic reward. It was this *spirit,* coupied with *rationality,* that was distinctive in nineteenth-century capitalism. Weber's hypothesis goes some way to explain the process of capital formation whereby some of the members of society forgo present consumption in favour of further capital investment, a process considered by many to be essential to the beginnings of capitalism. Work, to the ascetic Protestants and their secular descendants of Weber's study, was an activity rewarding itself and not for the material benefits it might bring. As a result, increases in wealth tended to be channelled into greater productive capacity rather than into increases in consumption.

On occasions, *capitalism* is used as though it were synonymous with such terms as *laissez faire, the free market, the profit motive, private enterprise,* etc. These usages, however, focus upon one characteristic of capitalism to the exclusion of others, and it is possible to conceive of having anyone of them within quite different kinds of economic institutional frames. For example, it is possible to have a free market without the institution of private ownership of production goods. The *profit motive* refers to the character of the motivation behind economic activity and, as Weber points out, is not peculiar to capitalism. The term *laissez faire* refers to an economic philosophy whose cry is for the removal of all restrictions, usually governmental, upon entrepreneurial activity.

To what extent political and other non-economic aspects of society are to be included within the notion of *capitalism* is a controversial point. Friedman, in *Capitalism and Freedom*, 1963, makes the point that 'econ-omic freedom is also an indispensable means towards the achievement of political freedom'. A view endorsed by F. A. von Hayek in *The Road to Selfdom*, 1944, Weber also suggested that democracy in its clearest form can occur only under capitalism. It is a matter of empirical fact that the particular configuration of social characteristics in Western Europe and the United States, which included a capitalistic type of economy, were found together with more or less democratic political systems. (See S. M. Lipset, *Political Man*, 1960.) However, this is not to demonstrate that a capitalistic form of economic organization is a necessary or sufficient guarantee of political freedom.

Capital Accumulation The process of accumulating reosurces for use inthe production of goods and services. Private capital accumulation takes place when productive capacity exceeds the immediate needs for consumption. For example, a farmer can accumulate capital (stored grains, improved equipment etc.) durignyearsof good harvests and good farm reveues. Generally, accumulationis directly linked to profitability: the resources used to make commodities can be replaced and augmented when the commodity is sold for a profit. Capital accumulation can also take place in the public sector,where, from a structuralist approach within a conflict perspective, the state is seen as performing the function of aiding inthe accumulation of private capital. this function may be performed by the state providing an educated work force (human capital), building rail lines into resource areas, maintaining a legal system to resolve contract disputes and providing tax incentives or tax breaks.

Case Study This is a practice derived from legal studies where a case is an event or set of events involving legal acts from the study of which the student derives both the principles and the practice of the law relevant to the case.

In social work and social administration a case is the

object of study in the sense that it requires a full description of the client, family or the administrative situation, so that all relevant matters affecting the issue or issues of interest may be discerned.

In sociology *case study* method is a holistic treatment of a subject where-by through the detailed examination of one instance information about a class of entities of which this is one may be obtained. The method has been criticized by social statisticians as incapable of providing methodologically sound results of a general nature, but on the other hand it may well be invaluable as a preliminary approach in order to discover the significant variables and provide useful categories which will lead to the formulation of hypotheses which then may be tested by reference to a number of instances. The subjects of case studies are usually families, organizations, social groups and small communities.

Caste A closed form of stratificationin which an individual's status is determined by birth and cannot be changed. (2) A status group, within a system of hierarchical social stratification, in which membership is hereditary. Caste differentiations are usually based on religious and mythical traditions and caste membership determines occupational roles, place of residence and legal and custmary rights and duties. Caste is maintained from generation to generation by the practice of within-caste marriage and strict formality insocial interaction with other castes.

category The term was first used by Aristotle in the logical sense that entities are classifiable according to that which may be significantly predicated of them. From Aristotle, Kant adopted the term *category* to denote the elementary concepts of the pure understanding. It is now little used as a term in logic. In non-philosophical contexts, category can be used interchangeably with, and has a similar meaning to, class, type or kind. Its use in sociology parallels that in the natural sciences where, since categories are supposed in general to be mutually exclusive, it is essentially classificatory. Every technical term and concept in the social sciences is a category, because they denote a class of entities of which predications may be made.

On another level, a central problem of the sociology of knowledge has been to give an account of the social causation of man's categories of thought. E. Durkheim and M. Mauss pioneered the attempt to seek for the social conditions which make for man's differential categorizations, and opposed both empiricist and rationalist explanations of man's categories. This French tradition has been continued by such anthropologists as L. Levy-Bruhl and C. Levi-Strauss. The main contention of this school is that differential social structures can be defined as the root cause of differential category structures.

The discussion of the source of man's categories has taken a central role in psychology. There are two main schools of thought in the con-troversy as to whether man's categories are innately or environmentally determined. They are represented by the Gestalt school, who favour at least partial inherent categorical capacities, and the behaviourist school who see man's categories as a purely learned phenomenon. Perhaps a more fruitful view of the problem can be derived from Piaget's work on language in particular and cognition in general; his position is less extreme than the more traditional schools of psychology.

Cause; Social Causation To say that one event *A* is the cause of a second event *B* may be to assert that the prior occurrence of an event of type *A* is a necessary condition for the occurrence of an event of type *B;* or that it is a sufficient condition for the occurrence of such an event; or that it is both necessary and sufficient. To formulate a causal law is thus always to formulate a connection between two classes of event, and thereby to furnish a recipe for producing events of the second kind by producing events of the first kind. Of course we are to the same extent furnished with a recipe for preventing events of the second kind from occurring. Whether or not we are able to make use of such recipes depends not only on the truth of our formulations of causal laws, but also upon the level of techno-logical achievement.

All causal explanation depends not only on our ability to formulate true generalizations about the connections between the events that consti· aute the causes and the events that constitute the effects, but also on our ability to formulate true generalizations about what would have happened if the particular cause had not operated. We understand the causal effect of a given agency only if we know the truth about certain unfulfilled conditions.

It is sometimes argued that in the social sciences causal explanation has a quite different role from that which it has in the natural sciences. Here a weaker and a stronger contention must be distinguished. The weaker contention is that in the social sciences no causal laws have in fact been established. But if by *causal law* we mean what has been meant so far in this article this contention is plainly false. What critics who advance this contention perhaps mean is that almost all the established generalizations in the social sciences lack convincing theoretical backing. That is, they are distinguishing between mere causal generalizations (All *A's* as a matter offact produce *B's)* and causal laws (All *A's must* produce *B's)* where the necessity embodied in the law consists in the deducibility of the law from a well-established theory. Yet it is clear that just this kind of backing for our generalizations is frequently supplied in economics, at least, and there seems to be no logical barrier to supplying it elsewhere.

The stronger contention is that not merely *have* no causal laws been established in the social sciences but that no such laws *could* be established. For the nature of human action is such that the regularities to be observed in human behaviour are of a different logical type from the regularities of cause and effect. On this view it is of the essence of human action that it is intentional and rule—guided, and the task of the social scientist is to observe and chart the rules and the concepts which inform the intentions by means of which the rules have to be expressed, and which define the way of life of a given society. Underpinning this view is the thesis that *because* human action is intentional and rule-governed, it cannot be causally explained. This thesis is false; it perhaps rests on the mistake of supposing that if two items are such that their descriptions are intentionally and conceptually related, as that of an action and that of its antecedents often are, then these two items cannot stand in an external, contingent causal relationship. But if this were true we could not for example enquire how often injuries and insults actually cause acts of revenge in societies where codes of vendetta prevail and formulate causal generalizations on the basis of observed correlations; which is clearly absurd.

The illusion that causality is unimportant in the social sciences may help to conceal the extent to which key concepts which are not themselves causal presuppose an ability to establish causal truths. So it is with the characteristically sociological notion of function. When it is said that the function of x is to produce y, although in the making of this statement the relationship asserted is not a causal one, the truth of the statement depends upon it being always or mostly true that the bringing about of x is the cause of the occurrence of y. Finally it is worth remarking that all causal generalizations can be expressed as probability statements; we often contrast the form of a causal law with that of a statement to the effect that if A occurs there is such-and-such a probability that B will occur but of course if the occurrence of A is sufficient condition for the occurrence of B, then if A occurs the certainty that B will occur is a limiting case of such probability.

Centrality; Centrality Index In any social group, considered as a structure of communications between people, it is possible to differentiate among the members according to their centrality. That is to say, each member, according to his or her position in a communication structure, possesses a certain advantage or disadvantage in regard to the number and frequency of communications he or she makes and receives in the group. For a group with a given communication structure, it is possible to calculate the number of communication links between a member and all other members. This may be expressed as a proportion of the total number of such com-munication links between each member and all other members totalled, whence one r.as obtained the centrality index of that member. Thus the centrality index of member *x* is the total number of communication links between group members divided by the number of communication links between *x* and all other members of the group. It follows that a high centrality index is indicative of a member's favourable position in a communication structure, and *ceteris paribus* such a person having a high centrality index may be said to be in a leadership position, for it is thus possible to estimate quantitatively the degree of influence members of a group may have by virtue of their position in the group.

Character Structure *See Personality*

Charisma; routinization of Charisma Charisma, which in Greek means 'divine grace' was used by Ernst Troeltsch and then adopted by Max Weber to designate the ability to lead and inspire by sheer force of person-ality and conviction without the aid of material incentives or coercion. A charismatic leader, therefore, is one who has no organized 'machine' at his disposal, whose power has not been obtained through institutionalized procedure, and who converts people to his message and secures their obedience by persuasion. The founders of doctrinal communities satisfied these criteria perfectly so long as they had acquired neither an apparatus of coercion nor wealth. Jesus, for example, was a purely charismatic leader. So was John Wesley,

Mahomet until he had organized an army, Gandhi before he acquired the backing of the party machine, and Lenin before his return to Russia. The power of the last three remained charismatic, but only partly. The opposite of a charismatic leader is a tyrant who rules through naked force and the fear which he inspires, or a ruler who is obeyed regardless of his personal capabilities and solely in virtue of the office which he holds.

As Weber pointed out, leadership can remain purely charismatic only so long as the number of the followers is small, that is to say at the very beginning of successful movements, because the creation of an admin-istrative machine and the acquisition of funds open possibilities of applying coercion as well as providing remunerative inducements. Moreover the mere duration of the hierarchy inculcates the habits of obedience to the office, which soon acquire a force of inertia independent of the personal qualities of the holder. A transformation of charismatic into institu-tionalized leadership is usually called its routinization, although 'adultera-tion' or 'dilution' might be a more illuminating term.

The term 'charisma' becomes superfluous and confusing if it is indis-criminately applied, as commonly happens, to such disparate phenomena as any kind of aura surrounding an office, the supernatural powers attributed to kings and priests, or even simple prestige or status; and the expression 'routinization of charisma' then becomes meaningless. With the exception of the founders of small sects, leaders can only be partially charismatic. For many of his admirers, de Gaulle has a great deal of charisma, but he also has a police force and the entire apparatus of the state at his disposal to enforce his commands. As the bloody purge in 1934 has shown, Hitler could not rely on his charisma alone, even in his relations with the party stalwarts. Nevertheless, his power over most of the Germans had a very large (though varying) charismatic element, although his power over the conquered nations and his political opponents was based on naked force.

Chronic Disease Disease of long duration, often not detected in its early stages, and fromwhich the patient willnot recover (such as high blood pressure or diabetes).

circulation of elites. See ELITES.

Civilization A term originally derived from the verb *to civilize* from *eivis* and *civilitas* describing the acquisition of qualities of politeness and amiability on the part of superiors to inferiors. The Encyclopaedists, however, contrasted civilization not with *barbarism* but with *feudalism*. Consequently, the term has the ring of the Enlightenment about it, for it suggests progress. This use of the term in the late eighteenth century was extended in early sociological writings to a theory of social development. This is clearly seen in Lewis Morgan's *Ancient Society: Researches in the Lines of Human Progress from Savagery through Barbarism to Civilization.*

A more modern use is to regard human history as being capable of analysis in terms of large units. A. J. Toynbee in *A Study of History*, 1933-1954, points to twenty-one civilizations in the known history of the world, each with its distinctive characteristics, but all sharing certain features or qualities which enable them to be distinguished as members of the same category. Sociologists, like many other people, use the term in a general and vague way as, for instance, in speaking of *modern civilization*, by which is usually meant contemporary urban and indus-trialized societies. In this respect there is a relationship between *civilization* and *culture*. In the example just given *civilization* tends. to be equated with high culture, but sometimes culture is not identified with civilization but instead is contrasted, in the sense that the latter is a more complex social phenomenon, including the organization of material and technological qualities as well as the beliefs, art forms, literature and the body of ideas and values of a people; which more specifically is spoken of as *culture*. An important contribution has been made to the comparative study of civilizations by Alfred Weber, who has analysed civilization as a process. For a synopsis see his *Einfuhrung in die Soziologie,* 1955.

Civil Society The sphere of social life that is separte from the intimate bonds of family and autonomous from regulation and scrutiny of the state.It generally refers to the social interactions between individuals as free makers of contracts acting with rational selfinteret ina society where all have equal legal status. teh concept of civil society alsoo implieslimits on the state's role inregulating social life and a generalized responsibility of individuals to act with due regardto the interests and collective life of the community.

Clan In modern British anthropological usage, a clan is a named, unilineal descent-group: that is, a body of persons claiming common descent from an ancestor (often mythical) and recruiting the children of either male or female members, but not of both.

The word derives from the Gaelic *clann* meaning children or descen-dants, and thus refers originally ~o a cognatic descent-group; anthro-pologists, however, have usually reserved the term for unilineal groups. An earlier usage favoured the Latin *gens* for unilineal descent-groups of this nature (see L. H. Morgan, *Ancient Society,* 1877), but because this referred, etymologically, to a patrilineal group, American authors tended to use *clan* for matrilineal descent-groups only, reserving *gens* for patri-lineal. Often *sib* was used as a generic term for both (see R. H. Lowie, *Primitive Society,* 1920). More recently, G. P. Murdock has suggested that *sib* be used to cover all unilineal groups, while *clan* is reserved for a localized descent-group including the spouses of members *(Social Struc-ture,* 1949). British usage is now standardized in the use of *clan* as the generic term, with *matri-clan* and *patri-clan* denoting the two varieties. Any grouping of clans is referred to as a *phratry.*

Classic works on clans include A. L. Kroeber, *Zuni Kill and Clan,* 1917; R. Firth, *We, The Tikopia,* 1936; M. Fortes, *Tile Dynamics of Clallship amongst the Tal/ensi,* 1945; E. E. Evans-Pritchard, *The Nuer,* 1940.

Class-consciousness Originally used in a Marxist context where the social system of Capitalism develops to a point where the Proletariat become increasingly aware of their class position *vis* II *vis* the Bourgeoisie, and hence gain cohesion in the face of their exploitation. Such a conscious-ness is the prelude to organization and training for the revolutionary conflict which brings about the Dictatorship of the Proletariat.

The term is often used in a loose and general way to indicate a group's self-awareness, and thus can mean a status group's self-identity, through the members sharing a common consumption pattern, in so far as members of the group are frequently aware that their consumption is related to their group membership.

Classificatory System A *classificatory* kinship system differs from a *descriptive* one in that certain collateral relatives are addressed or spoken of by terms which also apply to lineal relatives. Thus a man may address his father's brother *as/ather,* or his father's sister's son may be referred to as *brother.* A small number of kinship terms are thus used for a large number of relatives. The terms *descriptive* and *classificatory* were intro-duced into analyses of kinship by Lewis Morgan. A famous essay by A. R. Radcliffe-Brown on classificatory kinship systems is to be found in *Structure and Function in Primitive Society,* 1952. Radcliffe-Brown also proffered a structural theory to account for the differences and similarities between kinship systems.

Cognate; Cognatic Two persons are *cognates* when they are able to trace their descent from a common ancestor or ancestress regardless of whether the links are through males or females. Thus a *cognatic* kinship system is bilateral, observing no unilineal principle.

Collective Behaviour Some early social psychological writing was focused on crowd behaviour, for this seemed an important topic. People appeared sometimes to behave quite out of character in crowds, being emotionally swayed or abandoning restraints which w· re normally noticeable. Gustav Le Bon was one of the earliest writers on the subject *(La Psychologie des Joules,* 1895, translated 1896, *The Crowd: a Study 0/ the popular mind).* This kind of study concentrates on the unorganized aspect of collective behaviour, but of course many sociological studies are of organizational behaviour. It may be argued that the two are quite distinct, yet there are some aspects of organized collective behaviour partaking of the charac-teristics of crowd behaviour, e.g. fashions, financial cycles, morale in organizations and the expression of power in relations between organiza-tions. The theories which aim to explain collective behaviour may be classified into three groups: those which, like Le Bon's, explain crowd behaviour in terms of *contagion,* the rapid communication of moods and the uncritical acceptance of direction; those which describe collective behaviour in terms of *convergence* of people with similar predispositions, ideas and aims; and those which see collective behaviour as being regu-lated by a social norm which emerges in special situations, known as the *emergent lwrm* theory.

Collective Conscience This term is a translation of an expression used by Emile Durkheim, namely *la conscience collective,* but the difficulty remains of knowing if it should not rather be *consciousness* rather than *conscience,* i.e. should it have a psychological or a moral connotation? Durkheim's definition was that the totality of beliefs and sentiments common to average members of a society form a definite system; it is this system he is referring to when he speaks of *la conscience collective.* A second but related difficulty arises in locating it, for it would appear to be diffused throughout the society. Durkheim on occasion in his *De la division du travail social,* 1893, speaks almost as if there was a social mind in society, and for this reason the concept was not at first much liked in the Anglo-Saxon world, but perhaps we can appreciate its use if we regard it as largely synonymous with the concept *culture.* Thus, like culture, the collec-tive conscience provides the link between one generation and another, it is what is shared in the way of values and sentiments, it is what is upset and shocked by the commission of a crime; it is, says Durkheim, that which defines what a crime is.

Colour Bar A colloquial term not having a precise meaning in sociology. It generally implies an institutionalized restriction of access to certain places, amenities, privileges or opportunities according to a socially defined criterion of racial origin.

Community; Community Centre Originally the term *community* denoted a collectivity of people who occupied a geographical area; people who were together engaged in economic and political activities and who essentially constituted a self-governing social unit with some common values and experiencing feelings of belonging to one another. Examples are a city, a town, a village or parish. But the idea of community as a goal which people may achieve has become prominent. It arises from the greater mobility of people in modern industrial societies and also the prevalence of mass media of communication. Today industrial concerns spread into many areas and over many countries. Commodities are not restricted in con-sumption to local areas and there has been a vast increase in communica-tion. *Community,* although less all-inclusive, and slightly more specific in connotation, may be regarded as denoting a community of interests. In modern sociology it remains the case that the term *community* is used in a general and deliberately vague way. For an early attempt to analyse society making use of the concept.

The growth of towns and cities and their redevelopment to provide mass housing has led to an awareness of the lack of cohesion and identity of large sections of the population. In answer to this need *community centres* have sometimes been established to provide recreational and cultural activities for people, and to give an opportunity for democratic organiza-tion of the residents of an area. They were introduced into the U.S.A. before the First World War, but gained strength in Britain as a result of the work of the Association of Community Centres which has urged the wider development of this kind of provision in connection with new muni-cipal housing estates. Whilst having some cohesive qualities it has to be admitted that community centres can be divisive; they are of course associational in character and therefore limited in the ends pursued. The fact is that they are not communities, but they aim to foster community spirit. To this extent they are contradictory, for in fact a community centre is an association, and only in so far as it is deliberately an association with limited and specified ends can it serve the specific needs of a differentiated urban population.

Comparative Method The phrase refers to the method of comparing different societies or groups within the same society to show whether and why they are similar or different in certain respects. It was used by eighteenth-century philologists who compared different languages to show from their common characteristics (which also differentiated them from other sets oflanguages) that they must belong to the same linguistic 'family'. The phrase was subsequently used throughout the nineteenth century to describe the method of discerning similarities in social institu-tions so as to trace their common origins; however, the method as such was not new having been used by Aristotle in his study of political systems.

Both Montesquieu and Comte, often regarded as the founders of sociology, used or recommended comparison to establish and explain both differences and similarities between societies. Comte suggested the comparison of human with non-human characteristics, to show what was distinctive of the former, and the comparison of societies at the same and at different stages of social development to demonstrate the *laws of coexistence* and the *laws of succession* of social and mental phenomena.

Throughout the nineteenth century there was a strong link between the use of the comparative method and the evolutionist approach, particularly with the growing influence of Darwinism. However, some scholars were not content to establish common origins and to trace the 'natural history' of social phenomena, such as religion and the family, or to 'prove' some theory of the stages of social and mental development; for example, Tylor, like Comte, considered that one of the chief aims of comparison was to discover what he called cultural 'adhesions', or necessary correla-tions between two or more cultural phenomena, such as a rule of kinship behaviour and a rule of kinship terminology.

But the examples which typify the rather loose and unsystematic pro-cedures of the nineteenth and early twentieth century are to be found in the writings of Sir J. G. Frazer, who used countless illustrations from classical mythology, the Bible and contemporary ethnography to support his theories concerning the characteristics of the human mind and to confirm his hypotheses concerning the origins and development of in-numerable customs and beliefs.

It was J. S. Mill who introduced greater rigour into the discussion by showing that the comparative method was simply an application of the logic of science to ready-made cases, as opposed to experimentally con-structed ones; for, as he argued, the scientific method necessarily consists in the comparison of cases which are similar in some respects and dis-similar in others, to show whether certain characteristics are causally connected. However, Mill finally decided that the comparative method did not really accord with the inductive rules of science which he had formulated (*A System of Logic,* Book VI, 19(0).

This negative vi‑‑w was challenged by Emile Durkheim. In an early study Durkheim compared the legal systems of different societies at the same and at different levels of development and, using law as an index of the moral character of society, tested his hypothesis that an increase in the division of labour is accompanied by a change in the nature of social integration. Again, in his study of suicide, Durkheim compared the suicide rates both of different societies and of different groups within a society, to show that these rates varied inversely with the degree of social cohesion and with the degree of stability of moral norms; to do this he had also to compare selected indices and determinants of social cohesion and norma-tive stability, and chose types of religious organization, the form of community life, the state of the economy and the polity, and so on. Durkheim concluded, in criticism of Mill, that if comparison was carried out with true precision and control and yielded correlations (rather than invariant causal connections), it could qualify as a quasi-experimental method. Indeed, it has since been argued that Durkheim, particularly in his study of suicide, pioneered the method of *multivariate analysis* in sociology. For example, not content to compare the suicide rates of Protestant and Catholic countries and of Protestant and Catholic groups within anyone country, Durkheim compared the two sets of differences to show how far the factor of cohesion, as reflected in religious organiza-tion, did operate as an independent determinant of suicide.

A rather different method of comparison to that used by Durkheim is to be found in the work of Max Weber. His method consisted not so much in isolating factors or variables whose operations could be observed in a large number of cases, as in analysing many concrete features of different societies. He did this to show how characteristics, like those of bureaucracy, which are in some respects similar from one case to another are also in other important respects different, in so far as they are affected by other features of the unique historical configuration of which they are a part. Weber's recommendations included the use of *ideal types;* these described the universal characteristics of a social institution or system of beliefs as they would exist in their *pure* form, unaffected by those other elements which make up a unique historical complex. One type of comparison would consist in describing and explaining the variations around a particular ideal type, such as the forms of German and British bureau-cracy; another approach would lie in comparing different ideal types, such as those of Protestant and Hindu fatalism, to show how each corres-ponded to a different system of secular values. Weber demonstrated these; orrespondences not by establishing statistical correlations but by appeal-ing to a sense of meaningful relationship.

There have been numerous attempts to combine the comparative method .vith a broad survey of societies in the attempt to establish correlations. Hobhouse, Wheeler and Ginsberg tried in this way to establish a truly ~mpirical scheme of social evolution; they constructed a scale of techno-ogical development and then sought to correlate each level on it with)articular forms of social life, such as political institutions and moral 'ules *(The Material Culture and Social Institutions of the Simpler Peoples;* m *Essay in Correlation,* 1915). More recently, Gouldner has made a limilar attempt to correlate technological and moral development in his *Votes on Technology and the Moral Order,* 1962. Any defects of such Ichemes, particularly of the former, lie more in the theoretical assumptions .vhich underlie them, that is, in the idea that societies necessarily develop)ll all fronts in a well-defined direction, than in the comparative method tself.

Social anthropologists, in their reaction against Frazer and others like lim, did tend for a while to equate the comparative method with the worst :xcesses of the evolutionary approach, accusing the earlier scholars of tearing cultural items from their context' and so distorting their meaning. rhey recommended a *holistic* method and in so far as they did compare ocieties they did so either to classify them or else to demonstrate the larticular similarities and differences between a small' number of cases.

Thus sociologists, who have traditionally opted for comparison in the service of generalization, have come increasingly to accept that a more appropriate method for some purposes is that of comparative history, using certain general ideas about social structure to inform the analysis of a few cases, and to test hypotheses of a very limited range. On the other hand, a British anthropologist, E. R. Leach, has urged his colleagues to seek generalizations by abstracting a small number of variables from their wider context; but he has simultaneously warned them to understand the phenomena in their context before abstracting them. (See *Rethinking Anthropology,* 1961). In some ways complex societies lend themselves more to the methods of Durkheim, in that their component elements are less tightly integrated than are those of simpler societies, and can therefore be abstracted with less danger of contextual violation; on the other hand, complex societies are less stable, over time, than simpler ones, so that the process of abstracting certain enduring elements for comparison is more difficult and may therefore call for the methods recommended by Weber.

It is clear that the choice of method is governed by the problem in-vestigated. Furthermore, comparison does not in itself yield any particular type of theory or hypothesis, although it may suggest a line of theoretical enquiry, but is a method of testing hypotheses. However deficient it may be in this, it is as Durkheim said the only method available to the socio-logical disciplines.

Comte, Auguste (1798-1857) French philosopher, moralist and sociol-ogist; he collaborated with Saint Simon from

1817-23, and corresponded with J. S. Mill. He divided *sociology* into social statics and social dynamics. He elaborated the Law of the Three Stages of human thought: theological, metaphysical and positive, which he thought characterized the development both of human knowledge and of society, which correspondingly developed from a military to a legal, and finally to an industrial stage. His view was holistic and organic. The second keystone of his philosophical system was a theorem that the abstract theoretical sciences form a hierarchy, the crown of which is sociology; his synthesis of knowledge was to be the basis of the reorganization of society. Comte believed that social phenomena could be treated scientifically, his method being based on observation, experiment, comparison and history. He viewed the collective facts of history and society as subject to laws and not to individual volition.

Concept In general usage *concept* mainly means notion or idea. It may be defined as the name for the members of a given class of any sort, or as the name for the class itself. More simply, concept is a term referring to a descriptive property or relation.

A concept in sociology is generally regarded as being at a lower level of abstraction than a theory, but a necessary part of any theory, since theories are formed from the concepts employed. Concepts are not, of course, unchanging, and conceptual clarification and redefinition are continuing tasks for the sociologist. A useful discussion of the importance of analysis of concepts in sociology can be found in R. K. Merton, *Social Theory and Social Structure* (Revised Edition), 1957.

In sociology the prime interest is in the usefulness of concepts for the formation of theories relating to some problem area and the generation of hypotheses for testing. Amongst criteria that have been suggested for the selection of concepts, are precision, empirical anchorage, and usefulness for the formation of theories which have explanatory power for the problem under consideration. The choice and definition of concepts is crucial for the progress of sociology as a science, and the range of disagreement on basic concepts in sociology is still very wide.

Concrete; the fallacy of misplaced concreteness *Concrete* is best defined as anything that is specific or individual, as against general or abstract terms, which stress common characteristics or qualities considered apart from their specific setting. *World War II* is concrete whereas *war* is abstract.

A. N. Whitehead in his *Science and the Modern World*, 1925, has called the fallacy of confusing other types of entities with actually existing entities, *the fallacy of misplaced concreteness*. He suggests that this fallacy is pernicious, as it has been responsible for considerable error in philo-sophical theorizing. It is a fallacy which is inherent in language, for any entity can be the grammatical subject of a sentence and is thus readily treated implicitly if not explicitly as an actual entity.

Talcott Parsons in *The Structure of Social Action*, 1937, uses the fallacy of misplaced concreteness to identify the same error as Whitehead. Parsons has under consideration certain aspects of classical economics and r~tionalism. The point is that there is no objection to using propositions partially, provided that this is recognized and allowed for. They are then simply abstract formulations of certain aspects of the concrete situation. The fallacy is committed if these propositions are used in any sense as significantly complete representations of the situation in question. Parsons suggested that the rationalist scheme is in breach of the fallacy in that it has underestimated the role of the affective aspects of human behaviour.

Condorcet, Antoine Nicolas Caritat, Marquis de (1743-1794) French aristocrat, philosopher, revolutionary and social mathematician; his work covers the whole of the social science field. He collaborated with d'Alembert in the production of *l'Encyclopedie.* His chief work is the *Sketch of an Historical Picture of the Progress of the Human Spirit, 1795* (translated 1955), which traces the continuous development of mankind through nine epochs; the tenth, beginning with the Revolution, would see the ultimate perfection of humanity, and absolute equality of opportunity. He believed the basis of all progress to be popular education; he advocated state education for children, adults and the handicapped; he wanted co-education, and moral and physical instruction. Also, he favoured civil marriage, divorce, birth control, and the emancipation of women. He saw history's purpose as the discovery and application of the laws of social progress. His influence was widespread; his thought revolutionary.

Conflict: social conflict The mainstream of nineteenth-century socio-logical thought underplays the importance of social conflict. From Comte onwards sociologists were concerned to show what institutions were necessary from the point of view of achieving social integration and har-mony. Two types of theory were based on opposite assumptions. The Hobbesian tradition posited an initial social state of a war of all against all and this tradition was fortified by the Darwinian notion of a struggle for existence. And Marxists argued that there was a fundamental conflict of interests in society arising from men's differential relations to the means of production and leading to perpetual class struggle.

These disagreements over the role of conflict in social systems continue in contemporary sociology, both in the micro-sociology which studies social roles and relations and in the macro-sociology which studies social and cultural systems.

In the theory of Talcott Parsons, for example, attention is focused on what the author calls 'institutionalized social relations', i.e. social relations in which one actor has expectations of another's action and those expectations are understood and fulfilled. But clearly there are two other possibilities, viz. that in which expectations are not understood and that in which they are understood but not fulfilled. The latter case is the case of conflict at the level of micro-sociology.

Conflict may be of various kinds and it may be limited and regulated. When two individuals compete peacefully for the control of limited resources we speak of *competition* rather than *conflict* and when two individuals with conflicting interests haggle over the terms of an exchange we speak of *bargaining*. Where there is bargaining and free competition at the same time we speak of a *market situation*. But a market situation may break down if there is a restriction on competition and the parties to the market-bargain seek to compel compliance with their own interests by deploying sanctions. In these circumstances the market-situation gives way to a conflict-situation which is resolved on the basis of a balance of power.

Many sociologists, in accounting for the institutions of modern in-dustrial societies, have been inclined to emphasize the integration of social institutions and to posit a mutually sustaining system of such institutions recognizing only the possibility that some institutions rely upon the regulated conflict processes of the market. As against this, 'conflict theory' emphasizes that there may be conflict within an institution and between institutions and that the regulated and peaceful conflict processes of the market may give way to open and non-peaceful conflict.

The main attempt to systematize conflict theory emerges from the writings of Karl Marx. In Marxism the basis of conflict is to be found in the social relations of productions. Thus all supporting social institutions support the different 'sides' in this conflict and the unitary concept of a cultural and social system disappears. The political and economic insti-tutions of capitalist society are seen as representing 'the political and economic sway of the bourgeoisie' and as against this there is reference to 'the political economy of the working class'.. A conflict between classes in the social relations of production spills over to become a conflict in all spheres and the social system becomes one of 'two great warring camps'.

R. Dahrendorf, on the other hand, has suggested that intra-institutional conflicts occur about authority in all institutions and that there need not necessarily be any overlapping. In particular, he argues that industrial conflict has become institutionalized, i.e. confined within a particular institutional context. Lockwood has drawn attention to the importance of conflict between institutional sub-systems, e.g. there is no necessary harmony between industrial and educational institutions.

L. Coser and M. Gluckman have both argued that orthodox function-alist theory gives insufficient weight to conflict and that it should be revised to take this into account. Both argue that a number of cross-cutting conflicts which ensure that one's ally on one front is one's enemy on another make for social stability. Coser also argues that a looseness of institutional arrangements which permits the terms of some social rela-tions to be fixed after a trial of strength between the parties makes for greater stability than a more rigid structure.

The recognition of regulated conflicts of this kind as a permanent feature of all social structures is now widely accepted in sociology. They do not, however, adequately explain socially disruptive conflicts and in this sphere, the sociology of political revolution, a great deal of theoretical and empirical work remains to be done. Attempts to revise Marxism to give recognition to a greater number of classes by such writers as Karl Mannheim and C. Wright Mills point in this direction.

Connubium *Connubium* (from Lat., *connubium,* marriage) in anthro-pology refers to the right and obligation of members of a category of men to choose their wives from a prescribed category of women. The two groups are said to have or maintain connubium. Ties established between lineal descent groups on this basis form a *prescriptive alliance.* Such closed systems of marriage may be contrasted with Qpen, or preferential systems where, in theory, choice of a spouse may be made from a much wider range.

In Roman civil law connubium between the parties was a condition of marriage. The law specified the categories so linked.

Early uses of the term in sociological literature occur in E. Durkheim and M. Mauss, 'De quelques formes primitives de classification', *Annee Sociologique,* VI, 1903.

Consanguinity A social relationship based on descent from a common ancestor is described as a consanguinial relationship; Clearly, from the root the connotation is of a blood-tie, but in fact consanguinial relations may not be of this kind. Whilst normally referring to the lineal or collateral relatives of a person, the term may be extended to cover those linked by adoption or by fictional blood-ties, so that some relations arc considered consanguine whilst strictly speaking they are nothing of the kind. This difficulty led A. R. Radcliffe-Brown to argue that a better term to use is *kinship* and to differentiate between *kinship* relations (i.e. those based on descent from a common ancestor including fictional ones) from *affinal* relations such as marital relations and those following from marriage. For convenience, however, the term *kinship* sometimes includes affines.

Consensus *Consensus* is a variable property of social systems which range from groups of two or more members to whole societies. Consensus exists when the members of these systems are in a state of affirmative agreement about normative and cognitive matters relevant to their action towards one another, towards the central persons or roles in the system, and towards persons, roles, and collectivities outside the system. Consensus is, then, agreement about the rules which should govern their conduct concerning the goals of the system and the allocation of roles and rewards within the system. There is another element present in consensus: this is a solidarity formed by a sense of common identity arising from ties of personal affection, of primordial (ethnic, kinship, or territorial) charac-teristics, of a shared relationship to sacred things, or of a membership in a common culture or in a common civil community.

Consensus is consensus with respect to the centre of the system, which includes persons, roles, institutions, beliefs, and norms, and which the

Consensus affirms The element of solidarity can vary somewhat inde-pendently of the cognitive (beliefs) and normative (rules) elements in the consensus. A state of affective solidarity might obtain between sectors of a social system which are in dissensus with respect to particular issues.

The existence of consensus within any social system large or small does not necessarily entail a complete consensus embracing every member and governing every contingency which may arise within the system or in its environment. Thus, there might be more consensus on some issues than on others, and the sectors of the population participating in the consensus might vary so that lines of cleavage which separate the consensual from the dissensual sectors might shift from occasion to occasion. Furthermore, the intensity of the conflict or dissensus on a particular issue (i.e. the absence or suspension, in varying degrees, of consensus on the issue) might vary inversely with respect to the amount and coverage of con-sensus on other issues which accompanies it and in the strength of the affective element in the solidarity.

Consensus is a necessary component of macro-social order, meaning by 'order' a combination of relatively harmonious collaboration in the execution of agreed or accepted tasks, widespread acceptance of the allocation of rewards, and the relatively or mainly peaceful resolution of conflicts between corporate bodies, strata, and individuals. The importance of consensus to order does not mean that order is possible only on the basis of complete consensus. For one thing, order depends on other factors as well as consensus. But even the fullest consensus is never complete.

What is essential for order is that there should be sufficient consensus about the legitimacy of the central institutional system, about the legit-imacy of the mode of access of the incumbents of the major roles of the central institutional system, about the general rules and particular com-mands which they promulgate, and about the distribution of roles, rewards, and facilities which they influence or for which they are held responsible. If there is a moderate degree of consensus about some of these elements, and especially the first two, conflicts about the last can be contained and partially resolved.

In a narrow and literal sense, consensus can be conceived as the con-sensus of equals or subordinates in opposition to the central institutional and cultural systems. When we speak of consensus as a factor in the maintenance of social order, we are speaking of consensus between rulers and a substantial and relevant section of the ruled. It is more important for the maintenance of order that the elites of the different spheres and their proximate followings be in a considerable degree of consensus and that the counter-elites and their proximate followings, who are in-cluded among the ruled, likewise share in it, though the latter will naturally be less consensual *vis-a-vis* the elites than the various sectors of the elites will be among themselves. Where such a moderate consensus of elites and counter-elites is not present, the working of the central institutional system will be impeded and the hitherto prevailing order will be disrupted.

Complete Consensus is Impossible Diverse parochial attachments focused on internally relatively solidary subsystems of classes, ethnic groups, religious affiliations, and local and regional communities, as well as the divergent interests of occupations, professions, and classes, are inevitable in any differentiated society. Likewise, the diverse cultures of generations and of kinship groups continuously generate dispositions which are resistant to complete assimilation into a unitary society-wide consensus. The unequal distributions of authority, income, and deference make for resentment among some of those who are in the lower sectors of the distributions against those in the upper sectors. These separate cultures, divergent interests, and resentments are conducive to the denial of the legitimacy of what is done and enunciated by those in the higher strata who people the central institutional and cultural systems. Thus, even if the latter are fortunate in having a consensus of those strata or groups closer to the centre of society, they are not likely to receive an equal affirmation from the peripheral strata.

Besides this, in practically all large societies, including the mass societies of the present day, the processes of communication from centre to periphery are full of imperfections. Quite apart from the ecological hindrances to the saturation of society by communications from the centre, the unequal distribution of capacities, educational opportunities, resources, and aspirations means that certain sectors of the society, usually those at the lower portions of the distribution of income and deference, are bound to receive less of the central cultural values and beliefs. As a result, they cannot enter as fully into the consensual pattern as those in the upper portions of the distributions.

But all this notwithstanding, all societies normally do enjoy enough consensus concerning the distributions of authority, income, and deference to enable them to continue for very extended periods without civil war and revolution. For one thing, the very fact of effective coercive control tends to have a self-legitimating consequence, so that what often appears to be 'naked power' acquires the aura of legitimacy. If the incumbents of the key roles in the central institutional system are able to persist in their incumbency, with some modicum of effectiveness in maintaining themselves and in implementing their policies, they also succeed in imposing themselves on their societies and therewith in creating some measure of consensus around themselves.

Such consensus is never universally inclusive nor is it ever more than intermittent. Much of the life of any society is lived outside the consensus which focuses on the global distributions of authority, income, and deference. Many of the concerns of most members of any societies are focused on issues which seem not to involve the central institutional system. There are zones of social life which are neither consensual nor dissensual. They are practically irrelevant to the macro-social consensus. Ignorance, indifference, isolation, although they testify to the incomplete inclusiveness of consensus, are very important.in the maintenance of order. Hence, order in the society as a whole does not require continuous and universal consensus. Indeed, consensus of the sort under discussion here becomes pertinent only when issues referring to the global distri-butions emerge.

Nonetheless, even this partial, fluctuating, fragmentary, and inter-mittent consensus breaks down on occasion. When the central institutional system fails to maintain its normal level of effectiveness, when the elites fail to meet demands which they had previously satisfied, or when new demands cannot be met by the elites, the consensus concerning the legitimacy of their incumbency and their accomplishments undergoes attenuation at crucial points. The counter-elites then find greater support, and their refusal to collaborate within the framework of the previously operative consensus becomes stronger. Revolutions and secessions occur. Old elites are replaced, central institutional systems are remodelled, and then after a time a new consensus is formed to confront the same challenges and obstacles as those which preceded it.

Conspicuous consumption This term was much used by Thorstein Veblen in his famous book, *The Theory of the Leisure Class,* 1899, to describe the wasteful use of expensive articles, ostensibly because they have intrinsic value. Yet the very ostentation signifies a willingness to demonstrate wealth and position by identifying with the leisure class. Conspicuous consumption thus provides for invidious class distinctions because only those who belong to the leisure class can indulge in this behaviour, others can but be envious or else display pale imitations of this behaviour, or more usually be the one *and* do the other.

Conurbation Patrick Geddes in his book *Cities in Evolution,* 1915, coined this word to describe the towns which had grown together in South Lancashire. Today it is a recognized technical term used to describe urban areas formed by the fusion of towns through spreading industry and housing. Although containing open spaces such as parks and playing fields, conurbations are essentially built-up areas in which any agri· cultural land is only found in enclaves. A special report on the six major conurbations of England and Wales in the 1951 Census analysed Greater London, Tyneside, Merseyside, Manchester, West Yorkshire and the West Midlands, which together contain approximately forty per cent of the total population.

Cooley, Charles H. (1864—1929) American social philosopher and sociologist; greatly influenced by Schiiffie. Cooley's major works are *Human Nature and the Social Order,* 1902, *Social Organisation, 1909, Social Process,* 1918, and *Sociological Theory and Social Research, 1930.* The keystone of his sociology is his organic theory; he' viewed society as a whole, composed of differentiated, but 'systematically' related parts, each with a special function. Society is also a psychic entity, with a social mind manifested in organization and institutions. He considered society and the individual to be complements, 'the collective and distributive aspects of the same thing' (1902). He distinguished between *secondary* and *primary groups* which are 'those characterized by intimate face-to-face association and co- peration' (1909). Of the more inclusive groups, class and caste are most important. He developed the concept of *self* as developing in a social context and nurtured by primary groups.

Corporate Group Following Sir Henry Maine, a corporate group may be said to represent the case where there is a perpetuity of an estate, composed of rights over persons, over real, moveable, and incorporeal property, that is shared by an aggregate of persons. Usually corporate groups may be distinguished according to their typical activities and by the kinds of sanctions applied to their members; they may be economic, political, religious and so forth. Clearly, sometimes kinship groups are corporate groups in this sense. The nature of the corporate group was a particular interest of Max Weber, who saw in some of its modem forms the signifi-cant elements of modem industrial society. Thus its two chief mani-festations are the joint stock company and the political party.

It is difficult to discuss the corporate group without reference to property rights, especially rights over things. Thus the incorporated joint stock company is a group of persons who possess transferable rights to a share in the profits, together with rights' of control over the assets, although these latter rights may vary greatly from one case to another. It should be noted that shareholders are not merely owners of tangible property, but that they share in the less tangible, but primarily more important, legal personality of the group. In many cases, of course, ownership has in practice become divorced from control, especially in those instances where the corporate group consists of many members and where an individual's share is small in proportion to the whole.

Although one way of looking at the corporate group is

in relation to property, defined as rights over things, another way is to examine it in relation to authority. This was pre-eminently the view of Max Weber in his discussion of the concept *Verband* (translated as 'corporate group'). Weber considered corporate groups as internally differentiated into roles, played by the members, such roles being distinguished by their incorporation of authority to command or their duty of submission to persons playing other roles, themselves incorporating authority.

The subject of corporate groups, their nature, differences in types, and their evolution is one of the principal subjects of sociological investigation. Important contributions to the literature may be found in Max Weber's *Theory 0/ Social and Economic Organisation* (translated by T. Parsons), 1947, and A. A. Berle and G. C. Means, *The Modern Corporation and Private Property,* 1933.

Crime Funnel The image of a 'funnel' refers to the much lower number of crimes detected and punished by the criminal justice system than the number actually committed. This model implies that crime is an objective occurrence, it is thought to exist in the qualities of certain acts without needing to be recognized, identified and officially responded to. This is what is called a 'realist' assumption about crime. Symbolic interactionists and phenomenologists.

Criminology The study of criminal behaviour. The word seems to have been used for the first time in the writings of the French anthropologist P. Topinard towards the end of the nineteenth century. However, several major studies in penology and the treatment of offenders had been published considerably earlier, notably by Cesare Beccaria (1738-1794) and Jeremy Bentham (1748-1832). An analysis of the geographical distri-bution of crime in France, conducted by Andre Guerry, appeared in 1829, and in 1835 the Belgian mathematician Adolphe Quetelet published an ambitious study of the social distribution of criminal behaviour in France, Belgium, Luxembourg and Holland, under the title *Sur l'homme et Ie development de ses lacultes; essai de physique sociale.* In contrast to these investigations, which were essentially concerned with crime as a social phenomenon, the pioneer work of Cesare Lombroso (1835-1909) and his famous pupil Enrico Ferri (1856-1928), the leaders of the Positive School of criminologists, employed the methods of anthropology in the attempt to establish a biological theory of criminality. Modern criminology has its roots in the disciplines of sociology, psychology, psychiatry and law. It embraces studies of 1 the nature, forms and incidence of criminal acts, and of their social, temporal and geographical distribution; 2 the physical and psychological characteristics, histories and social origins of criminals (particularly, but not exclusively, of persistent offenders) and of the relations between criminality and other abnormalities of behaviour; 3 the characteristics of victims of crime; 4 non-criminal anti-social behaviour, especially that which is defined as criminal in some countries and not in others, such as homosexual conduct, adultery, prostitution and attempted suicide; 5 the procedures of the police and of the criminal courts, including sentencing practice, social influences upon the decisions of judges and juries, and certain problems of testimony and evidence; 6 methods of punishing, training and treating offenders; 7 the social structure and organization of penal institutions; 8 methods of preventing and controlling crime. (The last four fields of study are commonly grouped under the general name of *penology.*)

Some writers would also include within the purview of criminology the science of criminalistics (i,e. of methods of identifying crimes and detecting offenders) and studies of the origins and development of the criminal law and of public attitudes to crime and criminals.

The methods and strategies of investigation employed in criminology have, for the most part, been borrowed or adapted from one or other of its parent disciplines. (A comprehensive account of contemporary criminological research will be found in *Comparative Criminology*, by Hermann Mannheim, 1965, 2 vols.) *Statistical techniques* are extensively used in the analysis of the incidence of crime. Much basic information about the frequency, nature and geographical distribution of offences, and the age, sex and occupation of offenders, is derived from police records and other official sources. Intensive studies of particular classes of offence or offender, and area studies of the 'ecological' distribution of crimes in urban neighbourhoods, are also important sources of information about the patterns of criminal activity. *Studies of individual criminals* have been carried out by several distinct methods. Psychiatric case-studies, based upon prolonged unstructured interaction between investigator and subject, are mainly used to obtain a longitudinal case-history of the development of the criminal, although there are obvious hazards in retrospective studies of this kind. Psychometric investigations of particular groups of offenders (usually persistent criminals, or individuals convicted of certain categories of crimes) are usually directed to the discovery of individual differences which distinguish criminals from non-criminals or persistent offenders from others. Formal psychological tests, rating scales, objective-behaviour tests, physiological measures, or interview methods may be employed, or a combination of several of these. *Prediction studies* are a comparatively recent development, but promise to become one of the most valuable research strategies of the criminologist. They involve the compilation of 'experience tables', incorporating a wide range of information about a group of criminals and their offences; the subsequent analysis of this heterogeneous array of data in the light of the criminal careers of the sample group (or of their performance in a correctional regime) can yield valuable clues to the determinants of criminal conduct. Rather limited use has been made of *experiments,* although one or two major 'field demonstrations' in the prevention and contrvl of delinquency have been undertaken with rather equivocal results. Controlled experi-ments in correctional methods have become more common in recent years, usually involving random allocation of offenders between several alternative forms of training or treatment, with careful foHow-up evalua-tion of results. *Sociological* studies of neighbourhoods in which there are high rates of delinquency have thrown light on environmental correlates of delinquency and crime; similar techniques have been used to study the structure and organization of inmate groups in penal institutions.

Cross-cousin Cross-cousins are the children of siblings of opposite sex. Thus an individual's mother's brother's children and his father's sister's children would both be his own cross-cousins. The term has been used consistently in this way since it was introduced by E. B. Tylor. ('On a method of investigating the development of insti-tutions', *Journal of the Royal Anthl-opological Institute,* 1889). It is usual to distinguish the *matrilateral* cross-cousins (mother's brother's children) from the *patrilateral* (father's sister's children). The main issue in the study of the cross-cousin relationship has concerned the interpretation of prescribed or preferential marriage between such cousins which occurs in several societies.

An excellent summary and a provocative theory can be found in C. Levi-Strauss, *Les Structures Elementaires de la Parente,* 1949. This has been attacked in G. Homans and D. Schneider, *Marriage, Authority, and Final Causes,* 1955, and defended in R. Needham, *Structure and Sentiment,* 1962.

Culture *Culture,* in its broadest definition, refers to that part of the total repertoire of human action (and its products), which is socially as opposed to genetically transmitted. It used to be thought that *culture,* in the sense of a repertoire of learned behaviour socially transmitted, was the exclusive preserve of Man. Much research on Primates recently, however, has shown that social trans-mission plays a not inconsiderable part in their survival. (See Irven de Vore, *Primate Behavior,* 1965.) This also casts doubt on the 'critical point' theory of the origin of culture in Man. This states that'it was a develop-ment of the brain which gave rise to the 'capacity for culture'. (See A. L. Kroeber, *Anthropology,* 1923.) However, recent evidence has shown that the early hominid *australopithecus* is known to have made tools. Thus the advent of cultural activities predates the rapid growth of the human brain.

Most anthropological definitions of *culture* have been modifications of that of E. B. Tylor: 'Culture or Civilization is that complex whole which includes knowledge, belief, art, morals, law, custom, and any other capabilities and habits acquired by man as a member of society.' *(Primitive Culture,* Vol. I, 1871.) Several have placed stress on the fact that such behaviour is *learned,* and hence have made the learning process the central aspect of analysis. (See R. Linton, *The Study of Man,* 1936.) Others have seen the ideational aspects of 'social heredity' as crucial, as in the elaborate definition of A. L. Kroeber and Clyde Kluckhohn, ' ... patterns, explicit and implicit, of and for behaviour, acquired and transmitted by symbols, constituting the distinctive achievement of human groups, including their embodiment in artifacts; the essential core of culture consists of tradi-tional (i.e. historically derived and selected) ideas, and especially their attached values; culture systems may, on the one hand, be considered as products of action, and on the other hand as conditioning elements of further action.' ('Culture; A critical review of concepts and definitions', *Papers of the Peabody Museum of American Archaeology alld Ethnology,* Vol. 47, *No.1,* 1952.) Here artifacts are included as the 'embodiment' of culture, although they are more usually regarded as its products. Some-times anthropologists distinguish artifacts as *material culture.*

Yet other emphases on the ideational side are present in Robert Red-field's conception of culture as a body of 'shared understandings' *(The Folk Culture of Yucatan,* 1941), while for Malinowski, culture was essen-tially a response to human needs *(A Scientific Theory of Culture, 1944).*

Most sociologists have used the term explicitly with the ideational meaning, in order to distinguish culture from *society,* or *social structure,* which they consider to be their basic subject matter. Thus, for A. R. Radcliffe-Brown, culture is essentially a set of rules *(A Natural Science of Society,* 1957). Talcott Parsons and his collaborators in the Theory of Action school regard culture as essentially symbolic and evaluative. 'Cultural objects are symbolic elements of the cultural tradition, ideas or beliefs, expressive symbols or value patterns .. .' *(The Social System,* 1951). This view is shared by Pitirim Sorokin *(Society, Culture and Personality, 1947).*

Anthropologists, in contrast to sociologists, have usually taken their whole subject matter as culture, and have not confined its use to ideational aspects of behaviour. Thus the central concept has been that of *custom,* i.e. of traditional and regular ways of doing things. This refers to behaviour alone, while the other concept, *trait,* includes not only behaviour, but also material factors such as house types, weaving patterns, etc. Culture on this model is seen as a cluster of customs or traits. (See John Gillin, *The Ways of Men,* 1948; on traits see, for example, Leslie Spier, 'The Sun Dance of the Plains Indians', *American Museum of Natural History, Anthropological Papers,* 16, No.7, 1921.) Sociologically inclined British anthropologists have, in some cases, continued to recognize the central importance of custom in regulating behaviour (see M. Gluckman, *Custom and Conflict in Africa,* 1955). By and large, however, British anthropolo-gists have seen culture as either the *content* of social relations (R. Firth, *Elements of Social Organization,* 1951) or have seen social structure as one way of looking at culture. These distinctions have been discussed by Gregory Bateson in *Naven, 1936.*

The concentration on items of culture led to several

questions. The earliest of these concerned the origin and distribution of traits and customs. Thus, for example, many nineteenth century writers sought for the 'origins' of religion, the state, marriage, etc. (see, for example, H. Spencer, *Principles of Sociology,* 1876). There are two distinct theories in this field. One held that men were everywhere psychologically similar, and that similar problems called forth similar responses. This explained the widespread occurrence of similar customs throughout the world. (See Tylor, *op. cir.)* The other held that man's inventiveness was limited, and that most traits were invented once and then 'diffused' to. the other parts of the world. (See W. J. Perry, *The Children of the Sun, 1923.)*

Dissatisfaction with the above 'fragmentary' approaches to culture led to a concentration on *pattern* and *function* in the integration of cultures. Here we must distinguish between Culture, a property of the human race, and *a* culture, which is generally taken to be the distinctive way of life of a particular set of hwnan beings. (Note that a *sub-culture* is generally taken to mean a section of a *National* culture: e.g. The culture of an immigrant group.) The evolutionary and diffusionist approaches had taken the whole field ofhwnan culture as their subject matter. Malinowski, however, urged that understanding of specific cultures should be the aim of anthropology (see the article 'Culture', in the *Encyclopaedia of the Social Sciences).* He argued for an analysis of cultures through the 'function' of each element or custom in the total culture. (See his foreword to the third edition of *The Sexual Life of Savages,* 1932.) In America the same concentration on the integration of whole cultures was summed up in Ruth Benedict's *Patterns of Culture,* 1934. This stressed the idea of *cultural relativism,* that is, the principle that a culture can only be understood in its own terms, and that standards from other cultures cannot be applied to it. It also stressed the idea that culture moulded personality, and that ideas of normality and deviance were relative to particular cultures.

This idea has since been challenged by, for example, Robert Redfield in *The Primitive World and its Transformations,* 1953, and from being primarily concerned with cultural *differences* anthropologists have come to be interested in the possibilities of cultural *universals.*

The stress on the cultilral moulding of personality led to the develop-ment of a school of 'culture and personality' which concentrated on the development of the individual. It incorporated much of psychoanalysis (see Freud's *Civilization and its Discontents,* 1930). It received a stimulus from Margaret Mead (see, e.g. *Sex and Temperament in Three Primitive Societies,* 1935), and from the collaboration of anthropologist and psychiatrist in A. Kardiner and R. Linton, *The Psychological Frontiers of Society,* 1945. For a swnmary and assessment.

There has recently been a revival of interest in the evolution of culture-though not in terms of a search for origins. There are two branches, the 'ecological' represented by the work of Julian Steward *(Theory of Culture Change,* 1955) and the 'technological' as in the work of Leslie White *(The Science of Culture,* 1949). The latter has worked out an approach to cultural evolution which stresses the *autonomy* of culture (see also his *The Evolution of Culture,* 1959). Studies of long-run cultural changes figure in A. L. Kroeber's *Configurations of Culture C"owth,* 1944. An influential concept in this sphere has been that of *culture lag.* The central idea here is that various elements in a culture change at different rates, and so integration may be far from perfect. (See W. F. Ogburn, *Social Change,* 1922.)

A pre-occupation stemming originally from the trait approach to culture is that of *culture areas.* Here there is an attempt to mark out geo-graphical areas in which there is a high consistency of traits, and which differ recognizably from neighbouring areas. Thus, for example, in America, the *plains* culture area is distinguished from the *northwest coast*, the *northeastern woodlands*, etc. (See A. L. Kroeber, *Cultural and Natural Areas of Native North America*, 1939.) For South America, see J. Steward and L. C. Faron, *Native Peoples 0/ South America*, 1959; for Africa, G. P. Murdock, *Africa: Its Peoples and their Culture History, 1959.*

A more recent interest has been in the role of language in culture, stemming from the work of Edward Sapir (*Language*, 1921) and Benjamin Lee Whorf (*Language, Thought and Reality*, 1956). For a recent summary see D. H. Hymes (ed.) *Language in Culture and Society, 1964.*

The best discussion of the concept of culture is in Kroeber and Kluck-hohn, *op. cit.*, but this is difficult to obtain. There is a lot of discussion in A. L. Kroeber's *Anthropology* (1948 edition), and most text-books on cultural anthropology discuss the term. (See, for example, Melville J. Herskovits, *Cultural Anthropology*, 1955.) There are a number of useful papers in R. Linton (ed.) *The Science 0/ Man in the World Crisis*, 1945.

Custom The term *custom* refers to established modes of thought and action. This general term is used by anthropologists at various levels of abstrac-tion. By its use attention is directed to: the routine acts of daily life; the rules implicit in routine; the cultural patterns discernible in repetitive acts; and the distinctive nature of the whole culture. Let us take these in turn.

M. Fortes, stressing that 'the paramount concern of social and cultural anthropology is with tl:;le phenomenon of custom' avers that the research-er's 'main task is to observe and record the minutiae of custom and conduct in their context of social relations' (M. Fortes, 'Graduate Study and Research', in D. G. Mandelbaum, G. W. Lasker and E. M. Albert, 'The Teaching of Anthropology', *American Anthropological Association Memoir* 94, 1963). His emphasis is that of B. Malinowski who wrote of the 'im-ponderabilia of actual life', those daily routines, those conversational tones, those 'series of phenomena of great importance which cannot possibly be recorded by questioning or computing documents, but have to be observed in their full actuality' (*Argonauts 0l the Western Pacific,* 1922, p. 18). W. G. Sumner, \,.iting in 1906, regarded the formation of the folkways as due to 'the frequent repetition of petty acts' motivated by interset producing 'habit in the individual and custom in the group' (*Folkways,* 1960, pp. 18 and 19).

Malin'owski called for 'the study by direct observation of the rules of custom organically connected' and existing 'in the chain of social transac-tions' (*Crime and Custom in Savage Society,* 1926, p. 125. Cf. J. Beattie, *Other Cultures,* 1964, pp. 168-70). Sumner, too, emphasized the regulative force of the folkways, calling them mores 'when they include a judgment that they are conducive to societal welfare, and when they exert a coercion on the individual to conform to them'.

Cybernetics A branch of natural science concerned with the self-maintenance and self-control of systems, both mechanical and organic, through a feed-back process. It also includes the study of communication of information in such systems. This line of enquiry was advanced by the publication of N. Wiener's book *Cybernetics or Control and Communica-tion in the Animal and the Machine,* 1949. It has been described by G. T. Guilbaud in his book *What is Cybernetics?,* 1959. Its possible relationship to sociological research is discussed by D. G. MacRae in 'Cybernetics and Social Science', *British Journal of Sociology.*

D

Deconstruction A concept central to post-modernism, this is a process of rigorously analyzing and making apparent the assumptions, judgments and values that underlie social arrangements and intellectual ideas. Authors such as J. Derrida reject the idea that there is any correspondence between texts and truth, suggesting that tests (e.g.: the writing of Marx or Plato) have no objective links to external events. This being so these texts are not used to learn about the external events or to evaluate those events. Rather the text is only examined internally to search for the hidden text (or subtext) which given meaning.

Defining the Situation Refers to the process through which humans go when trying to comprehend the social situations in which they find themselves and deciding on what values and norms are relevant in guiding social interaction. If one contrasts macro-structural studies and symbolic interactionism, this conept is associated with the latter. The structural view tends rather to focus on the situation individuals are in, not on their definition of the situation.

Delicts In the sociological treatment of legal systems it is necessary to made a distinction other than that between criminal and civil offences, for what is regarded as a civil offence in one society may be a private matter in another, even although it is considered a wrong. A. R. Radcliffe--Brown in an article on 'Primitive Law' in the *Encyclopaedia of the Social Sciences,* 1933, introduced the distinction between the law of *public deliets* and the law of *private delicts.* This allows for a sociological dis-cussion of the different types of sanctions aroused by offences of each type, even when the actual offence may in one society be socially regarded as of a different category from that in another. Murder, for instance, is a public delict in modern Western societies, but among some people it is a private delict.

Delinquent An adjective commonly used to describe minor criminal acts and infractions of regulations (for example, failure to renew a ~ireless licence) and behaviour which, while not illegal, is generally regarded as anti-social or immoral (such as adultery). It is also applied to individuals in the same sense.

The expression *juvenile delinquent* usually refers to an individual who has been, or is liable to be, brought before a juvenile court, either because he has committed a criminal offence, or for some other reason within the jurisdiction of the court (for example, being 'beyond the control' of his parents or guardians).

Demography This word is defined in the United Nations *Multilingual Demographic Dictionary* (New York, 1958) as 'the scientific study of human populations, primarily with respect to their size, their structure and their development'. The word was probably first used by the French-man A. Guillard in his textbook, *Elements de Statistique Humaine.* W. F. Willcox *(Studies in American Demography,* 1940) quotes a number of different definitions of the word, varying among themselves, some of them more limited than the definition given above. Today the word is generally used to denote the study of phenomena connected with human popula-tions, such as births, marriages, deaths, migration and the factors which influence them. Very occasionally, the term is used by biologists in the study of animal populations. It is conventional to date the beginning of demography as a science in 1662. In that year John Graunt published his *Natural and Political Observations on the Bills of Mortality,* in which he used the returns of deaths in different parishes of London, to deduce some generalizations about human populations. He showed that the proportions of deaths attributed to certain causes tended to be constant, and attempted to study mortality by constructing a life table (or table of mortality) which follows a group of children born at the same moment of time, until the last of them has died. He was one of the first to recognize the existence of certain statistical regularities in human existence. His work on mortality was followed up by the medical statisticians of the seventeenth and eighteenth centuries who were interested in the study of health, disease and death. Interest in these subjects was probably stimulated by the development of life insurance during that period; moreover, in the conditions then pre-vailing, the level of mortality was probably the chief determinant of the rate of population growth. The principles underlying the construction of tables of mortality were already understood by Halley in the late seven-teenth century even though he lacked adequate data, and methods of constructing such tables were continually improved, until by the middle of the nineteenth century the methods of studying mortality had reached a stage of development which has changed but little since.

Developments in census-taking and vital registration in Europe, during the nineteenth century, led to a considerable improvement in the quality of basic data available to demographers, and stimulated the study of changes in population structure and of reproductivity. Mathematical methods came to be applied culminating in the development of the stable popula-tion model by A. J. Lotka in the early years of the present century. In this model, fertility and mortality rates are held constant over time, and it is shown that under these conditions a population tends towards 'stability', in the sense that the proportionate age composition of the population remains the same, and that the population changes at a constant annual 'stable' or 'intrinsic' rate. Whilst stable populations are not normally met with in present conditions, this model of development is useful in setting a norm against which the growth of actual populations can be studied. There is now a whole branch of the subject known as *formal demography* or *demographic analysis,* in which quantitative relations among demographic phenomena are treated in abstraction from their association with other phenomena.

Denomination A term used by sociologists to distinguish a type of religious organization. A *denomination* or church-type of religious organ-ization is contrasted to a sect-type. The word *Church* comes from the Greek word *ecclesia,* which in turn was used by Greek-speaking Christians to designate the reconstituted, Messianic, people of God. Such a local church was always conscious of its representative character, i.e. repre-sentative of the whole Church of God. To be sure it often displayed some sect-like qualities, in that it was often persecuted and to that extent represented people who were indifferent, if not hostile, to the prevailing social norms of the Roman world. Since the time of Constantine, when the Church acquired official standing, the connotation has altered somewhat, for its sociologically characteristic feature is an accommodation and association with other institutions. Denominations represent fragments of the Holy Catholic Church, but each displays church-like qualities, as distinct from sect-like ones. The membership is open, although there is a ceremony of initiation, tolerance towards other denominations is mani-fested, usually there is a professional ministry, although lay participation in religious acts of worship is permitted, and sometimes special tasks are given to selected laymen whilst others are retained exclusively by the professional ministry. In anyone local denomination there tends to be social compatibility among the members, but in theory and often in fact the denominational congregation is representative of the society at large.

Dependent Development A central concept of dependency theory. Rather than seeing the world's nations dividing economic labour and interacting as equal partners, dependent development suggests that some nations are able to impose unequal exchanges on others and thus retard the economic development of these nations or make their development dependent on stronger or more economically advanced nations. Dependent devlopment has typically involved the exporting of primary resources.

Descent *Descellt* is the term used to describe the recognized connection between a person and his ancestors, where the term *ancestor* denotes the person from whom one is descended. Such descent may be reckoned through the father's family or through the mother's family or through both families. In the first case we speak of *patrilineal descent* and in the second case of *matrilineal descent*. If it is either one or the other we speak generally of *unilineal descent*. Some writers use the terms *agnatic* instead of *patrilineal* and *uterine* instead of *matrilineal*. Where descent is counted through both lines we speak of *bilateral descent*. It should be pointed out that whilst descent is based on biological relationships, some such relationships may be stressed to the exclusion of others. Furthermore, sometimes fictitious biological relationships are assumed, and of course there is also the practice of adoption which may well include a person not biologically related in the descent system. .

Descriptive Systems *See Classification Systems.*

Deviancy, Social Deviancy In its widest sense this term may be applied to any behaviour which is not consonant with those expectations and norms for individual conduct which are shared and recognized within a social system. Most theoretical treatments of deviancy are concerned with behaviour which is both infrequent and dysfunctional; that is to say, in breach of mores or other social rules which are commonly regarded as necessary to cohesion and order within a social group. Idiosyncratic conduct is not always seen as deviancy; M. B. Clinard suggests that the term should be reserved for 'those situations in which behaviour is in a disapproved direction, and of sufficient degree to exceed the tolerance limit of the community'

(Sociology of Deviant Behaviour, 1963).

Early accounts of the origins of deviant behaviour (such as those of Thomas Hobbes and Sigmund Freud) reflected a belief in the existence of an essential conflict between the desires and impulses of the individual and the constraints imposed by membership of a social group. Deviancy was thus regarded as the result of partial failure of social controls to restrain the expression of natural impulses. In contrast, the modern sociological theory of deviant behaviour, exemplified by the work of R. K. Merton *(Social Theory and Social Structure,* 1949) treats it as the product of the pattern of institutions in a given society. Merton distin-guishes two key elements of the social structure: the goals and rewards which are recognized as appropriate and commendable objectives for individual striving, the attainment of which confers status, and those methods of achieving them which are regarded as legitimate. In some societies individuals located at diverse points in the social order are expected to pursue different goals, and their status depends upon the degree of success which they attain in doing so; in other social groups (particularly those in which a high degree of mobility obtains) similar goals and criteria of personal achievement are prescribed for all. But, for various reasons, opportunities for attaining these goals by legitimate means may be very unequally distributed in a society. High rates of deviant behaviour will be characteristic of those social groups in which access to legitimate ways of achieving success is limited but pressure upon the individual to pmsue socially-defined goals is high. Thus Merton describes aberrant behaviom as 'a symptom of dissociation between cultmally prescribed aspirations and socially structmed avenues for realizing these aspirations'.

Diffusion The term *diffusion* as used by anthropologists refers to the spread of elements of cultme, either singly or in a complex, from local group to local group. It is less frequently used to refer to dissemination within a group.

When we observe that a cultme trait occmring in group *A* is similar to a trait in group *B*, can we postulate diffusion and thus an historical con-nection between the two groups? Or were the traits developed indepen-dently? William Robertson (1721-1793) suggested criteria for estin1ating connection. Two groups, although remote from one another but found to be in similar climates, ' ... to be in the same state of society and to resemble each other in the degree of their improvement, . . . must feel the same wants and exert the same endeavoms to supply them ... the same ideas and sentimonts will arise in their ininds . . .' No connection need be assumed. On the other hand, there may be 'arbitrary institutions', not deriving from natural wants. If' ... a perfect agreement ... should be discovered one inight be led to suspect that they were connected by some affinity.'

For G. E. Smith (1871-1937) and W. J. Perry (1887-1949), taking an extreme position, there was but one *A* whose traits diffused to many societies. The culture of ancient Egypt, a veritable alpha, was deemed to be the radiant source of a world-wide diffusion. 'It can be shown that the first food-producing communities in all parts of the world outside the area of the Ancient East, especially those that could be reached by sea, possessed a culture so similar to that of Egypt in the Pyramid Age that little doubt can exist as to their mode of origin.' W. J. Perry, *The GrolVth of Civilization*, 2nd ed, rev., London, 1926, p. 76. See R. B. DixOD, *The Building of Cultures*, 1928, and R. H. Lowie, *The History of Ethnological Theory*, 1937.

Dilthey, Wilhelm (1833-1911) German philosopher; his new method-ology for the study of society influenced Max Weber in his notion of *verstehen*. He argued for a sharp division between natural sciences, aiming at external, factual description, and causal-law explanation, and social sciences, concerned with empathic, intuitive understanding of the inner meaning of cultural phenomena. The basis of the latter he held to be an analytical and descriptive psychology able to facilitate, through its systematic knowledge of consciousness, an understanding both of struc-tural (or organic) unity of individual and social life and of its historical development as manifested in cultural systems of art, science and religion; see, for example, *The Life of Schleiermacher*, 1870. He believed *Zeitgeist* determined attitudes of man as he develops through time.

Discontinuity; Social Discontinuity This term was used by Ruth Benedict in a paper she published in 1938 in *Psychiatry*, Vol. 1, and which was reprinted in *Personality il/ Nature, Society and Culture*.

Kluckhohn and H. A. Murray, 1949, revised edition 1953. Benedict contrasts continuities and discontinuities in cultural conditioning. Thus societies differ in the manner of instilling a sense of responsibility in their members; some do it regularly and gradually, others display sharp dis-continuities, requiring little responsible sense for a number of years and then suddenly requiring a great deal to be shown. Similarly, she pointed to differences in dominant and submissive behaviour and, again, she indi·cated contrasting sexual roles. In both these cases some societies display sharp variations in cultural conditioning and in some the discontinuity in conditioning is striking. Thus some societies that practise long and elaborate initiation ceremonies may display discontinuities, a boy being extremely submissive towards others before but dominant after the initiation. In our own society the bearing of responsibility may sharply change, and at arbitrary periods in a person's life, from a state where little responsibility is borne to one where a considerable amount is laid on a person. In modern industrial societies there are variations within the society, some of them according to social class membership.

Discrimination; Racial Discrimination Colloquially the term *discrimina-tion*, without the prefix *racial*, may be used to mean a simple differentiation between people or situations on the basis of an objective criterion, e.g. age-as a qualification for the franchise or measured intelligence and·attain-ment for entry to a University. Furthermore, certain types of discrimina-tory legislation may be designed to afford special privileges or protection to particular groups who are believed to be less able to defend their rights or interests than others, e.g. factory legislation governing hours and conditions of work for women and young persons. In colonial administra-tion legislation governing the ownership or Jale of land may discriminate in favour of an indigenous population to protect it (often too late) against economic exploitation by immigrant settlers. In sociology the term is used more often to mean the use, by a super-ordinate group, of its superior power to impose customary or legal restrictions and deprivations upon a subordinate group in order to maintain a situation of privilege and inequality. Such discrimination may be exercised by men against women, by dominant political, national, or religious groups or by one socially defined racial group against another. It may involve a restriction of franchise, enforced residential segregation, differential access to educational or employment opportunities and the imposition of other customary and legal disabilities. In the modern world racial discrimination is still widespread although increasingly resisted by its victims and condemned by liberal opinion. A full discussion of the situation in Britain and Commonwealth countries will be found in A. H. Richmond, *The Colour Problem* (rev. 00.) 1961, and concerning the United States in Gunnar Myrdal's *An American Dilemma* (rev. ed.) 1962.

Division of Labour The phrase refers to the division of a work process into a number of parts, each part undertaken by a separate person or group of persons. The expression *division 0/ labour* was used by Adam Smith in his *Inquiry into the Nature and Causes*

The specifically sociological use of the term was initiated by Emile Durkheim in his famous thesis *De la division du travail social, 1893,* translated *The Division 0/ Labour,* 1933.

In this work Durkheim almost equates it with social differentiation and points to the significance of the growth of this phenomenon for social evolution, as societies charac-terized by considerable division of labour differ from others in displaying an *organic* cohesion rather than a *mechanical* type of solidarity. The contrast is drawn sharply in Durkheim's thought. Moreover, the signifi-cance of social relationships in occupational groups for the development and maintenance of moral ideas is emphasized both in his preface to the second edition of this book, and in his later works.

Divorce In Western societies and in the United States of America, *divorce* has come to mean the process by which a marriage, recognized as valid, can be revoked in the lifetime of the partners who then revert to single status and are free to remarry. *Divorce* is thus distinguished (a) from *separation,* in which spouses are legally recognized as living in separate households but are not free to remarry since they retain their marital status, and (b) from *nullity:* the legal recognition that a marriage had not : u fact been valid. Not all cultures have so strict a concept of *divorce* and the concepts of *nullity, separation* and *divorce* often merge in the practice of some simpler societies. Nevertheless, it is quite clear that the vast majority of societies in all cultures do, in certain prescribed circumstances, allow the absolute dissolution of marital unions within the lifetime of the partners to the original contract and do allow subsequent remarriage.

The circumstances in which a divorce is granted differ a great deal from society to society and from one historical period to another. Among some peoples in eastern central Africa, the wife may divorce a husband who fails to sew her clothes. Until the eleventh century, according to Jewish law, a husband had the right to repudiate his wife at pleasure, whilst the wife had no right to divorce at all. In modern Israel, divorce by mutual consent is recognized by law, although it is vigorously resisted in England as almost certain to undermine the stability of marriage and the family.

It is, however, easier to point to the varying circumstances under which a valid marriage may be dissolved than to indicate the extent to which divorce is practised in any particular society. This arises partly through difficulties of precise definition of the concepts of both *marriage* and *divorce* in some societies and also from problems of interpreting crude statistics of divorce even in those societies where the concept is very precisely.

Dowry The wealth or possessions that a bride brings into the marrige. Thisis typicallya transfer of wealth from the bride's family to the husband.

Durkbeim, Emile Emile Durkheim was born near Strasbourg in 1858, graduated at the Ecole Normale, taught Sociology at the University of Bordeaux and then lectured on education and sociology in the Sorbonne from 1902 up till his death in 1917.

He was actively concerned with French politics throughout his life and particularly concerned to discover what values and principles should guide French education when it was placed on a secular basis. In these matters he inherited the collectivist tradition of social thought represented by de Maistre, St. Simon and Comte and reacted sharply against the individualist ideas of Herbert Spencer and the English Utilitarians. In his first major work *The Division of Labour* he reacted against the view that modern industrial society could be based simply upon contractual agree-ments between individuals motivated by self-interest and without any prior consensus. He agreed that the kind of consensus in modern society was different from that in simpler social systems but he saw both of these as types of social solidarity. The primitive form, mechanical solidarity was based upon the Conscience Collective, the modern form upon the Division of Labour, whose function was not the increase of individual utility or pleasure, but the imposition of a moral order.

The specific task of sociology according to Durkheim was to study not individual but social facts and the two main characteristics of social facts were (a) that they were external to the individual and (b) that they exer-cized constraint over his conduct. One of the main examples which Durkheim used in his *Rules of Sociological Method* to illustrate what he means by social facts is law and one of the features of law is that it has an existence separable from individual acts of law enforcement, so that it can be studied apart from the individual. But there are some social facts which do not have this obvious embodiment which is separable from study. In these cases the individual's conduct is influenced by a more diffuse 'collective current' and the best that the sociologist can do is to record its effects in the form of a statistical rate.

The danger of *anomie* and the importance society accords to preventing it is the mainspring of Durkheim's political writings. In his *Socialism and St. Simon* he sees the whole point of the socialist movement as lying not in a demand for common ownership but as a protest against the suffering of *anomie.* The restoration of a social order whose norms are meaningful to the individual who participates in it should, in Durkheim's view, be the main arm of modern politics. Thus in his *Professional Ethics and Civic Morals* he advocates a form of guild socialism.

As a teacher of education Durkheim was particularly concerned to analyse the nature of the constraint which the norms of society should exercise over the individual. His view of this changed and he came to think more and more, not of a blind external force, but of norms which became internalized. He saw the essence of the power of the norms to lie in their sacredness. In his final work *The Elementary Forms of Religious Life* he suggests that the whole concept of sacredness derived from the individual's experience of the social norms. What men called God was simply Society, which from a subjective point of view had all the character-istics normally attributed to the Deity.

To explain this Durkheim used ethnological evidence from the Australian tribes, amongst whom totems had the double characteristic of being regarded as sacred and being the badge or symbol of the clan.

Dual Career Damily Families in which both spouses are inthe outside labour force.

Due-Porcess Model An ideal type used to capture one side in the debate over the central values or practices of the criminal justice system. This model gives priority to values and practices that protect the rights of the offenders from the coercive power of the state. This protection would include strict regulation of police enforcement, independent and impartial judicial processes, and imposition of proportional and justifiable punishment.

Dysfunction *Function* has two dominant meanings in sociol-ogy. Its major use is to be seen in the following statement: 'The social function of religion is the maintenance of group solidarity.' *Herefunction* refers to the diagnosed objective consequence which a social phenomenon has for a wider system of which it is a part. *Manifestfunctions* are objective consequences for the system which are intended and recognized by the relevant participants; whilst *latent functions* are neither intended nor creognized. (See Robert K. Merton, 'Manifest and Latent Functions', in *Social Theory and Social Structure,* 1949, chapter 1). In order to distinguish between activities which contribute, on the one hand, to survival of social system patterns and, on the other, to their disturbance, a distinction is made respectively between *eufunctions* and *dysfunctions.* There are thus manifest and latent eufunctions and manifest and latent dysfunctions. Sometimes another possibility is invoked, namely that a set of activities may be of no particular consequence for the state of the system, and therefore, is neither eufunctional nor dysfunctional, as in William J. Goode, *Religion Among the Primitives.*

Function is also sometimes used as it is in mathematics.

When it is said that social phenomenon is a function of phenomenon *y* it is meant that *x* varies in proportion, as does *y*. Although this use must be distinguished from the first, the two are nevertheless related. This is because function as consequence for the state of the system implies that all social phenomena in a system are thought, at least initially, to be relevant to a consideration of its persistence. It is then but a short step to postulating that all pheno-mena in a system are interrelated and that a change in one area of a social system will have ramifications throughout the system. Thus function as consequence and function as related variation are often closely connected

E

Echo Generation Children born to the baby boomers. Those canadians born between 1980 and 1995.

Ecofeminism A set of ideas within the environmental movement. A basic assumption of this set of ideas is that patriarchal societies tend to associate women with nature and debase, or rape, both. Thus it is necessary for the environmental movement to overthrow patriarchal structures and ideologies in order to protect or enhance the natural environment.

Ecology; Social Ecology The word *ecology* is sometimes used as inter-changeable with *geographic environment* and, consequently, ecological studies are often limited to the study of the direct effect of environment on the material culture of peoples with simple technologies. But ecology is more than a study of man's material adaptation to his physical environ-ment. In botany, plant ecology is not only the study of plants in relation to soils and climate, but of plants in relation to plants and other living organisms in a particular environment. *Social ecology* is likewise con-cerned not only with the direct response to environment where tech-nology is unsophisticated, but also with the distribution and composition of groups necessary for the exploitation of natural resources, the indirect relationships which spring from these groupings, and the general concep-tualization of the cosmos associated with specific habitats. Conceived in these terms, *ecological studies* are extended to include modem urban societies; and such studies are concerned with the social relationship of people in relation to the constraints and permissiveness of urban habitat, and in relation to the environment of industry, its location, the limits it sets to domestic and local relationships, and the different types of social links associated with the various types of industrial technological processes.

Egalitarian;Eegalitarianism The word refers to a set of prescriptions of assumptions about desirable social relationships between individuals and groups. Egalitarianism, in more or less strong or weak forms, advocates equal treatment for equal cases and seeks to eliminate the use of irrelevant criteria in classifying cases. Examples of egalitarianism in social relation-ships are universal adult political franchise where race, religion, sex, wealth or educational level are held to be irrelevant criteria or the British National Health Service which, in principle, treats individuals equally according to the criteria of medical need and regards capacity or willing-ness to pay as irrelevant. Application of egalitarian doctrine varies according to the forms of inequality in different societies. In modern industrial countries the anti-thesis of equality is usually held to be social stratification. The principle of citizenship (with its claim to equality before the law, universal franchise and basic security against economic, physical and cultural deprivation) may be seen as the champion of equality against the inequalities of social class.

Eidos; Social Eidos *Eidos* is derived from Gregory Bateson's *Naven, 1936,* a book about a primitive people, and was used to denote the main features and characteristics of a body of ideas prevalent in that society. Charles Madge adapted it and refers to *social eidos* as 'that part of eidos which relates to social institutions and activities'.

Ego In anthropology this refers to the individual from whom the networks of kinship and family relationship and descent are reckoned and traced. In psychology the term is used to referto the self of the individual and the way they have constructed their personality and identity insociety. In Freud's psychoanalytic theory the ego is the outcome of th eindividual's struggle toadapt their basic drves (the 'id') to the imperative control of society and culture (the 'super ego'). Between their drives and the coercive influence of social expectation, individuals create a sphere of unique personality.

Elderly Abuse Acts of violence (or neglect) directed at the elderly (often by family members).

Elective Affinity The expression *elective affinity* was first used in physical science to refer to the property of a substance whereby it has a tendency to combine with one substance rather than another. J. W. von Goethe employed the term in a different context.

The term as used by Max Weber in his studies in the sociology of religion, denotes a view of society and culture allowing for greater weight being placed on the effects of human thought on social events than most other theories of human society. To begin with the theory holds that ideas are undetermined in their origin, but that only when circumstances are of such a kind as to render them relevant to public and social issues do they become popular and effective in determining social change. Some, like Max Scheler, have held that ideas are like platonic essences, existing in a realm of their own, but that they only become effective through the mediation of a few outstanding men of thought and action, or through an elite which adopts these ideas. (See his *Die Wissenslormen und die Gesell-schal t*, 1926.) Without being attached to Scheler's metaphysical views, Max Weber believed that the generation of ideas was not necessarily related to social and economic conditions, but was of the nature of an intellectual adventure. Yet he was convinced that for ideas to be influential appropriate social conditions must prevail. Thus a mutual accommodation between the incipient working class movements of the early nineteenth century and the availability of a socialist ideology is an illustration of elective affinity. Other writers who have been concerned with the subject include Karl Marx, Alfred Weber, Karl Mannheim and Alfred von Martin.

Empirical; Empiricism A widely used definition of *empirical* in sociology contrasts the term with *theoretical* and *analytical*. Here a field study, which mayor may not have an explicit theory, is seen as a different order of inquiry from that which either (a) sets out a conceptual language for analysing social relations, e.g. Talcott Parsons' discussion of social action is largely of this nature, or (b) outlines a theory or explanation of some aspect of social life without testing its truth or falsity. In a conceptual language the concepts are analytical in that they constitute decisions to use words in certain precise ways. The language is thus a structure of stipulative definitions. For example, Weber's distinction between class, as a logical category of people with similar 'life chances', and status group, as a group of people who view themselves as being equivalent in status or prestige, is such an analytical distinction. It is then a further task to see whether such a distinction is useful when dealing with social reality. In this view of *empirical*, therefore, a field study requires an additional pro-cedure, namely to define further these verbally precise concepts in terms of measurement operations, i.e. to 'operationalize' them. A theory, which consists not only of precisely defined concepts, as with a conceptual language, but of propositions asserting relations between the concepts and of deductively related propositions, similarly needs operationalizing and remains 'theoretical' until it is so brought into contact with social reality. This definition of *empirical*, therefore, amounts to a distinction betwecn inquiry, whether a thcory as such or simply a conceptual language, which has hoen operationalized and tested by the social reality, and that which lacks operationalization and whose usefulness or whose validity is therefore still in question.

While this first definition of *empirical* focuses on the specific notion of operationalization as a criterion of testability, a second use of the tcrm has a more gencral sense, meaning simply inquiry about the world in contrast to analysis which is asserting nothing about the world, namely pure mathematics and symbolic logic. In this view both natural and social science are empirical because they are asserting propositions and intro-ducing theories about social and natural reality, whose validity is testable by experience, Le. observed facts, whereas logic and mathematics are empty, deductive systems, whose propositions are necessarily true. In the sense that they do not apply specifically to one area of worldly inquiry, mathematics and logic have no content in themselves and it is their very emptiness, the fact that we can make the content of the symbols vary with our particular purpose, that allows them to be so useful to the sciences in explaining the nature of the world. It was to this empty symbolic quality of mathematics in contrast to substantive, empirical inquiry that Bertrand Russell referred when he spoke of a mathematician as being someone who never knew what he was talking about or whether what he said was true. This second use of the term *empirical* parallels the philosopher's distinction between synthetic statements which are about the world and whose validity depends on the world, and analytic statements, which are not about the world and whose validity is established solely by examining the logical structure of the statement.

A further use of *empirical* is central to the related term, *empiricism.* Here an empirical inquiry means one that lacks or has not made explicit the theory guiding its procedures. Such inquiry merely establishes an isolated proposition or empirical generalization, for example, that a greater proportion of manual workers vote Labour than vote Conservative at the General Election. This is not a theory or explanation of the behaviour pattern, but rather the problem to be explained.

Endogamy A practice of marrying within a defined group, e.g. a kinship category, a tribe, a social class or a religious denomination. As in the case of *exogamy* the practice may be preferred or prescribed.

Environmental Studies This term covers a number of recent develop-ments in several British universities. From the sociological standpoint, studies of the social and economic environment are implied; it is essentially centred on human beings whose welfare is related to housing and sanitation on the one hand, the size, spacing and characteristics of the assemblage of buildings in which they live, the resultant accessibility in respect of sources of goods, ideas and services, both within the urban or rural community, or externally over the country, to the capital or its ports. In some universities such studies are taken care of under the term 'urban geography'. Social psychology may be regarded by many as a function of the man-made environment, including not merely the buildings but also the cultural institutions and even the traditions and customs of the com-munity. Some would deem this to fall within the field of social anthro-pology.

In many training colleges and schools the term might best be translated as the study of local history, partly through field investigation which commonly takes the form of 'educative walks'; partly, through texts, documents, and population statistics; such studies can easily lead to simple-minded amateur sociology, or to those first stages of comparison which may encourage a student to probe more deeply.

To an architect or town-planner the study of the built environment is implied, with special regard to the efficiency with which its purposes appear to be fulfilled. This implies study of the internal environment and may overlap the domain of environmental physiology. In recent years the reactions of the human body to environment have been widely studied, largely through the need to maintain fitness and energy, both mental and physical, in wartime under stress; allied with this the study of the efficacy of methods of protection, whether through clothing, buildings, heating or air-conditioning, or protection against excess of damaging radiation.

The study of the characteristics and the changes that have taken place and are continuing to take place, and in the external, or outdoor physical environment makes yet another interpretation of a more fundamental character, involving as it does nothing less than the whole of that Quater-nary period in which intelligent modem man has evolved and in which he has developed his techniques, from the use of fire to that of nuclear energy. Essentially this makes a more objective approach which is the domain of the geologist, the ecologist and meteorologist, rather than the social anthropologist, the urban geographer or the sociologist.

Equilibrium; Social Equilibrium *Equilibrium* means a state of balance of a system, implying that there is a normal state with respect to both internal balance and the relationship of the system to its environment. The concept was diffused to the social sciences from mechanics, al-though similar notions, such as harmony and adjustment, had long been prominent among social analysts. The notion of equilibrium even has elevanco to the work of Karl Marx. Marx maintained that capitalist ocieties were inherently unstable, the instability residing in contradic-ions, i.e. lack of balance, between the technological spheres of such soci-:ties and the system of property ownership. In modern terminology, ;apitalist societies were regarded as being in a state of unstable equilibrium which, cumulatively, would lead to breakdown and the subsequent establishment of a non-contradictory social order, i.e. a state of stable equilibrium.

Equilibrium is a term used by economists, such as Alfred Marshall, and by sociologists, notably Herbert Spencer (*First Principles,* 1862, chapter 22) during the latter part of the nineteenth century. Its usage at that time was prompted by the desire to systematize the social sciences through the theoretical construction of models of the inter-relationships between social phenomena. Another inspirational source was the desire to depict the most efficient or ideal order of things. However, the most influential formulation of the concept of *social equilibrium* has been that advanced by Vilfredo Pareto in his *Trattato di soci%gia generale,* 1916, translated *The Mind and Society,* 1935, See Vol. 4. Pareto, who was both an economist and a sociologist and who had written a thesis on the equilibrium of elastic solids, said that a social system is in equilibrium if, when 'it is artificially subjected to some modification different from the modification it undergoes normally, a reaction at once takes place tending to restore it to its real, its normal state'. Three converging developments brought the concept of social equilibrium into the core of American sociology in the 19308 and 19408, firstly, among anthropologists, the shift towards the ahistorical analysis of stable interrelationships in the social structures of primitive societies; secondly, in the upsurge of interest in Pareto's work, notably at Harvard (see L. J. Henderson, *Pareto's General Sociology,* 1935). Finally, cross-fertilization from the work of biologists and physi-ologists led to a growing interest in the self-regulating properties of biological and social systems, for which the term *homeostatis* was coined.

Estates A form of stratification established by law.

Ethnocentrism A word coined by W. G. Sumner and used in his book *Folkways,* 1906, M a technical term for the 'view of things in which one's own group is the centre of everything, and all others are scaled and rated with reference to it'. Sumner used the term in connection with his distinc.-tion between in-groups and out-groups, and associated with it both patriotism and chauvinism.

Ethnocentrism, like several other terms coined by Swnner,

has been much used by sociologists and social psychologists, notably in recent years by T. W. Adorno *et alia* in *The Authoritarian Persoruzlity,* 1950, where a means of scaling the degree of ethnocentrism is presented. Sumner merely described the phenomenon as leading a people 'to exaggerate and intensify everything in their own folkways which is peculiar and which differen-tiates them from others'. Consequently, he observed, it therefore strength-ens the folkways. Adorno and his associates have shown that it may be regarded as a dimension of the personality and be subject to measurement.

Ethnography; Ethnology Today it is usual to refer to the descriptive account of the way of life ofa particular people as *ethnography.* However, since descriptive accounts are analytic as well, in Britain the term *.ethno-graphic monograph* has come to be used in a wider sense for the detailed studies by social anthropologists of the way of life of particular peoples. Whilst it is generally agreed that the sphere of ethnography is concerned with descriptive accounts and that of social anthropology with structural analysis, there is considerable overlap of techniques in many studies.

In the U.S.A., however, the overlap is with *ethnology.* In the first chapter of his book, *Man and His Works,* 1948, M. J. Herskovits sees the distinction between ethnography as 'the description of individual cultures', and ethnology as 'the comparative study of culture and the investigation of the theoretical problems that arise out of the analysis of human custom'.

Ethology A term used by J. S. Mill in his famous book, *A System of Logic,* 1843, to describe what he called a science of character. In the scheme of the social sciences Mill envisaged the need for a study of the human mind in relation to its environment, which would account for differences in men's characters or what is now called their personalities. The science did develop and is usually known as social psychology; the term ethology was not adopted by other sociological writers, although today it is used sometimes to refer to animal behaviour studies.

Eutrophication Oxygen depletionof water due to overfertilization.

Eugenics The endeavour to develop principles of good breeding is probably as old as man, but its scientific status was established with the publication of Charles Darwin's *Origin of Species*, 1859, and its application to human beings was attempted by Francis Galton a few years later. In his words, the science of eugenics is to study those factors which 'may improve or impair the racial qualities of future generations, either physically or mentally'. This endeavour was thought to be advanced in so far as it was possible to learn more of the laws of heredity, to study the factors underlying human marriages, to examine birth rates and to build up a body of knowledge based on case studies of families. The study of eugenics was later pursued by Karl Pearson, an early English social statistician.

The movement was popular in the pre-war period, but suffered by being associated with racial theories, especially those of Hitler Germany, and from a tendency to over-emphasize the importance of sound racial stock for human progress. In short, many of the ideas put forward by supporters of eugenics ran counter to egalitarian notions.

Euphoria; Social Euphoria A term used to denote a state of social well-being. It was used by A. R. Radcliffe-Brown in his discussion of primitive law in the *Encyclopaedia of the Social Sciences*, 1933. Here the distinction is made between a condition of *social dysphoria* which results from the commital of an offence by an individual in society. whereby some strong moral sentiment is outraged, and a state of *social euphoria* which can only be brought about, he argued, if the penal sanction is enforced and the offender punished. Only in this manner, it is maintained, can the com-munity be reconstituted. The theory owes much to Durkheim's analysis of repressive law.

Exogamy A practice of marrying outside a defined group. Such mar-riages may be preferential or prescriptive. The group may be a kinship group, a tribal segment or a village.

Expressive; Expressive Orientation It is in small group studies that the adjective *expressive* is mainly used. Thus R. F. Bales in his *Interaction Process Analysis,* 1951, and this author together with T. Parsons and E. A. Shils in *Working Papers in the Theory of Action,* 1952, use the term to denote behaviour of persons in groups in which emotional preferences are expressed, such as liking and disliking, or whero friendly or unfriendly remarks are made. This analytical term is used in connection with others such as *adaptive* or *instrumental behaviour.* Some groups are primarily task-oriented as in the case of a work group, a committee or a school class, whilst nevertheless displaying from time to time expressive be-haviour. Other groups have mainly an *expressive orientation* as in the case of a group of friends meeting for coffee; the term therefore assists in the analysis of group behaviour as may be seen in J. Klein, *The Study of Groups,* 1956, where the term is extensively used.

Exponential Growth A geometric rate of progression which has the potential of producing a very fast rise (or an "explosion") in the numbers of a population experiencing such growth.

External System In his analysis of *The Human Group,* 1951, Homans makes use of the concepts of the *external* and *internal systems.* Briefly, he argues that it is useful to consider the structure of a social group as consisting of an *external system,* which is defined as the elements of the system (activities, interactions and sentiments), and their inter-relationships in so far as they constitute a means of maintaining the system in its environment. Thus a group of workmen are gathered to-gether in a workshop to work, there is a procedure for carrying out tasks, some division of labour, a reward scheme which satisfies them enough to keep them at work, etc. These various actions, interactions and sentiments combine to constitute the external system. Yet over and above this there is an *internal system,* for there are other actions, interactions and senti-ments in addition which develop out of the external system, an elaboration of the system, in fact, and this system reacts back upon the external system to modify it. Thus a work group will engage in social activities, exchange information not relevant to the task, and develop sentiments of personal attachment among the members and so further social organization, of an informal type, develops.

F

Fabians The Fabian Society was one of the earliest socialist organiza-tions in England and has been one of the longest lived in the world. Its history has been largely that of a small core of its membership, and indeed could largely be told through the biographies of Sidney Webb (Lord Passfield), Beatrice Potter (Mrs. Webb), George Bernard Shaw, G. D. H. Cole and Margaret Postgate (Mrs. Cole). The influence of the Fabians as individuals, and on the whole they sought influence, not power, has been very great, but the influence of the Society has often been over-estimated. The socialism of the Fabians has always been gradualist, not revo-lutionary; bureaucratic rather than democratic; technical and research based rather than ethical or emotional; elitist rather than popular; Machiavellian more than liberal. Rather strangely the society grew out of a singularly utopian body, the Fellowship of the New Life. Dissidents from the Fellowship formed the Fabian Society in 1883, which Shaw joined in 1884 and Webb the following year. The society was called after Fabius who had commanded Roman armies against the Carthaginians, and who by delay and ruse had kept the armies of the republic in the field during a time of defeat, waging a war of attrition. The Fabians forgot or ignored that it had taken not a Fabius but a Scipio to vanquish Hannibal. From the beginning the Fabians repudiated Marxism. Webb rightly saw three great tendencies in the advanced capitalist societies of his time (N.B. he had direct knowledge of Imperial Germany and its social legis-lation), two of which the Marxists ignored or denied. These were (1) the increasing real income of wage workers over time, (2) the growth of administrative or bureaucratic regulation in industry and in local and national government, and (3) the increasing role of monopoly in industry, commerce and finance. Once Mrs. Webb became active in the Society they added to these concerns two further elements: (4) a reappraisal of the part played by the Trade Unions and Co-operative Societies in working class life and in the economy, and (5) a solid if limited concern with the conduct of social and economic research to increase the efficacy of their propaganda and the cogency of their programme.

From the first of these points they deduced the possibility of a gradual evolution of socialism within the framework of existing society. From the second they derived a contempt for much of the ordinary activity of politics, and the idea of the permeation of administration and admini-strators with Fabian ideas. Probably no group of comparable ability has ever so consciously believed in the capacity and ultimate power of bureau-crats and experts. From the third they derived the idea, by way of a formulation of Ricardo's theory of rent which Shaw brilliantly expounded, that socialism in the last resort was a matter of the public control of monopolies and the devotion of monopoly incomes to social purposes. Their appreciation of the growth and significance of working-class economic organizations helped them to the idea that a socialist party should have its foundations in these bodies. Their research interests gave rise to several hundred factual reports *(Fabian Tracts,* etc.) which did much to increase public knowledge of social conditions, but which have proved intellectually barren in as much as they were animated by no scientific and generalizing impulse. But this is not to deny their practical importance.

In 1889 most of these positions were taken up in *Fabian*

Essays, a collective, uneven, but still interesting volume. Their elitism was never very clearly expressed publicly, though neither was it concealed. It is accurately but unkindly mirrored in the pages of H. G. Wells, *The New Machiavelli* in which the Webbs appear as Oscar and Altiora Bailey. It finds constant, bitter expression in the pages of Mrs. Webb's voluminous diaries. It led the Webbs and Shaw in the end into a curious idolatory of the Russia of Stalin, in which they saw the Russian Communist Party as the equivalent of a group of upper-middle class higher civil servants, and the conduct of Soviet affairs as a rational and scientific bureaucracy.

Facility A *facility* is anything which is valued as a means to an end. A very general facility in the economic world is money, but other facilities include capital equipment, raw materials and so forth. In society generally all forms of property constitute facilities, in so far as property is trans-ferable. Discussion of the relation of facilities to other rewards may be found in H. M. Johnson's *Sociology: a systematic introduction, 1961*

Fact; Social Fact The problem of the facts with which the sociologist deals was first clearly raised by Emile Durkheim. Durkheim pointed out that not all facts about human behaviour are necessarily social facts. The fact that thirty per cent of the population have a particular hair-colouring, for example, is merely a fact about a mass of individuals. So also might be the fact that a small percentage of the population are extreme racialists. According to Durkheim, a fact is social only in so far as it exists externally to the individual and exercises constraint over him.

Unfortunately, such facts are not directly observable and sociologists are often tempted to substitute for a discussion of the forces which do constrain individual behaviour, a discussion of the forces which constrain them and which, they believe, should constrain all men. Durkheim there-fore insisted that social facts must be treated 'as things'. This injunction is somewhat misleading since it appears to imply that the constraining social forces can be directly observed. If all that is meant is that such facts must be studied objectively, however, it is acceptable. The problem of theory and method in sociology then becomes one of showing how hypotheses about these external constraining forces can be treated. Such hypotheses will be sociological, i.e. about a social subject matter, pro-vided that they make reference not simply to the biological and psychological constitution of an individual, but to the demands made upon that individual by social norms and other people.

Family Although sociologists are convinced that the family is the basic unit of social organization, the term itself remains one 'of the most loosely defined in their vocabulary. In large measure this arises from a curious reluctance on the part of sociologists, as distinct from anthropologists, to study the institution itself and a perhaps less surprising reluctance on the part of the members of the advanced societies which sociologists study to allow close investigation of a group whose structure and viability so intimately affects their lives. E. W. Burgess and H. J. Locke, in their book *The Family,* 1953, attempted a definition in the following terms: 'The Family is a group of persons united by the ties of marriage, blood, or adoption; constituting a single household, interacting and intercommuni-cating with each other in their respective social role of husband and wife, mother and father, brother and sister; creating a common culture.' What-ever shortcomings this definition itself may have, it is a good deal prefer-able to that of Kingsley Davis who defines *the/amity* as a 'group of persons whose relations to one another are based upon consanguinity and who are therefore kin to one another'. This would be an inadequate definition even of the family in the contemporary West, where *pater* and *genitor* are usually one and the same person; for even here, adoption is a perfectly well known and recognized basis of family membership. In some simple societies, that bonds of family require social recognition and do not rest merely on the facts of procreation is underlined by the practical require-ment that a man should acknowledge himself to be a child's 'father'. In parts of Melanesia, for example, the family to which a child belongs is not determined by the physiological act of birth, but depends on the per-formance of some social act; in one island, the man who pays the miciwife becomes the father of the child, and his wife the mother; in another, the father is the man who plants a leaf of the cycas tree before the door of the house. There are societies in which apparently the physiological role of the male in reproduction is not understood, so that a notion of the bio-logical connection between father and offspring is not part of the cultural ideology. There are other societies in which the connection is understood but little or no significance is attached to it, the husband simply regarding a child born to his wife as his own.

Among simpler peoples and in some non-industrial societies, the *nuclear family* is more often incorporated in or subordinated to some larger, composite family structure. N. W. Bell and E. F. Vogel, in their *Modern Introduction to the Family,* 1960, define 'any grouping broader than the *nuclear family* which is related by descent, marriage or adoption' as the *extended family.* More usefully, however, G. P. Murdock in *Social Structure,* 1949, distinguishes between two major forms of composite family. An *extended family,* he states, 'consists of two or more *nuclear families* affiliated through an extension of the parent-child relationship ... i.e. by joining the *nuclear family* of the married adult to that of his parents'. This family form is distinct from the polygamous family which 'consists of two or more *nuclear families* affiliated by plural marriages, i.e. by having one parent in common'.

To make confusion more confounded, however, *extended family* is sometimes used not merely to include but as a synonym for *joint family.* It is more useful to restrict this last term to a form of family which has a number of distinctive characteristics: co-residence, commensality and often joint property and some common family cult.

Feud A *feud* is a perpetual state of hostility between two corporate groups, marked by homicide or violence whenever members of the groups meet. Certain pre-requisites are necessary if a feud is to occur. Relation-ships between feuding groups cannot be of such urgency that hostilities would continuously interfere with the ordinary run of everyday life; they must be of a kind which permit controlled and sporadic outbreaks of hostilities. It follows that feuding groups are highly discrete. As territorial units they are separate, and their economic activities are of a kind which do not require co-operation for productive purposes. Members of groups are concentrated territorially, because dispersal would mean that men could be held to ransom in the territories of other groups. And marriage rules are of a kind which do not compel a wide dispersion of affinal links. This latter condition is best satisfied where parallel cousin marriage is permitted, as among Arabs, for then wives can be recruited from within the vengeance group itself. Demographically, some marriages have perforce to be made outside the vengeance group, but since a significant number can be made within it, the relatively small number of external marriag~ can be deployed in such a way that affinal alliances are made with only a few groups, leaving others unconnected. Exogamy tends to make for a greater dispersion of linkages, but if this dispersion can be res'ricted, feud is theoretically impossible; although it is true to say that where exogamy occurs, economic, territorial, political and ritual links tend to militate against feuding relationships.

In societies where discreteness of groups allows the appearance of feud, it is to be seen, essentially, as the competition for the capture of resources of some sort or other, and the outbreak of hostilities mark the calculated efforts of a group to expand its power domain at the expense of another.

Vengeance, as an act of homicide, is part of the feud, but it is to be distinguished from it in that it occurs between closely linked groups, and in this context it can be used to achieve a termination of hostilities, on the basis of a life for a life.

Feudalism Sociologists do well to treat the term *feudalism* and its school-book synonym *the feudal system* with some caution, since there was nothing very 'systematic' about feudalism. Though lordship and vassalage were universal features of feudalism, there was everywhere a diversity of practice and custom in every lordship, hence it is impossible, with even the most scrupulous care, to give any brief account of feudalism without conveying the wrong impression.

With this caveat in mind, it is nevertheless generally recognized that developed feudalism was based on a number of principles and relation-ships, however variously interpreted, one of which we have mentioned already. Fundamentally, the relationship between a vassal and his lord rested on the concept of the fief, which was usually land, although it could be any desirable thing such as an office, revenues in money or kind, the right to collect tolls, etc. To accept the grant of rights and title to a fief was to become the vassal of the benefactor, to whom was given in return pledges of loyalty and service, the faithful performance of which guaran-teed the continued right to the fief. The obligations of the vassal were not primarily intended to be economic but political and moral. Hence the obligations of military service and court servict>—the duty both to help the lord to form a court and to submit to the judgments of the lord's court and none other. In addition to these two sets of obligations there was a third, made up of financial obligations to the lord, of which the most important were *relief-the* sum paid by a vassal's heir for the lord's recognition of his succession to his father's fief; aid-money paid on a few occasions determined by custom when a lord was put to unusual expense, for example ransom or the knighting of his eldest son; and the ward-ship and rights of marriage of a vassal's orphans who were not yet of age to inherit their father's fief.

This third set of obligations served as a practical emphasis of the essen-tial characteristic of developed feudalism, *tenancy.* Although a son might inherit his father's fief, he inherited rights of tenancy, not of ownership. Every holder of a fief was a tenant of one higher than himself; hence one man's lord was another man's vassal. Not until the highest were reached was there any conception of *ownership* and even the most exalted were sometimes seen as owing obedience to something higher than themselves -Providence.

Ideally, feudalism covered Europe with a network of obligations which linked the highest to the lowest through a series of intermediate tenancies, but nowhere was there in practice a fixed gradation of authority. A knight might hold a fief directly from the king; a bishop might hold a fief from an abbot. Hence the model of *the feudal pyramid* gives only the crudest indication of the structure of feudalism.

It has been said of feudalism that in its developed form, 'private law had usurped public law' and it is certainly true that all sorts of services that men ordinarily owe to the public or to one another were translated into a form of *rent* paid for the use of land and defined and enforced by a private contract between the lord and his vassal. Thus the tendency to political centralization, the rise of a professional judiciary, the increasing circulation of money and better communications were all to contribute to its downfall at the end of the thirteenth century.

Folkways The term *folkways* was introduced into sociological literature by W. G. Sumner in a book of that title published in 1906. Classifying social norms in an evolutionary framework, Sumner distinguished *folkways* from *mores* largely in terms of the severity of the sanctions applied to those who offend. Mild ridicule or ostracism follows an infringement of a folkway, severe disapproval an offence against the mores. Folkways, he believed, result from the frequent repetition of acts i.e. they are habits in .the individual and custom in the group. They are unconsciously acquired and those who act in terms of them believe them to be right and true. 'When elements of truth and right are developed into doctrines of welfare, the folkways are raised to another plane.' Thus, do mores emerge from folkways, and in turn laws and institutions emerge from mores.

Formalism; Formal School of Sociology A view of sociology which empha-sizes the importance of the analysis of the form of a social relationship and the comparative study of cases which differ whilst the form remains constant. Georg Simmel was one of the principal exponents of this view. At the turn of the century he had already carried out studies of such formal relationships as co-operation, competition, sub- and super-ordinate relationships and so forth. He was followed in this endeavour by other German sociologists, notably Alfred Vierkandt and Leopold von Wiese. The influence of these men, known collectively as the Formalists, or the Formal School of Sociology, extended to the United States, where E. A. Ross and Albion Small were interested in Simmers ideas, and where later Howard Becker introduced v. Wiese's ideas in their joint publication *Systematic Sociology,* 1932. Relevant aspects of Simmel's work are to be found in K. Wolff's translation entitled *The Sociology of Georg Simmel,* 1950.

Frazer, Sir James George (1851-1941) British classicist and 'armchair' anthropologist; his interest in anthropology was stimulated by *Primitive Culture,* 1871, by E. B. Tylor; in turn, Frazer greatly influenced anthro-pologists and allied workers until the decline of classical evolutionism.

His major work, *The Golden Bough,* 1900, was a reconstruction of the gradual evolution of human thought and custom through the successive stages of Magic, Science and Religion; science he viewed as a return to the age of magic-but with the correct premisses and techniques to manipulate nature. Religion he understood as 'a propitiation or concilia-tion of powers superior to man which are believed to direct and control the course of nature and human life.' *Totemism and Exogamy,* 1910, is another important work, which shows the influence of L. H. Morgan. Other works include *Garnered Sheaves,* 1931, and *Anthologia Anthropologica,* 1938-39.

Frazier, Edward Franklin (1894—1962) American negro sociologist, he was a member of the Chicago school contributing descriptive studies of negro family life in the large cities. His best work is *The Negro family in* 80 *the United States,* 1939; a later work *Black Bourgeoisie,* 1955, aroused some controversy. He was a popular teacher with a wide experience of educational institutions. He had a tendency to write in a satirical manner.

Function *Function* has two dominant meanings in sociol-ogy. Its major use is to be seen in the following statement: 'The social function of religion is the maintenance of group solidarity.' *Herefunction* refers to the diagnosed objective consequence which a social phenomenon has for a wider system of which it is a part. *Manifestfunctions* are objective consequences for the system which are intended and recognized by the relevant participants; whilst *latent functions* are neither intended nor creognized. (See Robert K. Merton, 'Manifest and Latent Functions', in *Social Theory and Social Structure,* 1949, chapter 1). In order to distinguish between activities which contribute, on the one hand, to survival of social system patterns and, on the other, to their disturbance, a distinction is made respectively between *eufunctions* and *dysfunctions.* There are thus manifest and latent eufunctions and manifest and latent dysfunctions. Sometimes another possibility is invoked, namely that a set of activities may be of no particular consequence for the state of the system, and therefore, is neither eufunctional nor dysfunctional, as in William J. Goode, *Religion Among the Primitives,* 1951, pp. 1-55.

Function is also sometimes used as it is in mathematics. When it is said that social phenomenon *x* is a function of phenomenon *y* it is meant that *x* varies in proportion, as does *y*. Although this use must be distinguished from the first, the two are nevertheless related. This is because function as consequence for the state of the system implies that all social phenomena in a system are thought, at least initially, to be relevant to a consideration of its persistence. It is then but a short step to postulating that all pheno-mena in a system are interrelated and that a change in one area of a social system will have ramifications throughout the system. Thus function as consequence and function as related variation are often closely connected.

Functionalism The antecedents of functional orientations in sociology are illustrated by a dictum of Voltaire, to the effect that if there were no God, it would be necessary for man to invent one; meaning that Voltaire regarded belief in God as functionally indispensable to man. The real impetus to the employment of the term function came with those nineteenth century sociologists like Auguste Comte and Herbert Spencer who regarded groups of societies or individual societies as being very similar to bio-logical organisms in the way in which they worked. Emile Durkheim in turn argued that any sociological explanation should consist of the discovery, firstly, of a phenomenon's cause and, secondly, of its function; 'We use the word "function" in preference to "end" or "purpose", precisely because social phenomena do not generally exist for the useful results they produce. We must determine whether there is a correspon-dence between the fact under consideration and the general needs of the social organism, and in what this correspondence consists, without occupying ourselves with whether it has been intentional or not.'

These earlier functionalist tendencies were mediated to modern soci-ology through two major developments during the 1920s and 1930s. First, the 19208 witnessed a reorientation among cultural and social anthr ›pologists. This sprang particularly from the work of Bronislaw Malinowski, who was instrumental in establishing an approach which emphasized the importance of analysing primitive societies as socio--cultural wholes, accounting for institutions in terms of their relations to other institutions in the same society and their significance in satisfying and meeting the basic needs, notably the biological needs, of individual members. However, Malinowski was less important than A. R. Radcliffe-Brown with respect to the elaboration of the theoretical ramifications of a thoroughly *social* functionalism. (c.f. *Structure and Function in Primitive Society,* 1952, chapters 9 and 10.) Radcliffe-Brown frankly advocated the analogy between social life and organic life; although he tried to avoid Durkheim's emphasis on the 'needs' of the social organism and spoke instead of 'necessary conditions of existence'. This was because he wished to avoid teleological implications, such as the notion of some 'guiding spirit' or mysterious force in social life. However, it should be stressed that Durkheim, probably the most important single influence on modem functionalism, did not adhere to such teleological notions as this, nor was he straightforwardly committed to the biological analogy in the way in which Spencer and Radcliffe-Brown were. Radcliffe-Brown's work involved a distinction between social morphology, the analysis of the network of social relationships constituting social structure, and social physiology, the study of the working and persistence of all interrelated social phenomena in a society.

Secondly, in sociology the same period saw an increasing interest in an abstract conception of social systems, one which did not take as its point of departure concrete, historically isolatable societies. Rather, human societies were regarded as consisting of a series of interlocking social systems. Since Talcott Parsons' *The Structure of Social Action*, 1937, this focus has been increasingly prominent, and it is in Parsons' 'structural -functional' theory that sociological functionalism has attained its most systematic and rigorous formulation. In one of his earliest outlines of this theory, written in 1944, he argued that the significance of the concept of function inhered in its potential for the linking of the structural categories of sociology. Without such a concept the analyst was prone to give a static impression of social systems. A functional approach would produce criteria of the importance of factors and processes and their interrelation-ships within the system as a 'going concern'.

Parsons has openly described his scheme as being teleological, although his use is more restricted and rather less controversial than older meanings of this term. By teleological he simply means a means-end relationship; either activities or conditions contribute to the maintenance or development of a system, or they are dysfunctional, and thus detract from inte-gration and effectiveness. The principal features of structural-functionalism are as follows: (a) The delineation of boundaries between the social and other relevant systems, notably the cultural, personality and biological systems; (b) An abstract and transhistorical delineation of the major structural units of the social system, and a heavy emphasis upon the normative relationships between these units; (c) An overriding concern with the conditions of stability, integration and maximum effectiveness of the system as abstractly depicted. The functional orientation runs through all these characteristics, one of its most influential aspects being the idea of *functional imperatives*. Deriving in part from experiments on small groups, the term refers to the four basic 'problems' of a social system, problems which all social systems face and which must be adequately coped with if the system is to be adequately maintained. Particularly since Merton's 'Manifest and Latent Functions' (1949), there have been two major variants of sociological functionalism. Merton helped to precipitate the establishment of a perspective which was less committed to the stability, consensus, and integration foci of structural -functionalism. Thus whilst most sociologists are social functionalists in respect of their concern with systems comprising interdependent parts, and their interest in the unintended social consequences of social action and organization, and also their refusal to reduce the analysis of social life to the psychological level, only structural-functionalists base their work on the highly abstract conception of the normatively integrated system.

G

Gang An informal group of individuals that engage in common activities, many of these activities may be outside the law.

Geddes, Sir Patrick (1854-1932) Scottish biologist, he was influenced by members of the Le Play school on a visit to France and slowly began to develop an interest in social problems and the quality of urban life. His interests were wide, covering sociology, economics, social reform, art criticism and civic design. With Victor Branford he founded the Sociology Society of London, largely as a vehicle for his own ideas. He was prom-inent in the town-planning movement which helped to bring about legis-lation in 1909. He travelled widely, taught in many universities, but failed to obtain the newly established chair of sociology at London University. He was an enthusiastic polymath, impatient and sometimes tactless, he talked too much and whilst mentally exhilarating he was also exhausting. His endeavour to relate sociological studies to urban development is his abiding achievement.

Geiger, Theodor (1891-1952) Born in Miinchen, Geiger in later life lived and taught in Denmark and visited Canada. He was Professor of Sociology at the University of Aarhus. Influenced by the formalist tradi-tion in German sociology, he later developed a broader interest in macro-sociology, both with respect to the sociology of knowledge and social stratification. Among his early writings may be mentioned *Die Masse und ihre Aktion,* 1926, *Fiihren und Folgen,* 1928, *Allegeine Soziologie, 1930.* His later works on social stratification and mobility include *Die Soziale*

Schichtung des deutschen Volkes, 1932, *Die Klassengesellschaft im Schmelz-tiegel,* 1949, and *Soziale Umschichtungen in einer Danischen Mittelstadt,* 1951. An article in English on the origins and structure of the Danish intelligentsia ap.peared in the *British Journal of Sociolog.*

Gender Gap According to Toennies, social organization based on close and personal ties and traditional norms and values.

Gender Socially defined behaviour regarded as appropriate for the members of each sex.

Gemeinschaft A German term used extensively in sociology, although sometimes translated as 'community', but usually nowadays left un-translated. *Gemeinschaft* and *Gesellschaft* are contrasting types of social order. The contrast was made by F. Tonnies in his book, *Gemeinschaft und Gesellschaft,* first published in 1887, but which ran to several editions. Tonnies also wrote an essay of this title in the *Handworterbuch der Soziologie* in 1931. In a society characterized by Gemeinschaft relation-ships there is what he called a 'community offate'. People share both the benefits and misfortunes of life, although this should not necessarily imply that they do so equally. There is usually a marked involuntary element in such relationships, e.g. as between parent and child, or monarch and subject; there is no instrumental factor, but rather the relationships constitute an end in themselves. *Gesellschaft,* usually translated as 'associa-tion', represents relationships that are specific, partial and utilitarian. Thus a contract is indicative of *gesellschaftlische* relationships. The contrast pointed by Tonnies has been made by many nineteenth-century writers preoccupied with the emergence of an industrial civilization; usually there was a tendency to see Gemeinschaft relationships as being destroyed by modern social developments; a somewhat similar contrast was made by Sir Henry Maine in distinguishing between societies based on status and those based on contract. Others, like Spencer and Durkheim, also pointed to it. The contrast is not entirely satisfactory for there are elements of *Gemeinschaft* in all *Gesellschaft-type* organizations, but if there are no concrete empirical referents for these terms it must still be added that they have proved most influential in sociological thought. Tonnies' book was translated by C. P. Loomis and published in the U.S.A. under the title *Fundamental Concepts of Sociology,* 1940, and in the United Kingdom under the title *Community and Association, 1955;* the latter includes a translation of the essay in the *Handworterbuch.*

Genotype *Genotype* is a term used to denote the organic structure as it is determined by heredity, precisely the genes. It is used in contrast to the term *phenotype* which denotes the organic structure as determined by genetic factors *and* other factors, which will be environmental.

Giddings, Franklin Henry (1855-1931) American sociologist; important for combining psychology with his sociology and his emphasis upon the need for quantitativism. His major works are *Studies in the Theory of Human Society,* 1922, and *The Scientific Study of Human Society, 1924.* The keystone of his sociological system is 'ConscioUllness of Kind' (later reformulated as 'Pluralistic Behaviour') which unites individual minds which, responding to common stimulation, act upon one another through suggestion, example and imitation to produce a social mind. Giddings' system was a complex and logical scheme; he distinguished between social statics (concerned with structure), social kinetics (concerned with function), and social dynamics (change, development, evolution). Also, he distinguished between ethnic and demotic social compositions (cf. *Gemeinschaft)* and social constitutions or associations for particular ends (cf. *Gesellschaft).* He formulated a law of social change: a community endeavour to perfect its type in compliance with prevailing conceptions of the ideal good.

Globalization A comprehensive world-wide process of the internationalisation of communication, trade and economic orgaisation. In the economic sphere it can be seen in international trade agreements, vast increases in the volume of international trade and growing economic inter-dependency. It is also marked by the expansionof the size and power of multinational corporations and the development of the American entertainment industry's domination of international cultural communication. Generally the process is seen as driven by the growth of international capitalism and involving the transformation of the culture and social structures of non-capitalist and pre-inddustrial socieites.

Green Revolution Refers to the great rise in agricultural productivity brought about by new plant hybrids, fertilizers and agricultural chemicals in the 1950's and 1960's. Advocated by the developed nations as a way to make developing nations food sufficient, there is now a concern that this enforced transformation of agricultural ethods has harmed the environment, diminished local control and erased local methods of production.

Green House Effects A term from environmental science referring to an increase in the average temperature of the earth brought about by the effects of atmospheric pollution. The pollutants are suspended in the lower atmosphere above the earth and retard the loss of heat by convenction from the earth's surface.

Group; Social Group The American sociologist, Albion Small, in 1905 85 defined a group as 'any number of people, larger or smaller, between whom such relations are discovered that they must be thought of together'. This definition has come to be seen as too broad a one. Today it is necessary to distinguish an aggregate or category of persons possessing some common features, e.g. the same sex, or the same income, which thus group them in a statistical sense, from a number of persons between whom there are relationships based on interaction. Thus to reinforce the distinction many sociologists use the prefix 'social' for the second use of the term. Very often the expression *social group* is applied to a small face-to-face group of persons, or what C. H. Cooley called a *primary* group.

Group Dynamics The study of group dynamics, strictly speaking, is the investigation of the manner in which adjustive changes, occurring in a small social group as a whole, are the product of the changes in any part of the group. The term, however, has come to denote the study of small social groups generally. Small group studies gained impetus during World War II, but may originally be said to have been inspired by the writings of C. H. Cooley and Georg Simmel. Cooley distinguished be-tween *primary* and *secondary* groups. The former were defined as face-to-face groups which enjoy feelings of solidarity, groups that are productive of the moral norms operating in adult lives, or groups that reinforce these norms and the stability they produce in human society. Thus the family was regarded by Cooley as the main primary group, but others would include the work group, the club, the college fraternity and so forth. Secondary groups, on the other hand, are the larger aggregates like social classes. Indeed, categories of people rather than social groups proper were included by Cooley, but especially if they are bound by a normative order and display interaction among the members, in which case they constitute an associational kind of secondary group; examples are the trade union, a learned society, the Automobile Association. The study of primary groups is a well-developed feature of sociological investigation; its history has been documented by E. A. Shils in 'The Study of the Primary Group' in *The Policy Sciences,* edited by D. Lerner and H. D. Lasswell, 1951. Simmel's work consists of brilliant essays on aspects of societal relations. He explored the implications of dyadic relationships and compared them with triadic ones, he discussed the nature of super-ordinate and subordinate relationships, the characteristics of secret societies, and other social phenomena at the micro-sociological level.

Work on small groups gained strength during the last World War, the military organizations of the Allies having come to appreciate the small group as a major factor in maintaining the morale and hence the military efficiency of the soldier. Pioneer work in this field was carried out by S. A. Stouffer in the U.S.A., many of his findings being published in *The American Soldier,* 1949, and by a number of British psychologists em-ployed by the War Office, some of whom later helped to staff the Tavistock Institute of Human Relations in London. Experimental work has been a prominent feature of small group studies. Kurt Lewin's influence has been strong in this respect, and together with R. Lippitt and R. K. White he carried out work with children's groups having different kinds of leader-ship; this was reported in 1939. Since then more rigorous experimental work has been done to discover the relationship between task performance and communication structures in small groups, notably by H. J. Leavitt in 1951 and by L. S. Christie, R. B. Luce and J. Maeya year later. These studies showed differential degrees of efficiency according to both the nature of the task and the type of communication structure involved. At the same time G. A. Heise and G. A. Miller also added some experi-mental reflnements with consequent theoretical improvements to the subject. These studies are reported and discussed by J. Klein in *The Study of Groups,* 1956. Many other studies have been made, mostly by students of Lewin and many of them at the Centcr for Group Dynamics at Ann Arbor in Michigan. Two major contributions to the theoretical develop-ment of Group Dynamics are those of G. C. Homans, who in his book *The Human Group,* 1950, showed the usefulness of a systematic scheme of thought of a functionalist character by comparing various group studies, and by R. F. Bales, who provided a scheme for the observation and analysis of small group activities in his book entitled *Interactioll*

Process Analysis, 1951.

The main topics of concern to students of small groups are probl cms of cohesion, communication, the influence of the group on individual members' perceptions, group morale and leadership. Distinct advances may be claimed in answcring some of thc fundamental sociological questions about these subjects. Theoretically, in fact, sociology has made considerable strides in this micro-sociological ficld, although it is un-certain how far generalizations may be extended from small face-to-face groups to larger social organizations. The application of small group theory may be seen in relation to work groups, school classes, therapeutic groups in mental hospit.118, and generally in social work.

Guerrilla Movement A non-government military organisationthat engages in fighting or harassment.

GumpJowicz, Ludwig (1838-1909) A Polish sociologist, who being both a Jew and a Polc was inclined to be interested in racial, national and social conflict. He was an adherent and modifier of Social Darwinism. He belicved that social and cultural evolution was a result of the survival of the fittest in a struggle between (successively) racial groups, states and classes. The ultimate cause of this struggle he held to be the polytenetic nature of the human species and the universal hatred between distinct racial and social groups, but the proximate cause he believed to be the desire for cconomic improvcment. The state evolved when economic exploitation replaced extinction as a policy to be adopted towards sub-ordinated I;roups. Legal and political institutions were developed by dominant groups to maintain their power. Syngenism and amalgamation are, he believed, secondary factors in social life. Gumplowicz tried to formulate sociological laws as a result of his attempt to define the role of sociology as a scientific subject.

Gurvitch, Georges (1894-1965) Russian sociologist who taught in Russia at the time of the Revolution but left in 1921 to spend three years in Prague before eventually settling in France, where he became a natural-ized Frenchman. Whilst retaining a strong Russian accent he lectured at the Sorbonne and later as a professor at Strasbourg University where he succeeded Maurice Halbwachs. He founded the Centre d'Etudes Socio-logiques de Paris, becoming its first Director, and in 1948 became Professor of Sociology at the University of Paris and Director of L'Ecole Pratique des Hautes Etudes (6th section). In 1946 he founded the successful journal *Cahiers Internationaux de Sociologie,* to which, from time to time, he contributed articles. From 1960-63 he was the President of the Com-mission of sociology and demography at the Centre National de la Recherche Scientifique.

H

Harm Reduction A term often used in the discussion of drug users, prostitutes, etc. Rather than taking a moralistic approach, perhaps focusing on punishment or rehabilitation, the system tries to reduce the harm that comes to such offenders. For example, provide drug users with clean needles, or perhaps with a safe place to shoot-up, or even to provide them with standardized heroin. Or the community could provide a safe area for prostitutes to work, provide free testing for infectious diseases, etc. All of this will reduce harm to the 'offenders' but in the long-term should also reduce harm to the community.

Hawthorne Effect An increase in worker productivity observed at the Chicago Hawthorne plant of General Electric in the 1920's and 1930's attributed to improvements in worker-management communIcation and increased involvement of workers with each other. The term is now used more generally to refer to improvement of worker productivity that does not result from any objective change in working conditions or work organization, but seems to arise from workers having more positive psychological feelings about the workplace.

Health Maintenance Organizations (HMOs) An organization that provides health care to patients in return for a fixed annual fee. HMOs therefore have an interest in limiting the cost of treatment per patient (see also Managed Care).

Heart Street language for having courage.

Hegemony A concept of Italian Marxist Antonio Gramsci (1891-1937) which refers to the way that the political and social domination of the bourgeois class in capitalist society is pervasively expressed not only in ideologies but in all realms of culture and social organization. The comprehensive expression of the values of class divided society in social life lends this form of society an appearance of naturalness and inevitability that removes it from examination, criticism and challenge. While arising in the analysis of a class divided society the term is also used in discussion of a patriarchal society or a colonial society.

Heritability The extent to which a characteristic of a living organism is genetically determined, rather than shaped by the surrounding environment. In the social sciences, this term is chiefly associated with debate about the heritability of characteristics such as intelligence, criminality, gender behaviour, aggressiveness: are each of these (however measured) shaped most by biological (genetic) inheritance or by the influence of environmental factors like culture, socialization and physical nutrition?

Heterosexuality An orientation in sexual activity towards people of the opposite sex.

Heuristic Device An abstract concept or model useful for thinking about social and physical phenomena. For example, sociologists use of the concept social structure to help them in defining and analysing aspects of society that create patterns and regularity in the everyday roles and activities of individuals. Sociologists do not imagine that individuals mechanically and automatically act in precisely prescribed ways within social structures or that social structures are unchanging or fixed, but the concept of structure and regularity is an essential tool for understanding how social life itself is possible.

Hidden Curriculum (1) Behavior or attitudes that are learned at school but which are not a part of the formal curriculum. For example, aspects of classism can often be "unintentionally" conveyed in learning materials. (2) The norms, values and social expectations indirectly conveyed to students by the styles of teaching, unarticulated assumptions in teaching materials and the organizational characteristics of educational institutions. Social scientists find that the influence of the hidden curriculum on educational outcomes is equal to or greater than the overt or intended curriculum.

Hierarchy A structuring of social statuses and roles within an organization or society ranked according to differentiations of power, authority, wealth, income, etc. Related terms are ranking or stratification.

Higher Education Usually refers to education beyond high school level, often in colleges or universities.

High-Trust Systems Work settings in which individuals have a great deal of autonomy and control.

Hiss, Alger A lawyer who rose to become a significant public official in the United States through the 1930's and 1940s. In 1948 a magazine editor, who confessed to being a communist, accused Hiss of assisting in the transmittal of documents to the Russians. Hiss denied any involvement but was found guilty in his second trial and sentenced to five years in prison. Many did not believe his pleas of innocence and the case stimulated support for Senator McCarthy and the hunt for communists in places of influence in American society. It is now widely believed that Hiss (who was probably wrongfully accused) was the scapegoat for the loss of China to the Communists and the Russian development of the atomic bomb. Americans found it difficult to believe that either of these events could have happened without duplicity and thus looked to subversion, spies, lack of loyalty and moral degeneration as explanations for these world developments. See: Mccarthyism.

Historical Materialism (1) Marx's interpretation that processes of social change are determined primarily (but not exclusively) by economic factors. (2) The central concept of social analysis in the work of Karl Marx (1818-1883) and Frederick Engels (1820-1895). The core idea is that the political and intellectual hist~ry of human societies is shaped most importantly by the social and technical organization of economic production and exchange. This view suggests that it is not principally intellectual ideas and knowledge that shape the structure and cultural values of social life, but rather the shape of social life, especially in the social organization of economic production, that chiefly shapes intellectual ideas and knowledge. See: Dialectical Materialism.

Homogamy Marriage between individuals who are, in some culturally important way, similar to each other. The similarity may be based on ethnicity, religion or socio-economic status. Canadians, for example, tend to be homogamous, with marriage partners usually having quite similar social and economic status and ethnic affiliation. This is a descriptive concept only and does not refer to rules or customs about mate selection. See: Endogamy.

Homophobia Fear, hatred or loathing of homosexuals. (2) Literally an uncontrollable fear of homosexuals and of homosexuality, but the term is generally used for a negative and contemptuous attitude to same-sex sexual relationships and to those who participate in them.

Homosexuality Having sexual preference for persons of the same sex.

Horizontal Integration The expansion of a corporation to include other previously competitive enterprises within the same sector of goods or service production. For example, one candy maker may take over anuther candy maker. This process is characteristic of capitalist economies which have a marked tendency to sectoral concentration into fewer and fewer enterprises and business conglomerates. See: Conglomerate.

Housework (Domestic Labour) Unpaid work carried on in and around the home such as cooking, cleaning and shopping. Studies show that the bulk of this labor is carried out by women despite the predominance of dual-income families.

Hudson's Bay Company The Hudson's Bay Company was incorporated in 1684 by Royal Charter of the King of England to exercise political and economic control over all the lands and the sea around Hudson's Bay and the entire area which drained its lakes and rivers into Hudson's Bay. The Bay's main interest was to monopolise the extraordinarily profitable fur trade, particularly in the beaver pelts that were prized by European hat makers. The extent of the Bay's territory ran from Edmonton in the west to north of Ottawa in the east and from south of the present border with the United States to Baffin Island in the north. Over this vast territory the Bay wielded unchallengeable political and economic power and was for almost 200 years the effective government of this area. After confederation the new government of Canada determined immediately that the Bay must be shorn of its monopoly domination of trade and resources and of its quasi-governmental powers. In 1869, under pressure from the British government, Canada and the Bay reached an agreement by which the Bay surrendered almost all its territory. The company retained great tracts ofland, however, and for another hundred years exercised extensive powers and influence in Canada's remote northern communities. In 1987 this role in the north was ended when the Bay sold its northern stores and the company then became similar to any large corporate retail organization.

Human Capital The talents and capabilities that individuals contribute to the process of production. Companies, governments and individuals can invest in this 'capital' just as they can invest in technology and buildings or in finances.

Human Rights See: *Bill of Rights / Charter of Rights and Freedoms / Universal Declaration of Human Rights.*

Humanism An ethical doctrine that asserts the central importance of human life and experience on earth and the right and duty of each individual to explore and develop their potential. Humanism is, to some extent, in opposition to religious doctrines, like Christianity, that diminish the importance of earthly life and assert that human existence is merely a stage of preparation for heavenly life after death. In the social sciences humanism is evident in those groups who argue that social theory must conceive of the human actor as a subject rather than an object.

Hunter Gatherer Society The earliest form of human society and still persisting to some extent in remote regions of the world. These societies have an economic base that rests on the use of the naturally occurring animal and plant resources of the environment. They do not practice agriculture or raise and herd animals. Social structure is usually egalitarian with little economic and gender inequality. Private property is minimal. In Canada the Inuit and many First Nations communities were hunter-gatherer societies prior to Ew·opean contact. This aboriginal life style had generally disappeared by the second half of this century, but many communities are now attempting to recover traditional ways.

Hunting and Gathering Societies Societies whose subsistence is based primarily on hunting animals and gathering edible plants.

Hutterites An Anabaptist (opposed to infant baptism) group which emerged in central Europe in 1528 under the leadership of Joseph Hutter. The basic components of their religious beliefs are communal ownership of property, communal living, nonviolence and commitment to adult baptism. A large number of Hutterites emigrated to Canada in 1918 and the majority now live in the prairie provinces and retain traditional styles of dress and custom. Mennonites originated at approximately the same time as the Hutterites but arrived in Canada from the USA in 1786. See: Sect.

Hypothesis (1) A tentative statement about a given state of affairs that predicts a relationship between the variables, usually put forward as a basis for empirical testing. (2) A testable statement (i.e., it may be true or false) of a specific relationship between or among variables. In the classic model of science this testable statement is deduced from a theory. See: Hypothetico-Deductive Model of Science.

I

Iatrogenic Disease caused by the physician in the course of treating the patient.

Id Concept of Sigmund Freud (1856-1939), founder of psychoanalysis. The id is the unconscious drives and psychic energies of humans as biological organisms. As such, it is untouched by culture and social learning and encompasses all that is primitive, natural and pre-civilized in human passions and energies. Freud seems to have assumed that the human struggle to achieve self consciousness against the ungoverned and unconstrained passions of the id, remained deeply buried in the unconscious minds of all human beings. See: Ego / Superego.

Ideal Type (1) An abstract model of a classic, pure, form of social phenomenon. It is a model concept and does not necessarily exist in exact form in reality. An example is Ferdinand Tonnies's dichotomy Gemeinschaft and Gesellschaft. Tonnies described two opposite, or polar types, of social association, one personal and committed (community) one impersonal and unemotional (society-association). These two formal types then provide a benchmark for the analysis and comparison of actually existing societies. Max Weber also used this method of analysis with his ideal types of bureaucracy, authority and social action. (2) Weber's construct of a 'pure type', constructed by emphasizing logical or consistent traits of a given social item. The traits are defining ones, not necessarily desirable ones. Ideal types do not exist anywhere in reality, rather they are "measures" that we can use in comparing social phenomena. One example is Weber's ideal type of bureaucratic organization (which are anything but desirable). More widely used (and understood) examples would include "ideal democracy" and "ideal capitalism."

Idealism A perspective that asserts the independent causal influence of intellectual ideas on social organization and culture. It is contrasted to materialism, which focuses on concrete aspects of social organization as causative of particular intellectual ideas and values. Max Weber can be said to have given an idealistic explanation of the growth of capitalism by linking it to the emergence of a 'Protestant Ethic'. See: Historical Materialism.

Identity Politics Thought to be a central aspect of postmodern politics and communities in which the legitimacy of a unitary public identity or an overarching sense of self has diminished and in its place the previously private identities of citizens (based on their race, ethnicity, sexual preference, physical state, or victimization) compete for public recognition and legitimation. Some theorists fear that this will lead to private values and identities coming to take precedence over public involvement as citizens. See: Citizen.

Ideographic Explanations of specific events, phenomenon or behaviours which are sought in the careful examination of specific preceding events. For example, why did Mary murder the butler? Or, What caused World War I? For the most part clinical psychologists and historians are interested in ideographic explanations. Other disciplines, like sociology, are interested in explanations of classes of events or behaviours and seek these in a careful examination of a few general categories or classes of preceding events. For example, why do men murder their partners? Or, What are the causes of international violence? These explanations are known as nomothetic explanations.

Ideological Hegemony A situation where a particular ideology (see definition) is pervasively reflected throughout a society in all principal social institutions and permeates cultural ideas and social relationships.

Ideology (1) A linked set of ideas and beliefs that act to uphold and justify an existing or desired arrangement of power, authority, wealth and status in a society. For example, a socialist ideology advocates the transformation of society from capitalism to collective ownership and economic equality. In contrast, a liberal ideology associated with capitalist societies upholds that system as the best, most moral, most desirable form of social arrangement. Patriarchal ideology also has this characteristic of asserti!lg claims and beliefs that justify a social arrangement: in this case, male social domination of women. Another example is a racist ideology claiming that people can be classified into distinct races and that some races are inferior to others. Racist ideologies are used as justifications for systems of slavery or colonial exploitation. Although there is often a dominant ideology in a society, there can also be counter-ideologies that advocate transformation of social relationships. See: Dominant Ideology Thesis / Hegemony. (2) Shared ideas or beliefs which serve to justify and support the interests of a particular group or organizations.

Ignorance of the Law is No Excuse A fundamental principle of criminal law is that individuals may not offer the legal defence that they were unaware that their acts were designated as criminal under the law. All citizens are presumed to know the law.

Immigration (1) The movement of peoples into a country or territory (movement of people within countries is referred to as migration.) Immigration has played the central role in the development of Canada from the first permanent European settlements in the mid 1600's to the 1990's where 16% of Canadians were born outside Canada. The birth rate of Canada's population - the number of children born to a woman in her fertile years - is about 1.6, much lower than the 2.1 that would be needed to maintain a stable population. The prospect of a declining and aging population has led to some calls for increased immigration to Canada. Economic recession, the demands on public services resulting from the concentrated patterns of immigrant settlement and concern about inter-ethnic tensions, have more recently led to controversy about levels of immigration. A special mention should be made of Quebec, where the population increased, until the 1960's, mostly through a high birth rate. In history, Quebec had one of the highest birthrates known in any world society. Although there has been immigration of Francophones to Quebec, chiefly from old French colonial territories, the great majority of the Francophone population has descended from the approximately 60,000 people who lived there when the French empire over Quebec ended in 1759. (2) The settlement of people into a country in which they were not born.

Imperialism (1) Domination by one or more countries over others for political and economic objectives. It can be effected by force of arms or through the economic and political power exercised by state and corporate agencies. Imperialism is sometimes organized in a formal empire, with a ruling nation and colonized territories, but it can also exist where one nation or region exercises dominant influence over international trade and investment, patterns of economic development and mass communication. See: Colonialism / Metropolis-Hinterland Theory. (2) The establishing .of colonial empires in which domination is both political and economic.

In Vitro Fertilization The fertilization of a human egg outside of the womb (usually in a laboratory dish). The fertilized egg is then implanted in the womb where normal development occurs.

Incapacitation A philosophy of incarceration that argues that some offenders might have to be incarcerated not for what they have done but to prevent future harm to the community. This depends on the community's ability to identify those that might re-offend. Some also argue that it is unfair to punish people for what they might do, rather than for what they have done. Selective incapacitation is provided for under dangerous offender legislation.

Incest. Sexual intercourse between individuals who are culturally regarded as too closely related for sexual intimacy to be legitimate or moral. Incest rules vary cross culturally, but generally all cultures forbid intercourse between parents and children, betwe~n siblings and between grandparents and grandchildren. Rare historical exceptions to the rules are ancient Egypt and traditional Hawaii where siblings were favoured marriage partners among the royal family and probably other members of the aristocracy and the wealthy. Many cultures have mythical or religious stories that warn of the terrible consequences of violating incest rules.

Incidence A contrasting term to prevalence. Incidence tells us the frequency of occurrence of some event during a particular time period. For example there were 581 criminal homicides in 1997, or the rate of crime for one year is higher than for the previous year.

Income Payment of wages usually earned from work or investments.

Independent Immigrant One of three classes of immigrants to Canada (the other two being family class and refugees). The independent class do not require sponsorship - they apply on their own - but they are rated on a point system which tends to give points to education and training, labour market demands, age and having family in Canada. See: Sponsored Immigrant.

Independent Variable Causal research examines the world in terms of variables (those things which reveal variation within a population). An independent variable is typically the cause, while a dependent variable is the effect. The independent variable is that variable assumed to be the causal variable. In experimental research it is the variable the investigator manipulates. The effect (the dependent variable) is dependent on the causal variable. If unemployment is thought to cause crime rates to increase, unemployment is the independent variable (it can vary between high and low) and crime rates the dependent variable. Something which is an independent variable at one time can be a dependent variable at another.

Index Many of the concepts social scientists study are quite complex and cannot adequately be measured by a single indicator. In these cases researchers develop several indicators and in some case will give different weights to each indicator. This combination of indicators and weights is an index. Socio-economic status is difficult to measure and typically the indicators of income, occupation and education are used. If occupation is seen as more central it may be given more weight. An index of socio-economic status is developed.

Indexicality As used by ethnomethodologists refers to the contextual nature of behaviour and talk. Talk for example is indexical in the sense that it has no meaning without a context or can take on various meanings dependent on the context. As we construct talk or listen to talk we all must engage in the interpretive process of constructing a context. With this context we give the talk a sense of concreteness or definiteness. There is no way to avoid indexicality, however, nor a way to remove it, since talk about context itself is also indexical. For this reason constructing a sense of reality is an ongoing accomplishment of social members.

Indian Act The British North America Act (1867), creating the nation of Canada, gave responsibility for the Native peoples of the new nation to the federal government. Federal legislation governing Natives was first passed in 1868 and in 1876 the first Indian Act was passed. This Act provides a legal definition of 'Indian' and for those covered by the designation provides a framework in which their activities are governed. From the outset the Act espoused the goal of assimilation and in the name of this end authorized many repressive actions by the state. The Inuit (until recently referred to as 'Eskimo') of the North were not included in the Indian Act and a court decision in 1939 was required to declare them a federal responsibility. The Act has been described as a 'total institution' since the lives of Natives covered it are entirely lived out within its rule. The Act has been a powerful instrument for the colonization of Indian lands and peoples. Since 1970 there have been suggestions that the Indian Act be removed and Native peoples become similar to other citizens in Canada. See: total institution; reserve; Potlatch;

Indictable Indictable offenses are the most serious category of crime, carry substantial criminal penalties, and are usually tried in higher courts often before juries.

Indigenous Peoples Those people inhabiting a land prior to colonization by another nation. In Canada this would include the Indians and Inuit but would probably not include the Metis who are of mixed European and aboriginal descent. See: Aboriginal Peoples.

Individual Pathology A term used to refer to biological or psychological explanations of criminal or deviant behaviour by individuals. The assumption is that the deviant behaviour of individuals can be at least partly explained by some physical or psychological trait that makes them different from normal law abiding citizens.

Individualism A value system, central to classical liberalism and capitalism, which upholds choice, personal freedom, and self-orientation. See: Classical Liberalism.

Individualistic A theory which focuses on explaining the behaviour of individuals and using factors or features of the individual in explaining this behaviour. An alternative to this approach would be to explain the behaviour of a group (the crime rate of Canada) in terms of characteristics of this group.

Individuation Unlike individualism which refers to an individualistic value system, individuation refers to the process by which individualism is accomplished, the breaking down of obligatory ties and responsibilities to other people or to institutions so that the individual is freed from social bonds. Such a process must also lead to the adoption of the value of individualism. See: Individualism.

Inductive Reasoning Developing a theory or reaching a conclusion after consideration of several empirical observations. See: Grounded Theory.

Industrial Democracy Democratic participation in the workplace.

Industrial Production Economic production carried on through the use of machinery driven by inanimate sources of power.

Industrial Relations A general term referring to workplace relationships between workers and management. Industrial relations has become an important professional and academic discipline, since successful management of industrial relations is closely linked to workplace productivity and product quality. There have been many different approaches to the management of industrial relations in modern capitalist societies, but they generally share the characteristic that they seek to discipline, motivate and engage workers in processes of production or administration without making any fundamental change to the structure of ownership or direction of the workplace. At the end of the 19th century scientific management became increasingly popular as a means of workplace direction and this approach relied upon" close and systematic control of the work process and of the methods of work employed. Beginning in the 1920's and 1930's, a new movement in industrial relations began to focus instead on the management of human relations in the workplace after it was demonstrated that creation of a positive communicative atmosphere at work was capable of stimulating worker productivity. In more recent years, the idea of quality control circles, where workers take direct responsibility as work groups for productivity and work quality has become popular following successful use of this approach in Japan. There have also been numerous schemes to increase worker participation in the workplace, either through enhanced workplace communication, consultation and co-operative worker-management planning or through worker representation and participation directly in management. See: Scientific Management/Alienation.

Industrial Revolution The production of goods for trade and profit using machines to enhance the productivity of labour. The term is used to describe the profound technological changes that began in England in the mid 18th century. Before the 18th century there was very little power machinery except wind and water mills and production was carried out with hand tools and hard human labour. The industrial revolution introduced technologies that could employ power from water, steam, gas, coal, electricity and oil to replace or enhance human labour. This made possible a level of economic productivity that had never before been achieved and it initiated a process of unending technological transformation and social change. Socially, the industrial revolution is associated with the rational organization of work, a transformation from a society of self sufficient producers to a society of employed wage workers and the spread of a market-driven system of allocation of resources. In Canada these changes occurred in the 19th century. Social scientists continue to be interested in how this technological transformation affected social relations, politics, community life, family structure, and women's role in society. Many people argue that the computerization of society is bringing with it a set of changes equal in importance to the industrial revolution.

Industrialization of War The application of industrial production and bureaucratic organization to warfare.

Industrialization (1) The continual expanding application of sophisticated technology designed to efficiently draw energy and raw materials out of the environment and fashion them for human use. (2) The process of developing an economy founded on the mass manufacturing of goods. Industrialization is associated with the urbanization of society, an extensive division of labour, a wage economy, differentiation of institutions, and growth of mass communication and mass markets. Many western societies are now described as post-industrial since much economic activity is based on the production of services, knowledge or symbols.

Inequality of Condition Where individuals have very different amounts of wealth, status and power. This is a characteristic of all complex modern societies, however equality of condition is often present in small-scale, hunter-gatherer societies. See: Class.

Inequality of Opportunity Where differences in individual possession of wealth, status and power result in definite advantages and disadvantages in the pursuit of personal success.

Infant Mortality Rate The number of infants who die during the first year of life, per thousand live births. Infant mortality rates have declined dramatically in industrial societies.

Inference. The logical process of moving from an indicator or observation to a conclusion or general rule.

Inferential Statistics Statistical tools or techniques used to draw inference about a population on the basis of research evidence from a sample. For example, estimating the frequency of value for a particular variable within a population. This is found commonly in reports of public opinion polls when it is noted that 'a sample of this size is accurate to within +/- 3.2% [note, this number will vary], 19 times out of 20 (i.e., 95%)'. See: Statistics / Descriptive Statistics.

Inferiorization Refers to the process of imposing a stigmatized or inferiorized identity on a group of people. The people stigmatized tend to adopt a sense of inferiority that leads to a sapping of confidence and ability, inhibits political organization and results in a host of personal and collective social problems. This concept can be linked to the theory of a 'culture of poverty'.

Informal Economy Also known as the 'underground economy', or the 'hidden economy', refers to those economic activities which are carried on outside the institutionalized structures of the economy. For most purposes this means they are transactions not reported to the taxation department, office of unemployment insurance, worker's compensation or municipal governments. Usually these transactions are based on cash exchanges but they may be bartered for goods or servIces.

Informal Relations Relations in organizations developed on the basis of personal connections. These ties are often '..lsed to pursue organizational goals instead of the formally recognized procedures.

Infrastructural Determinism The major principle of sociocultural materialism (borrowed and modified from Harris' cultural materialism). "The mode of production and reproduction (probabalistically) determines primary and secondary group structure, which in turn determines the cultural and mental superstructure" (see also Mode of Production, Mode of Reproduction, Primary Group, Secondary Group, Superstructure, and Feedback Loop).

Infrastructure (1) In Marxist theory or political economy theory, refers to the base or economic foundation of society upon which the culture and social institutions of society are built. The concept of 'infrastructure' is similar to 'mode of production' and would include the forces of production and the relations of production. See: base; mode of production. (2) The interface between a sociocultural system and its environment. In sociocultural materialism it contains the principle mechanism by which society regulates the amount and type of energy from the environment (see also Mode of Production, and Mode of Reproduction).

In-Group A social group an individual belongs to and identifies with.

Inherent Right to Self-Government A right claimed particularly by Native peoples in Canada. By declaring that this right is inherent there is rejection of the notion that the right is bestowed by the government of Canada. Rather the right existed prior to Canada becoming a nation and therefore acknowledges that Native peoples were, and perhaps still are, nations with the right to fully make decisions for themselves. See: Nation.

Inner City The areas composing the central neighborhoods of industrial cities which are subject to dilapidation and decay, the more affluent residents having moved to outlying areas.

Institution, Social A pattern of social interaction, having a relatively stable structure, that persists over time. Institutions have structural properties - they are organized - and they are shaped by cultural values. Thus, for example, the 'institution of marriage', in western societies, is structurally located in a cohabiting couple and regulated by norms about sexual exclusiveness, love, sharing, etc. There is not full agreement about the number or designation of social institutions in a society but the following would typically be included: family, economy, poljtics, education, health care, media.

Institution, Total A social institution which encompasses the individual, cutting them off from significant social interaction outside its bounds. These institutions are frequently involved in the process of resocialization whereby individuals are detached from their previous sense of identity and re-shaped to accept and absorb new values and behaviour. Examples include religious orders, prisons and army training camps.

Institutional Capitalism A condition that exists when large institutions such as pension plans, banks, and insurance companies hold large shares of capitalistic enterprises.

Institutional Completeness The condition of a group within a larger society where the major institutions -economy, politics, family, schooling, - are reproduced thus enabling the smaller group to have little social connection with the larger group.

Institutional Discrimination Accepted social arrangements that place minority groups at a disadvan tage.

Institutional Racism Accepted social arrangements that exclude on the basis of race.

Institutionalization Where social interaction is predictably patterned within relatively stable structures regulated by norms. For example, seeking a diagnosis for a physical illness or obtaining advise or a cure is institutionalized within the 'health care' institution. Conflict over values or interests is institutionalized within the 'political system'; sexual access and raising children is institutionalized within the 'family'.

Instrumentalist Marxism A view ofthe role of the state from a conflict or Marxist perspective. The state is seen as an instrument of the dominant class of the society and is assumed to operate at its behest. This approach stresses the importance of the intimate connection of the capitalist class to the state power apparatus and argues that it is this interconnection that explains political and economic policies in capitalist societies. This view has now been largely displaced by a structurally-focused analysis. See: Structuralist Approach / Relative Autonomy.

Insurrection An organized revolt against civil authority in an attempt to replace that authority with another.

Integration, Social (1) The joining of different ethnic groups within a society into a common social life regulated by generally accepted norms and values. This process need not involve the obliteration of distinct ethnic identity, which would be assimilation, but it implies that ethnic identity does not limit or constrain commitment to the common activities, values and goals of the society. Canada's official policy of multi-culturalism assumes that social integration can be achieved without the elimination of the cultural di5tiilctiv'",il",55 of ",thiJ.ic giOUpS. (2) In the work of Emile Durkheim (1858-1917) the term refers to the density of connection between individuals and social institutions. He assumes that a society requires intense individual participation in a wide range of institutions for it to maintain social integration and provide individuals with a sense of meaning and belonging.

Intelligence Level of intellectual ability in an individual. Also refers to the gathering of information (defensive, offensive, and industrial capabilities) about one nation by another.

Intensification The application of ever greater amounts of technology and labor techniques to increase productivity. Refers to the growth in the complexity of the mode of production (greater energy expenditures as well as energy produced/consumed), and population over the course of social evolution (see also Bureaucratization, and Rationalization).

Interest Group (1) A group of individuals and organizations linked together for the purpose of active promotion of particular values and objectives. Interest groups are usually associated with the political process through which they seek support and resources for their objectives. Interest groups encompass those with issue specific goals (e.g.: opposition to nuclear energy) as well as those seeking to regularly defend and advance their goals and objectives (e.g.: the Canadian Federation of Independent Business, the Canadian Labour Congress). Pluralist theory upholds the view that political process and political decision making is best thought of as consisting of open and competitive interest group interaction and advocacy within a framework of democracy. (2) Groups organized to pursue specific interests in the political arena. The interests of these groups is often' economic, but many are organized around moral concerns. The major activity of interest groups is lobbying the members of legislative bodies (Congress as well as state legislators), contributing vast sums to political campaigns, and increasingly running their own propaganda campaigns to affect the legislative process.

Intergenerational Mobility Movement up or down the social hierarchy from one generation to anvther. Internal Colonialism. The economic exploitation of a group within a society whereby their labor is sold cheap and they are made to pay dear for products and services.

Internal Validity A standard or criteria against which research results are judged. To be internally valid the results of an experiment or of a survey are considered to be accurate indications of the manipulation of an independent variable in the case of an experiment, or of the attitudes or knowledge of respondents in the case of a survey. If the results, however, can be seen as produced by the way the experiment *ot* survey was conducted then the results are internally invalid. Something internal to the research process produced the results, so researchers are no longer measuring what they claim to be measuring. Selection bias in the allocation of subjects to the experimental and ~ontrol groups may contaminate the results as can questions in a survey which elicit socially desirable answers. Placebos and double blind procedures in experiments are used to enhance internal validity. See double blind procedure; external validity; validity.

International Division of Labour The interdependence of countries wbich trade on global markets.

Internment To segregate and confine those considered suspicious persons. Internment camps were used in Canada during both world wars. During the first war (1914-1918) nationals of Germany and of the Austro-Hungarian (this includes Ukrainians) and Turkish empires were interned. During the Second World War, enemy nationals and Canadian citizens were interned, including Germans, Italians and Japanese Canadians. A total of 720 Japanese-Canadian citizens were interned. Another 20, 000 were removed from their homes and relocated away from the Pacific coast until 1949 when they were allowed to return. See: War Measures Act.

Interpersonal Violence The use of force between individuals to kill, injure, or abuse.

Interpretive Theory A general category of theory including symbolic interactionism, labeling, ethnomethodology, phenomenology and social constructionism. The term is typically contrasted with structural theories which claim to remove the subjectivity of the actor and the researcher and assume that human behaviour can best be understood as determined by the pushes and pulls of structural forces. Interpretive theory is more accepting of free will and sees human behaviour as the outcome of the subjective interpretation of the environment. Structural theory focuses on the situation in which people act while interpretive theory focuses on the actor's definition of the situation in which they act. See: Definition of the Situation.

Intersubjectivity Sociologists who reject the assumption of the objective nature of social reality and focus on the subjective experience of actors have to avoid the fallacy of reducing the world only to personal experience. The concept of intersubjectivity achieves this: ordinary people as well as sociologists assume that if another stood in their shoes they would see the same things. We all constantly make our subjective experience available and understandable by others as well.

Interval Measures See levels of measurement. Invisible Hand of the Market. A phrase associated with the great classical economist Adam Smith (1723-1790) referring to the self-regulating capacity of free markets. Free markets, through the mechanism of supply and demand, are assumed to provide the optimal allocation of scarce economic resources to alternate uses without the need for any conscious direction or control. See: Market Economy.

Involvement The degree to which an individual is active in conventional activities. In Travis Hirschi's work, aspects of the 'social bond'.

IQ (Intelligence Quotient). A score attained on tests of sYmbolic or reasoning abilities. Most social scientists (excluding psychologists) do not put much stock in the validity of IQ tests.

Iron Cage A phrase associated with Max Weber who wrote that the new emphasis on materialism and wordly. success that arose with Protestantism had imprisoned human society in an iron cage of self perpetuating rationalization and depersonalisation.

Iron Law of Oligarchy First defined by German sociologist Robert Michels (1876-1936), this refers to the inherent tendency of all complex organizations, including radical or socialist political parties and labour unions, to develop a ruling clique of leaders with interests in the organization itself rather than in its official aims. These leaders, Michels argued, came to desire leadership and its status and reward more than any commitment to goals. Inevitably, their influence was conservative, seeking to preserve and enhance the organization and not to endanger it by any radical action. Michels based his· argument on the simple observation that day-to-day running of a complex organization by its mass membership was impossible. Therefore, professional full-time leadership and direction was required. In theory the leaders of the organization were subject to control by the mass membership, through delegate conferences and

J

Jekyll and Hyde The primary characters in the 1886 story by Robert Louis Stevenson (Dr. Jekyll and Mr. Hyde). Jekyll was the stereotypical member of the middle class - repressed and moralistic. Through the ingestion of a drug Dr. Jekyll becomes his mirror opposite - vital, egocentric, a sexual predator and ferocious. While expressing a Christian dichotomy between good and evil the two characters are also seen as expressing the conflict within the self between 'ego' and 'id' as well as the conflict between 'culture' and 'nature'.

Judeo-Christian Ethic Refers to broad moral precepts associated with the Jewish and Christian religions. Among these are the idea of responsibility for one's own actions and of redemption of the criminal or sinner through just punishment and repentance.

Jung Originally associated with Freud, Karl Jung developed a distinctive tradition within psychoanalysis, known as analytical psychology, that focused on the idea that all humans share in a collective unconscious mind that is exhibited in the classic forms - or archetypps- of different cultures and in the thoughts, experiences al'.d behaviour of individuals.

Juristic Person The legal concept that corporations are liable to the same laws as 'natural persons'. Treating corporations as individuals raises practical difficulties for legal enforcement and punishment.

Juvenile Delinquents Act First enacted in 1908, and replaced by the Young Offenders Act in 1984, the JDA provided a welfare response to youthful delinquents. The Act was guided by the principle of attending to the best interests of the child and had the power to declare youths to be in a state of delinquency for violating the criminal code of Canada as well as a host of provincial or municipal statutes and bylaws. Certain behaviours such as incorrigibility, sexual promiscuity, and truancy could also be declared delinquent. Legal challenges to the Act in the 1960's questioned its constitutionality (asserting that it was welfare legislation rather than criminal legislation and thus touching on provincial jurisdictions) but these were unsuccessful and the Act was declared to be criminal legislation. Changes to the Act were initiated in the 1960's but a successful compromise was not found until 1984 after many of its provisions were found to be in violation of the Charter of Rights and Freedoms (introduced in 1982).

K

Keynesian Economics The economic theory of John Maynard Keynes (1883-1946) associated with a stress on the necessity of active government intervention in the direction and control of the economy. The most central idea is that the business cycle of capitalist economies, irregular alternations of boom and bust, can be smoothed out by government creation of credit, investment activity and income transfers during economic contraction and the raising of revenue surplus during periods of expansion. This approach, in Keynes' theory, offered insurance against the human cost of mass unemployment and the wastage of productive capacity by economic instability. For several decades, beginning in the 1930's, this was the dominant model for the economic policies of western governments. Since the mid 1970's, monetarism has challenged and, to some extent, displaced Keynesian economics as the framework for public policy and academic work. Keynesian economics is linked to a strong public policy, the welfare state and active state involvement in the economy, while monetarism supports a non-interventionist state, privatization and reliance on the self-regulating forces of the market. See: Monetarism.

Kinsey Report Two volumes on the Sexual Behavior of the Human Male (1948) and the Sexual Behavior of the Human Female (1953) by researcher Alfred C. Kinsey (1894-1956). These two volumes stirred a storm of criticism as the results about the frequency of sexual activity such as premarital intercourse and masturbation were seen as alarming. Further, the report provided what was the first scientific enumeration of homosexual activity and suggested that this sexual preference was very common and must be regarded as normal.

Kinship Structure A term referring to the way social relationships between individuals related by blood, affinal ties or socially defined (fictive) connection are organized and normatively regulated. Kinship is the central organizational principle of many traditional societies, since it is through the kinship structure that social placement, cultural transmission and many functional necessities for life will be met. Extent of relevant kinship connection differs greatly from society to society. Kinship bonds are generally defined more broadly and extensively in traditional societies than in modern capitalist societies.

Kinship The network of social relationships which link individuals through common ancestry, marriage, or adoption.

Komagata Maru The name of a ship chartered by a group of Sikhs and used to sail to Vancouver, Canada, in anticipation of immigration being granted. At the time of its sailing, 1914, Indians could only come to Canada if they sailed continuously (or directly) from India to Canada, although there were no such regular routes. All others were to be prohibited entry to Canada, a method to restrict immigration of people from the Indian sub-continent. The Komagata Maru sailed from Hong Kong with 376 Punjabis on board. On arrival at the port of Vancouver they were denied entry and were kept on board for two months while negotiations proceeded. These negotiations eventually failed and the ship returned to Calcutta where 20 of the passengers were killed in clashes with authorities who were suspicious of the politics of the travellers.

Kula Ring A complex system of visits and exchanges among the Trobriand Islanders of the western Pacific first described by Bronislaw Malinowski in 1922. Necklaces were exchanged in one direction among the residents of a chain of islands and armbands exchanged in the opposite direction (hence the notion of a ring). These exchanges did not serve primarily an economic function but served to create social obligations among peoples which could be depended upon at various times in an individual's life. The person who gave the most gifts would create the most obligations and in this sense create the most wealth by forming a relational net which could be depended upon.

L

Labeling Theory A social theory that holds that society's reaction to certain behaviors is a major factor' in defining the self as deviant. People become 'deviant' because certain labels (thief, prostitute, homosexual) are attached to their behavior by criminal justice authorities and others. The resulting treatment of the individual pushes them into performing the deviant role. Also called "societal reaction" theory.

Labeling Theory A theory which arose from the study of deviance in the late 1950's and early 1960's and was a rejection of consensus theory or structural functionalism. These approaches to deviance assumed that deviance could be understood as consisting of behaviour that violates social norms. Deviance is therefore something objective: it is a particular form of behaviour. Labeling theory rejected this approach and claimed that deviance is not a way of behaving, but is a name put on something: a label. Law is culturally and historically variable: what is crime today is not necessarily crime yesterday or tomorrow. For example in 1890 it was legal to possess marijuana, but illegal to attempt suicide. Today, the law is reversed. This shows that deviance is not something inherent in the behaviour, but is an outcome of how individuals or their behaviour are labeled. If deviance is therefore just a label it makes sense to ask: where does the label come from? How does the label come to be applied to specific behaviours and to particular individuals? The first question leads to a study of the social origins of law. The second question leads to an examination of the actions of labelers such as, psycl1iatrists, police, coroners, probation officers, judges and juries. See: Amplification of Deviance / Secondary Deviance / Moral Entrepreneurs.

Labour Theory of Value A fundamental component of the economic and social theories of Karl Marx (1818-1883) and of his analysis of capitalist exploitation. Marx argues that the value of any commodity is determined by the socially necessary labour time that goes into its production. Marx uses the term 'socially necessary labour time' because the labour time required to create a commodity depends on the society's levels of technology and craft. In Marx's theory, commodities should in principle be exchanged in the market place for prices that exactly correspond to the necessary labour time embodied in them. When a commodity is exchanged- or sold - for more than its labour value, a surplus value is realized. This theory of value provides the foundation of Marx's claim that labour is exploited in a capitalist society: the capitalist, through the power of capital ownership, is able to pay the worker less than the market value of the commodities produced and the surplus value is captured by capital and largely re-invested to augment the means of production.

Laissez Faire Literally, 'to leave alone'. This is the economic doctrine that government should not interfere in the economic or social regulation of society unless absolutely necessary. It assumes that the competitive system of free markets is the best means of allocation of scarce resources between alternative uses. Government intervention in the market place to regulate economic activity is seen as illegitimate and inefficient. This doctrine lost popularity in the middle of the twentieth century, with the rise of the 'welfare state' and extensive public ownership of parts of the economy, but has regained favor in the 1980's and 1990's. See: Classical Economic Theory / Invisible Hand of the Market.

Laissez-Faire One of the main doctrines of capitalism that asserts that government should not interfere with commerce.

Lament for a Nation The title of Canadian philosopher George

Grant's 1965 prophetic book in which he argues that Canada's national autonomy was lost to the creeping forces of continentalism. See: Continentalism.

Land Claims See: *Comprehensive Land Claims / Specific Land Claims / Calder Case.*

Latchkey Children Children who spend a part of the day unsupervised, usually the period from the end of school until a parent returns from work.

Latent Functions The unintended consequences of one part of a sociocultural system. For example, the reform of big city political machines had a lot of unintended consequences on the govern ability of American cities (see also Manifest Function).

Law (1) A body of rules or norms passed by a legislated authority and enforced by an authorized and specialized body. Law clearly identifies the defining characteristic of the state - the ability to establish and legitimately use coercion to enforce a framework of social regulation and direction. The state, by passing law and having the authority to force compliance, can coerce citizens to act in particular ways (or leave the country). Not all societies have law. While all large-scale, modern societies have law it was not found among hunter-gatherer, pastoral or horticultural societies. In these societies social life was regulated primarily by custom and tradition. (2) A written rule established by a political authority and backed by government.

Ledain Commission Gerald LeDain was the chair of the 1969 Royal Commission on the Non-Medical Use of Drugs, investigating the role the government and courts should play in prohibiting and regulating drugs used largely for recreational purposes. The Commission produced numerous published volumes, which rank among the most thorough and accurate assessments of drugs and drug policy in the world, but none of the recommendations were legislated. The Commission stimulated the new sociology of deviance in Canada through its sponsorship of research.

Left Realism A criminological perspective emerging in Britain in response to the rise of neo-conservatism. The right-wing politics of Prime Minister Margaret Thatcher made it clear that left-leaning criminology had little impact on social policy and was going to have little significance in the future. Some critical criminologists struggled to make their work relevant and did so by focusing on the working class as victims of street crime, state and corporate crime and women as victims of male crime. They asserted that official studies of crime underestimated victimization of the working class and women and supported community controlled research as a method of getting at the 'reality' of their experience. Social policies to reduce victimization of marginal communities, involve communities in crime prevention, return political control to local communities and increase police accountability follow from this beginning point. Left realism can be contrasted with left idealism, which, while also believing that the structure of capitalism is the culprit in crime, tended to see working class crime as acts of rebellion or political resistance. This can be seen as a somewhat romantic or idealistic view.

Legitimacy The generally held belief that a particular social institution is just and valid.

Legitimation Crisis A condition during which a political order, or government, is unable to evcke sufficient commitment or sense of authority to properly govern. The government, or those in authority, is no longer seen as legitimate. Low levels of voter turnout in the United States, for example, may be seen as an indicator of a legitimation crisis as may the massive rejection of the Charlottetown accord in Canada when acceptance was recommended by most of the established political leaders in the nation. From a political economy perspective the major source of the legitimation crisis is the economic transformation of the world in conjunction with what is termed 'globalization'.

This transformation raises the possibility that citizens will see the economic system with its growing class polarization and impoverishment as illegitimate as well as the governments that attempt to regulate this new world economic order. See: Globalization / Exceptional State.

Legitimation Crisis The lack of sufficient commitment on the part of members to a particular social institution for that organization to function effectively. Governments that lack legitimation often rely on repression to continue their rule (which is very inefficient). Legitimation crisis in other institutions produce parallel responses on the part of administration.

Leninism Refers to the ideas of Vladimir Ilich Lenin (1870-1924) leader of the Russian Revolution (1917) and founder of the Soviet Union. Lenin's ideas were mainly derived from Marxism but he had a distinctive view of the importance of leadership in creating a working class revolution. He advocated the organization of the working class by a disciplined and centralised Communist Party believing, unlike Marx, that class consciousness could only develop under the guidance and direction of party leadership. Many historians have argued Lenin's focus on the dominant role of the party and of its central leadership led directly to the establishment of Stalin's dictatorship and to millions of deaths in the attempt to establish Soviet- style communism. Lesbianism. Sexual activities and emotional attachments between women.

Level of Measurement In quantitative social science concepts are measured in order to provide a frequency count for each value of a variable. Not all measurements have the same qualities and some statistical tests require particular levels of measurement. There are four levels of measurement: nominal, ordinal, interval and ratio. Nominal measures only allow for the placing of the subjects into categories, e.g.: female and male. Ordinal levels of measurement allow the researcher to rank respondents, e.g.: strongly agree and agree. Interval measurement allow the researcher to specify the distance between respondents, John has 10 less units of intelligence than does Mary. A ratio level of measurement allows the researcher to express various scores as ratios and this requires an absolute zero. For example, Mary has twice as many siblings as does John. Complex statistical tests require interval or ratio measurements.

Leveraged Buy-Outs A corporate takeover in which the purchaser finances the acquisition almost exclusively by incurring debt, rather than from corporate profits and income flows. Typically the acquiring corporation will issue shares and corporate bonds that are not backed by any significant collateral property or obligation. Bonds issued in these circumstances are popularly called 'junk bonds'.

Liberal Democracy Refers to those societies based on some form of democracy coupled with capitalism.

Liberal Feminism A form of feminism which argues that the liberal principles of equality, freedom and equality of opportunity must be fully extended to women. This form of feminism does not call for specific structural changes to society. Neither patriarchy nor capitalism are identified as the enemies of women, rather the restricted reach of liberalism is identified as the problem. See: Feminism / Royal Commission on the Status of Women.

Liberalism An ideology that upholds private property, individual rights, legal equality, freedom of choice and democratic government. Liberalism suggests that the essence of freedom is to be free from constraint. Liberalism is an ideology that supports capitalism and advocates the principle of free markets, left largely undirected by governments. While liberalism upholds free markets, it also places great value on equal of opportunity and is strongly opposed to ascriptive processes in society, since they restrict individual choice and deny equal access to satisfaction. In the twentieth century, a more active view of the state's role in creating improved equality of opportunity in society became important within liberalism. (This trend in liberalism was also a reaction to the development of trade unions and of socialist and populist movements.) There was a massive expansion in state - provided education, social programs etc. from the end of the 19th century until the 1960's and 1970's. In the 1980's and 1990's a more classical view of liberalism has returned to prominence, one that advocates a much smaller role for the state and increased reliance on the workings of the free market. In making this argument, classical liberals claim that intervention in the market rarely, if ever, promotes choice, but frustrates the market adjustments that ultimately improve efficiency, the wealth of society and the ability of individuals to make choices.

Liberation Theology A mixture of Christian belief and political activism usually derived from a Marxist analysis of social inequality. Acceptance of this theology encourages priests to assume a political posture in the pulpit and in their activities with the community. This has led to many confrontations between churches and corporate interests and the religious hierarchy has been urged to restrict the political activity of priests.

Lihertarianism A philosophy or belief system which gives priority to the liberty of the individual. May be associated with classical liberalism regarding economic matters or the protection of those negative liberties which declare the right of the individual to be free from interference by the state, or the community, unless the actions of the individual constitute harm to others. For example, the individual has the right to freedom of speech, freedom of association, freedom of religious expression, freedom of contract. Libertarianism is related to individualism and contrasted with communitarianism: *See: Communitarian.*

Life Expectancy The number of years a newborn in a particular society can expect to live. Also refers to the number of further years which people at any given age can, on average, expect to live.

Life-Span The maximum length of life that is biologically possible for a member of a given species.

Lifestyle Changes Often called for when treating chronic disease. Rather than curing the disease, the patient makes changes in lifestyle (nutrition, exercise, smoking sessation, weight reduction, alleviating stress) that help to control the disease process.

LifestylelExposure Theory A theory of victimization that acknow ledges that not everyone has the same lifestyle and that some lifestyles expose people to more risks than do other lifestyles. If you go to bed early you are less at risk than if you like to visit the bars many nights a week.

Limited War Warfare fought principally by a relatively small number of soldiers to reach specific and politically limited objectives (see also Total War).

Literacy The ability of individuals to read and write. Local Knowledge. Knowledge of a local community possessed by individuals who spend long periods of their lives in them.

Lone-Parent Family Used by Stati$tics Canada to refer to single-parent families.

Longevity A long duration of life. Or, a long tenure in an organization.

Longitudinal Studies These measure relationships between variables over a period of time. For example, one might follow a group of males from birth to age 30 to measure their involvement with the criminal justice system over time ann relate this information to their parents' socio-economic status. A series of cross-sectional investigations taken over time will provide a longitudinal study.

Looking Glass Self Developed by C.H. Cooley (1864-1929) to describe the social nature of the self and the link between society and individual. In this formulation social interaction is like a mirror, it allows us to see ourselves as others see us. This was an early formulation of symbolic interactionism but less influential than that of George Herbert Mead.

Lorenz Curve Developed by Max O. Lorenz in order to describe the extent of inequality in a society. Imagine a graph in which the cummulated income (expressed as a percentage) is placed on the vertical axis and the cumulated number of households (expressed as a percentage) is placed on the horizontal axis. If there was perfect equality (so that the first 10 per cent of the households received 10% of the income and 20% of the households received 20% of the income, etc.) a diagonal line would be drawn across the graph. When actual income distributions are depicted on this graph the line (a curve) departs from the line of perfect equality. For example, the bottom 20 per cent of households may receive only 4.5% of the total income. This line is the Lorenz curve and can be expressed mathematically. The Gini coefficient is an expression of the ratio of the amount of the graph located between the line of perfect inequality and the Lorenz curve to the total area of the graph below the line of equality. See: Gini Coefficient.

Lower Canada Established upon the division of the province of Quebec in 1791 as a result of the Constitutional Act, this territory was to eventually become the province of Quebec. See: Lower Canada / Constitutional Act (1791).

Lower-Class Culture It has been argued by some that the lower class have developed and transmit to their children, a different set of cultural values and expectations. They argue further that this culture is a barrier to their success in society. Used in this way it is associated with the 'culture of poverty thesis'. More recently sociologists have rejected this emphasis on values and argue that structural barriers create the conditions which might generate these values and expectations. If this is so, the solution is to transform the structures and not to blame the poor.

M

Macho, or Machismo The public display of characteristi-cally (and usually exaggerated) masculine behaviour.

Macro-Perspective The perspective, or the form of analysis, which focuses on the structure of society and provides a way of seeing society as a unified whole. In this perspective minimal attention is given to the individual or the subjectivity of actors - the structures of society are thought to be primary and responsible for shaping the individual.

Macrosociology The study of large-scale organizations, sociocultural systems, or the world system of societies.

Mafia Originally used to identify a specific Sicilian crime group, is now commonly used to identify any ethnic or regionally based crime organization.

Magic (1) Rituals which attempt to influence supernatural beings to help achieve human ends. (2) The performance of routines, usually in a fixed or rigid manner, designed to influence the future, persuade the 'gods' or shape fate. The ball player who believes that wearing the same sweater or eating the same meal before a game will determine whether the teams wins or not is performing magic.

Majority In sociology this term does not refer to a numerical majority. Rather, it refers to that group(s) which has power. In South Africa, the Blacks were the majority numerically, but a minority in terms of power. All this of course began to change with the inclusion of Blacks in the electoral process and the election of Nelson Mandela.

Male Inexpressiveness The difficulties men have in talking about their feelings to others.

Malthusian Crisis Refers to the ideas of Thomas Malthus (1766-1834) who argued that while populations grow exponentially the rate of increase in the food supply is much less. This creates a natural limit on populations and produces miserable conditions for society and inevitable mass starvation, unless of course individuals practice birth control. Malthus didn't advocate contraceptives, rather he advocated reducing sexual intercourse. See: Demographic Transition / Exponential Growth.

Malthusianism Thomas Malthus' theory of population dynamics, according to which population increase inevitably comes up against the 'natural limits' of food supply. Population grows geometrically (1, 2, 4, 8, 16, . . .) while food supply grows arithmetically (1, 2, 3, 4, 5, ...). The debate rages on, there are neo-malthusians and anti-malthusians among us today!

Man in the House Rule A regulation of most Canadian provinces, declaring that a woman who lives with a man can not receive welfare in her own right. The assumption being that she must be dependent on the man.

Managed Care The reorganization of the health care delivery along corporate lines (see also Health Maintenance Organizations).

Managerial Capitalism A change in the control of capitalist enterprises from owners (which predominated in Marx's day) to control by (very well) salaried managers.

Managerial Revolution Traditionally, manufacturing enterprises had been owned and controlled by individuals or families. In the mid 19th century however, joint-stock companies began to emerge and over time increasing numbers of investors held a share of ownership and received a portion of the profits. These companies no longer had a single owner and managers emerged to control business operations. It was assumed that this new breed of salaried workers would transform the workplace: values other than profit would enter into business calculations and there would be greater harmony between workers and executives. Since most managers have become large stock holders (and thus owners) the significance of the -:nanagerial revolution has been called into question.

Manifest Destiny A belief found among the early American colonies that held it to be the destiny of the colonies to stretch from the Atlantic to the Pacific and as far south as the Rio Grande river. In the early 19th century this belief was behind the decision to reclaim the territories of Texas, Oregon and California. Bring the country into conflict with England and Mexico. Canadian politicians were concerned that this belief also held that the American state should eventually occupy the territories to the north and much Canadian policy can be seen as an attempt to cut off American territorial and market expansion. *See: Continentalism.*

Manifest Function The intended and known consequences of one part of a sociocultural system. For example, the reform of big city political machines had the intended consequence of limiting (relatively) corruption by city officials (see also Latent Function).

Market Economy An economy in which goods and services are freely exchanged without obstruction or regulation and where decisions about production and consumption are made by many separate individuals each seeking satisfaction of specific needs and desires. Sometimes used interchangeably with 'capitalist economy', but this is an error since a cooperatively based economy could also be operated on market principles. See: Invisible Hand of the Market.

Marketing Boards Used frequently within Canada, bodies which attempt to regulate the marketplace so as to soften the harmful activities of a free market. For example, the Canadian Wheat Board (the 33rd largest firm in Canada and the fifth largest exporter) requires that Canadian grains be sold to the Board at a set price and the Board then sells the grain on the international market. Similarly marketing boards may regulate the number of commercial producers of eggs or chickens. These activities are thought to provide a stable market for products, guarantee the producer a reasonable return, limit foreign control of commercial activity and prevent major fluctuations in supply and prices. In recent years there has been growing pressure within Canada, as well as from international producers, to remove marketing boards and let the production of goods and their prices be set by the free market.

Marriage A socially approved sexual and economic relationship between two or more individuals.

Marsh Report Published in 1943 the Report on Social Security for Canada was written by Leonard Marsh and resulted from his work as research adviser on the federal government Committee on Post-War Reconstruction. Although the Marsh report was largely ignored it does provide the intellectual foundation for much of the welfare state which was developed over the next 25 years. Marsh was born in London, England and emigrated to Canada in 1930. After the war he taught at the University of British Columbia. The Marsh report can be compared to the Beveridge Report in Britain.

Marshall Inquiry A Royal Commission of Inquiry initiated in September of 1987 to· investigate the wrongful conviction and imprisonment of Donald Marshall Jr. for the 1971 death of Sandy Seale in Sydney Nova Scotia. Marshall, a Micmac, spent 11 years in prison before he was found to be innocent.

Marxism (1) Contemporary social theory deriving its main elements from Marx's ideas. Marxist theory strongly emphasizes class struggle and material causation. (2) The body of philosophical, political, economic and sociological ideas associated with Karl Marx (1818-1883) and his lifelong collaborator Frederick Engels (1820-1895). The term is also used more generally to refer to work in the social sciences and humanities that employs key ideas and concepts from Marx and Engels' original writings. The core of Marxist ideas is the claim that each historical period has a distinct mode of production that rests upon particular forces - or technological organization - of production and distinct ways of organizing social relationships between people in the economy. This mode of production then exerts the primary influence in shaping social relations within the society in general as well as its politics, law and intellectual ideas.

Marxist Feminism A form of feminism which believes that women's oppression is a symptom of a more fundamental form of oppression. Women are not oppressed by men or by sexism, but by capitalism itself. If all women are to be liberated, capitalism must be replaced with socialism. In Frederick Engels' (1820-1895) writing, women's oppression originated with the development of private property and of regulated family and marital relationships. Men's control of economic resources develops with settled society and the development of separate spheres of life for the two sexes. In capitalist societies, women become segregated into the domestic sphere and men into the outer world of paid work. Economic and social inequality between the sexes is increased and women's' subordination in marriage, the family and in society in general is intensified. Engels assumed that socialist revolution, through which the means of production would become common property, would result in the development of equal access to paid work for both men and women and the consequent disappearance of gendered inequality between the sexes. See: Liberal Feminism / Radical Feminism.

Masculine Female By mixing the notions of gender and sex this term identifies those of the female sex who demonstrate features of the masculine gender.

Masculinity The characteristic forms of behavior expected of men in any given culture.

Masculinization A term central to the critique of traditional academic discussions of the female offender and of popular depictions of female criminality. The term refers to the attribution of male characteristics to women in an attempt to understand their behaviour rather than locating women's behaviour in female experience or structural location. Freda Alder, for example, argued in 1975 that the women's liberation movement would lead to an increase in female crime because liberation would make women more like men.

Mass Culture A set of cultural values and ideas that arise from common exposure of a population to the same cultural activities, communications media, music and art, etc, Mass culture becomes possible only with modern communications and electronic media. A mass culture is transmitted to individuals, rather than arising from people's daily interactions, and therefore lacks the distinctive content of cultures rooted in community and region. Mass culture tends to reproduce the liberal value of individualism and to foster a view of the citizen as consumer. See: Popular Culture / Mass Society.

Mass Media (1) Forms of communication designed to reach a vast audience without any personal contact between the senders and receivers. Examples would include newspapers, magazines, video recordings, radio and television. (2) Sociologically speaking in modern times the 'community' has been replaced by a 'mass', a set of autonomous and disconnected individuals, with little sense of community. The mass media then is that media (radio, television, newspapers, etc,) which are targeted at the mass rather than at specific groups or communities,

Mass Society Refers to a society with a mass culture and large-scale, impersonal, social institutions. Even the most complex and modern societies have lively primary group social relationships, so the concept can be thought of as an 'ideal type', since it does not exist in empirical reality. It is intended to draw attention to the way in which life in complex societies, with great specialization and rationalized institutions, can become too anonymous and impersonal and fail to support adequate bonds between the individual and the community, The concept reflects the same concern in sociology - loss of community - that Tonnies expressed in his idea of Gesellschaft, See: Mass Culture,

Massey Report Vincent Massey, the first Canadian-horn Governor General of Canada, was chairman of the Royal Commission on National Development in the Arts, Letters and Sciences (1951). This report recommended the creation of the Canada Council and federal government spending on university education, a provincial responsibility. The Commission was an early expression of the need for Canadians to strengthen their cultural institutions in order to avoid being dominated by American cultural influences.

Master Status (1) A position that is so central to the identity of the individual that it overshadows all other statuses. (2) A status that overrides all others in perceived importance. Whatever other personal or social qualities the individu~l possesses they are judged primarily by this one attribute. Criminal is an example of a master status that determines the community's identification of an individual. A master status can also arise from other achieved or ascribed roles.

Materialism The view that 'material conditions' (usually economic and technological factors) have the central role in determining social change.

Matriarchy (1) A society or family in which women possess most of the power and authority. While there is some dispute among social scientists, there is no clear evidence of matriarchal societies existing in the world in either the past or the present. Individual families, however, have frequently exhibited matriarchal structure with women clearly possessing dominant authority and control. The term must be distinguished from matrilineal which refers to the system of tracing descent through the blood lines of women and which exists in a number of world societies. See: Matrilineal

Societies (2) Social organization in which females dominate males.

Matrilineal Descent The tracing of kinship through only the female line (see also Patrilineal Descent).

Matrilineal Societies Societies in which descent is traced through mothers rather than through fathers. In such societies property is often passed from mothers to daughters and the custom of matrilocal residence may be practiced. In such systems, the descendants of men are their sister's children and not their own, who belong to their mother's matrilineage. Matrilineage is sometimes associated with polyandry or group marriage where women have a variety of sexual partners and lines of male descent are uncertain. See: Patrilineal Descent / Bilineal Descent.

Matrilocal Residence The custom or practice of a new husband moving to his wife's village or household after marriage. Tends to be found among matrilineal societies. See; patrilocal residence.

Matrilocality A family residential pattern in which the husband is expected to live near to the wife's parents (see also Neolocality).

Maturational Reform The observation that involvement in crime tends to decrease as people age. A visit to any prison confirms this as would the tracking of 10 year olds crime involvements as they go through adolescence and into adulthood.

Mccarthyism Joseph McCarthy was elected Senator for Wisconsin and rose to public attention when in a 1950 speech he claimed to have in his hand the names of 205 individuals who were active members of the communist party, many within government itself. From this point on he campaigned against communists and others described as subversive to

American interests. In 1953 he became chair of the Senate's permanent committee of investigation and turned the committee's attention to the pursuit of communists and subversives (including homosexuals). Although in control of this committee for a short time many people were named, marly reputations damaged and public expression of dissent was silenced for a decade.

Mcjob A low paying, low status job usually performed on a part-time basis and having no career potential. In the past, these jobs were usually the first work experiences of new entrants to the labour market, but economic changes are now thought to have made them a long term destination for growing numbers of workers. See: Generation X.

Mcworld A concept developed by Benjamin Barber (1995) to describe the new globalised world where nation states have little power and citizenship has become meaningless as a cornerstone of democracy. This new world is ruled by corporations (multinational corporations or in Barber's 'terms antinational corporations) which see everyone simply as consumers. In this new world citizens can no longer effectively use democracy to enhance or protect social values because this would interfere with the marketplace. The assumption is that the actions of countless consumers will best satisfy the social needs of communities. See: consumer culture; multinational;

Me A concept of George Herbert Mead (1863-1921) referring to the aspect of personal identity or self that is aware of and has internalized the expectations of others. The 'me' is guided and shaped by the culture of an individual's society or group, which is internalized and acts to direct and control behaviour. In social interaction, each individual's behaviour is shaped by the interaction of their socially shaped 'me' and their more spontaneous and ego-focused T. See: I.

Mean (1) A measure of central tendency for data at the interval or ratio level of measurement, commonly called an average.

Determined by summing the values or scores in a distribution and dividing by the number of values or scores. See: Median / Mode. (2) A statistical measure of 'central tendency' or average based on dividing a total by the number of individual cases involved. The mean is very sensitive to extreme scores. For example, the average life expectancy for people in a society with high infant mortality would be a misleading me2.sure (see also Median).

Means of Production Marx's term referring to the means whereby the production of material goods is carried on in a society. Marx included in this concept both technology and the social relations among the producers (based on the ownership of that technology).

Means Test A policy for the provision of social assistance or services which determines access by considering whether the applicant has the means to provide the service from their own resources. Legal aid in most provinces, for example, is means tested; legal aid is provided without charge to those unable to pay while others pay part or all of the cost of the service. A policy of universality is opposed to this and is one in which all citizen have a right to assistance or service without charge. In the past, for example, the 'baby bonus' was offered to all mothers of children. Similarly, health care is now offered to all citizens without charge regardless of their income. There is a growing tendency towards means tests, however. Old age income support is now 'clawed back' from seniors with incomes over a certain amount, for example, and in the future will only be given to those with income below a set amount.

Measure of Crime All science at one point or another must deal with measurement. One can think of measuring the weight of a friend, measuring the height of all three year olds, etc. The question is: what tool or method to use in the measurement? In the above examples it seems obvious; use a bathroom scale or perhaps a medical scale, or use a tape measure. It is much more difficult to decide how to measure crime. Do we rely on police records, do we find the number of people incarcerated, or do we use a victimization questionnaire ? Whatever the tool or measurement one uses it must be asked: Is this measurement reliable? Is it valid?

Mechanical Solidarity A term used by Emile Durkheim (1858-1917) to refer to a state of community bonding or interdependency which rests on a similarity of beliefs and values, shared activities, and ties of kinship and cooperation. See: Organic Solidarity / Ideal Type.

Mechanization The use of machinery to replace human labor.

Median (1) A measure of central tendency for data at the interval or ratio levels of measurement. When a set of values or scores are arranged in ascending order that value which divides the sequence in half; half of the values or scores are greater than the median and half are less than the median. A median is frequently superior to a mean as a measure of central tendency when there are some scores or values which are significantly higher than all others in the distribution. The median gives these high scores the same emphasis as all other scores while a mean gives them much greater weight or emphasis. See: Mean / Mode. (2) The number that falls halfway in a range of numbers-the score below which are half the scores and above which are the other half. The median is a way of calculating 'central tendency' which is sometimes more useful than calculating a mean (particularly when many extreme scores are in the distribution). Medicaid. Government program (federal and state) to provide medical care to the poor.

Medical Model The application of the medical perspective in explaining and treating troublesome human behavior.

Medicare Government health insurance for those over sixty-five.

Medieval Period Also known as the 'middle ages' this term was developed in the 18th and 19th centuries to refer to the period of European history between the decline and fall of the Roman empire and the Renaissance: approximately 500 to 1500.

Medium is the Message A central idea of communications theorist Marshall McLuhan (1911-1980) who demonstrated that each media (print, speech, television) is connected with a different pattern or arrangement among the senses and thus results in a different awareness or perception. Although the literal message of a radio report of a disaster and the television coverage of the same event may be identical, the event will be perceived differently and take on different meaning because the two media arrange the senses differently. In this sense the medium (the singular for the word media) is the message; this message is often more important than the literal message.

Meech Lake Accord An agreement by the Prime Minister of Canada and the ten provincial premiers, signed June 3, 1987, to amend the Constitution of Canada to provide for: explicit recognition of Quebec as a 'distinct society'; increased provincial power over immigration; limitation of federal government spending power; recognition of Quebec's right to veto further Constitutional change; provincial participation over appointments of Supreme Court Of Canada judges.

The Accord required assent from Parliament and all ten provincial legislatures, but did not receive final ratification in either Newfoundland or Manitoba before the June 23, 1990 deadline. Principal components of the Accord were later included in the Charlottetown Agreement (August 28, 1992), a further attempt to amend the Constitution of Canada, which was defeated in a national referendum.

Megalopolis A vast unbroken urban region consisting of two or more central cities connected by their surrounding suburbs.

Member A central term in ethnomethodological theory and replaces terms like 'status position' or 'role' in structural theories. From a structural perspective an . individual actor is examined according to their structural characteristics (gender, age, ethnicity, class) and is assumed to behave in accordance with these structural characteristics. The subjectivity of the actor is insignificant. Ethnomethodology on the other hand, attempts to highlight the subjectivity of the individual actor and thus needs to identify the person in a way that acknowledges their knowledge, competence, engagement, commitment, or ability to make sense. The term 'member' accomplishes this. Ethnomethodology also refers to membership categories (things like teacher, mother, employee) and identifies membership categorization devices and rules of application (things like the economy rule and the consistency rule) as a form of ethnomethodological analysis.

Mens Rea Criminal intent. An act must be blameworthy. It must be done with criminal intent or be an act of gross negligence or recklessness. Canadian courts have traditionally favoured an objective definition of mens rea using the test of what a reasonable person would have thought and done in the situation. Recently a more subjective view has been adopted. See: Beaver Decision.

Mental Disorder The inability to psychologically cope effectively with the demands of day-to-day life. Psychiatrists recognize two general types of mental disorder, neurosis (milder forms of illness, such as anxiety states) and psychosis (more serious forms of disturbance, in which individuals lose touch with reality). The organic and sociocultural basis of various mental disorders are disputed matters.

Mental Superstructure Sociocultural materialism term used to refer to conscious and unconscious motives for human behavior. Borrowed from Max Weber, there are four basic motivations for human behavior: wertrational (or value oriented rationality), affective action (action motivated by emotions), traditional action (action motivated by what Weber calls the "eternal yesterday"), and zweckrational (goal oriented rational action). (See also Superstructure, and Cultural Su perstructure).

Mercantilism An economic theory that preceded the modern concept of a market economy regulated by the forces of supply and demand. Ml3rcantilist ideas were quite varied but a common theme is the importance to any nation of maintainir.g a favorable balance of international trade, ideally leading to net inflows of precious metals. To attain this end it was appropriate for the state to intervene in the market place by vigorous economic regulation backed by state authority. Among classic mercantilist policies were laws requiring colonial territories to trade only with the imperial power, imposition of monopolies in merchant shipping and trading rights and the establishment of physical quotas to manage and regulate trade. In Canada's early history, trading monopolies of both French and English origin - like the famous Hudson's Bay Company - were an expression of mercantilist policies and they played a central role in the exploration and economic development of Canada.

Meritocracy Rule by those chosen on the principle of merit. The principle of merit is consistent with liberal theory and assumes equality of opportunity and occupational advancement based on achievement rather than ascription. Emile Durkheim's notion of the 'spontaneous division of labour' and the argument of Kingsley Davis and Wilbert Moore (1945) on the function of inequality both depend on the belief that in a liberal society people will be rewarded on the basis of talent or merit and that the more talented and thus meritorious will come to occupy the more important positions in society. See: Autocracy / Plutocracy *I* Democracy.

Meta-Analysis There has been so much research on specific topics (i.e., the effectiveness of corrections, the effects of divorce on children) that it is possible to do analyses of a collection of research results - this is meta -analysis.

Metanarrative A story, narrative or theory which claims to be above the ordinary or local accounts of social life.

Postmodernists claim that the majority of the writings of Marx, Durkheim, Weber are offered as metanarratives, presented as capturing universal properties of social life and thus superior to local or more grounded stories. Postmodernist social theorists argue for a return to the local, the rejection of grand theory and a privileged position for science and its narratives, and an acknowledgment of the inherently political nature of all narratives.

Method Is the tool or instrument one uses to measure crime (or height). One method might be to go to the police department and go through all of their files.

Another might be to use the data provided by the Centre for Justice Statistics, and yet another might be to design a questionnaire to be given to people asking if they have ever committed a crime or been a victim of a crime. The method one might use to measure weight is to step on the bathroom scale. There are obviously other methods for measuring weight. There are many methods for measuring crime.

Methodological Holism An orientation in research and analysis where the aim is to understand the phenomenon under investigation in its totality as unique and apart from its component parts, rather than to seek to fragment it into known or familiar components. The key idea, in essence, is that the whole differs from the sum of the parts not only in quantity but in quality.

Methodological Individualism The belief that all sociological explanations can be reduced to characteristics of individuals who make up the society. This position is also known as 'psychologism': explaining social phenomenon in terms of the psychological dispositions of members of society. This is a rejection of macro-structuralists working in the tradition of Emile Durkheim or Karl Marx who assumed that the characteristics of individuals need not be considered. They argued that social facts (society) had an existence of their own and that it was these which sociologists were interested in. See: *Psychologism.*

Methodology The study or critique of methods. There are many philosophical issues around the use of a particular method or about positivism or measurement itself.

Metis Refers to people who have a mixed biological and cultural ancestry. These were usually mixtures of French and Indian or British/Scottish and Indian. Originally the term referred to the French-Indian people who settled in the Red River area of Manitoba, a group who saw themselves as having a distinct cultural and political position in society and their history is important in understanding Canada. This group is now represented by the Metis National Council. The Native Council of Canada acknowledges other people of mixed ancestry as being Metis. *See: Red River Rebellion.*

Metropolis-Hinterland Theory A theory of social and economic development that examines how economically advanced societies, through trade and colonialism, distort and retard the economic development of less developed societies and regions. A metropolis is identified as the centre of political and economic power, as having a more advanced labour market, more skilled and educated workers, an abundance of value-added production, higher standard of living, etc. A hinterland would be less able to withstand the political and economic interference of the metropolis, would have an abundance of resource extraction industries, fewer skilled and educated workers, a lower standard of living and in many ways would emulate the culture of the metropolis. For more than a century Ontario, or even more narrowly the Toronto region, was seen as the metropolis to a vast Canadian hinterland and the United States has been seen as the metropolis for a Canadian hinterland. See: Dependent Development / World Systems Theory.

Micro-Perspective A perspective, or form of analysis, which focuses on the individual and their subjectivity, rather than focusing on the structures of society thought to be external and constraining on the individual. This perspective is found in symbolic interactionism, ethnomethodology, labeling theory, interpretive theory.

Microsociology The study of small scale patterns of human 'interaction and behavior within specific settings.

Middle Class (1) A social class broadly defined occupationally as those working in white-collar and lower managerial occupations; is sometimes defined by reference to income levels or' subjective identification of the participants in the study. (2) There have been several different approaches to defining this term. (1) In Karl Marx's (1818-1883) analysis of class, the middle class is the 'petite bourgeoisie' who are in small scale independent business or craft or who have special skills that provide' an income outside the wage system of employed labour. Marx assumed that this class would diminish in number as capitalist enterprises developed, consolidated into larger units and eliminated small-scale competition. (2) The term can also be used statistically to define a group of individuals who occupy an intermediate position in a society's income strata: for example those who earn between 66% and 133% of a society's average family incomes. These are attempts to define the 'middle class' objectively, by some standard of measurement, but a more subjective view is possible: the middle class are those individuals who orient themselves to the values and expectations they consider normative for average members of their society. This approach is useful for understanding why most Canadians irrespective of occupation, wealth or income identify themselves as middle class.

Middle-Class Measuring Rod A phrase suggesting that children and young people from the lower class often find themselves in situations in which they are measured against middle-class standards. The school, for example, rests on the middle-class values of reading and writing and the teachers are primarily middle-class. Lower-class children often realize they are never going to 'measure up' so anticipate failure, become frustrated, or drop out of school. They may also begin to move towards other marginal students in the school and become engaged in deviant or criminal activity.

Migration The movement of people from one country or region to another in order to settle permanently.

Military Rule Government by military leaders. Military-Industrial Complex. A reciprocal relationship (such as the interchange of personnel) between select business firms and the armed forces of a society, based on common interests in weapons production.

Millenarianism Beliefs held by the members of some religious movements that cataclysmic changes will occur in the near future (often centered around the year 2000 and the second coming of Christ) heralding the arrival of a new epoch in human affairs.

Millennium Literally, a period of one thousand years or a thousandth anniversary. In Christian tradition the Millennium refers to the one thousands years of peace that will accompany the second coming of Christ. Christ's coming is portended by growing strife and conflict (an apocalyptic vision). Millenarianism, refers to the belief in the doctrine of the Millennium (the coming of Christ). These ideas have come together to suggest that the end of a thousand years will be associated with social breakdown, despair and turmoil and will be followed by new energy and confidence. The non-religious beliefs of Millenarianism have been associated with the end of one hundred year periods (the end of the 18th century or the 19th century).

Ministerial Responsibility Associated with Parliamentary systems of government, this is the convention that a minister is answerable to Parliament for the conduct and actions of his or her ministry's personnel. Originally, the responsibility was quite strictly imposed on a minister and resignation might be demanded even where the minister did not have, and could not reasonably have been expected to have, knowledge of improper or negligent acts or omissions by officials. In recent times, this idea has been abandoned and it is rare for a minister to accept responsibility and resign.

Minority Group (or Ethnic Minority) (1) A group of people who are defined on the basis of their ethnicity or race. Because of their distinct physical or cultural characteristics, they are singled out for unequal treatment within a society. (2) A group distinguished by being on the margins of power, status or the allocation of resources within the society. 'Visible minority' refer to those racial or ethnic groups in a society which are marginal from the power and economic structure of society, not to those which are few in number. In South Africa, Blacks are the statistical majority but were for countless decades a social minority. Women can also be identified as a social minority group.

Miscegenation Sexual intercourse between individuals of differing racial groups. At various times and places (including the American south and South Africa under apartheid) there have been laws prohibiting both sexual intercourse and marriage between racially mixed couples. The Supreme Court of the United States struck down miscegenation laws in 1967.

Mixed Economy Economies which have major elements of both capitalism and socialism (such as many economies of Europe).

Mobility, Social The movement of an individual or group from one class or social status to another. Usually, the point of reference is an individual's class or status of social origin and social mobility occurs when later class or status positions differ from those of origin. Social mobility would be high where individuals have equal opportunity to achieve new statuses and low where there are inequalities of opportunity and processes of status ascription. See: Demand Mobility/ Open Class Ideology.

Mode of Production (1) The dominant form of social and technical organization of economic production in a society.

Historically a variety of modes of production can be distinguished based on both technology and the structure of social relationships. Historical modes of production include hunter-gatherer with very simple technology and common ownership; ancient, with more advanced technology and slavery; feudal, with simple technology and landowning lords and bonded serfs; and capitalist with sophisticated technology, private ownership of capital and a wage system. See: State Capitalism. (2) The technology and the practices employed for expanding or limiting basic subsistence production, especially the production of food and other forms of energy., Examples would include the technology of subsistence, technological/environmental relationships, and work patterns (see also Mode of Reproduction, and Infrastructure).

Mode of Reproduction The technology and practices employed for expanding, limiting, and maintaining population size. Examples of variables included are demography, mating patterns, fertility, natality, mortality, nurturance of infants, contraception, abortion and infanticide (see also Mode of Production, and Infrastructure).

Mode (1) A measure of central tendency useful for data at any level of measurement. The most frequently occurring number in a set of scores or values. In a series of numbers there is frequently more than one

mode Other measures of central tendency are the median and the mean. See: Mean / Median. (2) The value that appears most often in a given set of data. This can sometimes be a helpful way of portraying central tendency (see also Median, and Mean).

Modeling A form of learning that occurs as a result of watching and imitating others.

Modernization Theory A theory of social and economic development, following functionalist or consensus assumptions, that societies need to have harmony among their component parts. This assumptions leads to the belief that modern economies (capitalist) demand special characteristics in their culture and the structure of social relationships. For example, family systems are assumed to change towards a narrow conjugal form, and away from extended structure, in order to accommodate the individualism and occupational flexibility that is demanded by a modern complex economy undergoing continual transformation.

Modernization The process of general social change brought about by the transition from an agrarian to an industrial mode of production.

Monarchy, Constitutional A system of government in which the head of state is an individual usually acquiring the position by hereditary descent. In earlier times in history, monarchs were often absolute in their effective power and were unconstrained by either legal or political limitations. Britain's system of monarchy, from which Canada's is derived, has been subjected to formal constitutional limitation since the Magna Carta issued in 1215 by King John of England. The Magna Carta was demanded from the King by England's landowning aristocracy who wanted definite and permanent legal limitations on royal power. Over the centuries, England's monarchical system became academic economics and public policy. It is closely associated with neo-conservatism, a version of liberalism that stresses free markets and individualism rather than the 'welfare state' vision that had become dominant in most western societies. There is controversy over the role of monetarist policies in the current deficit problems of most of the worlds' largest economies. See: Fiscal Crisis / Keynesian Economics.

Monetary Policy The use of monetary levers - interest rates, money supply, foreign exchange rate - by governments to achieve some control over the performance of the economy. See: Fiscal Policy.

Monogamy A form of marriage that joins one male and one

female at any given time.

Monopoly (1) A situation in which a single producer dominates in a given industry or market (see also Oligopoly). (2) A situation in which one company has gained control of the market for a particular good or service. This is in direct conflict with the values of liberalism which emphasize competition among numerous producers.

Monotheism Belief in a single devine power. *Monozygotic Twins*. Commonly known as "identical twins" they are from a single egg that has divided after fertilization to create two embryos, consequently they share exactly the same genetic material and are of the same sex. Monozygotic twins who have been separated in earliest infancy and raised apart have provided a classic research situation for social scientists because their genetic identity, yet different social experience, makes it possible to disentangle the separate effects of heredity and social environment.

Montreal Massacre On December 6, 1989, Marc Lepine entered the Ecole Polytechnique in Montreal and killed 14 women students before taking his own life. This event has been a rallying point for women's groups who see the killings as reflective of generalized devaluation and violence against women in society. December 6 has become a National Day of Remembrance and Action on Violence Against Women.

Moral Development Theory Refers generally to theories of individual psychology that investigate how moral reasoning emerges and develops as the individual matures.

Moral Economy The central characteristic of economic activity in a tribal society. Rather than economic exchanges being motivated by self-interest, greed or profit, exchanges are driven by moral obligations created by kinship relations, gift giving, and rituals. A hunter or food gatherer may by obliged to give much of the food to a network of relations, thus accounting for the distribution of food within the community. It was the final collapse of economic exchange as moral obligation that Karl Marx (1818-1883) bemoaned when he described the 'cash nexus' that has become the central medium and motivator of exchange in a capitalist society. See: Gift, The / Potlatch.

Moral Entrepreneurs To be in the business of persuading the society to make policy from particular moral viewpoints. In symbolic interactionism (or labeling theory) social policy is not seen as the' implementation of a shared consensus about what is best. Rather the society is viewed as consisting of a plurality of understandings of what is best. In order for social policy to arise, some individual or group has to initiate a social movement whose task is to articulate a definition of a social problem such that a desired social policy is consistent with this definition of the problem. These individual or groups are referred to as moral entrepreneurs. MADD (Mothers Against Drunk Driving), the pro-life movement, the gun lobby, anti-

Mortality Rate The number of deaths that occur in a particular population in a specified period of time (usually a year).

Motivated Offenders To be motivated is to be ready to engage in a particular experience or action. You may have been motivated to attend college by your upbringing or by a particular role model. Others are motivated to offend perhaps because they have a drug dependency, are poor, lack self-control, or any number of other reasons. It is argued that something has to happen to turn this motivation into action. Perhaps you had to get a scholarship or the offender has to see a car with the keys in it.

Multiculturalism A term having two distinct but related meanings. On the one hand it refers to a condition of cultural pluralism and the attitudes of tolerance which make this possible. On the other hand it refers to a set of federal government policies designed to 'assist all Canadian cultural groups ... to grow and contribute to Canada' as well as to assist members of all cultural groups 'to overcome cultural barriers to full participation in Canadian society'. While there is little debate about the first of these meanings there is great debate about the implications of the second.

Multilinear Evolution An interpretation of social evolution that not all societies pass through predetermined stages of evolutionary development-there are varying paths of evolutionary change followed by different societies.

Multinational Corporation A company which has operations in more than one nation. The development of these corporations has challenged the belief of liberal Caada. It is noteworthy that Quebec refers to its legislative house as the NationalAssembly while other provinces use the term Legislature.

N

Nation A word somewhat similar to society in that it includes all those persons who share common descent, language and history and close association with each other. For Canadians, the term reflects a major debate about the nature of Canada. In English, the term nation implies a community of people who have political autonomy and who occupy a distinct territory. In French, in contrast, the term is closer in meaning to a community of people sharing common origins and ties of interrelationship. Thus when French speakers refer to Quebec as a 'nation' they tend to mean Quebec as an historic community of people, rather than necessarily implying that Quebec is, or ought to be, completely politically autonomous and detached from

Canada It is noteworthy that Quebec refers to its legislative house as the National Assembly while other provinces use the term Legislature. There are approximately 170 nation states in the world but there are 15,000 nations in the second sense of the word.

National Party A short lived Canadian federal political party started by nationalist publisher Mel Hurtig in 1993. The party advocated repeal of the Free Trade Agreement with the United States, increased public involvement in political decisions making and major reforms to fiscal and taxation policy. In the 1993 federal general election the party received almost 200,000 votes, but failed to win any parliamentary seats. After the election, the party was weakened by internal controversy and it ceased to be an active political force.

National Policy Associated with the second Conservative government led by Sir John A. Macdonald, elected in 1878, which imposed tariff protection from foreign manufactures. The policy was intended to promote the development of Canadian manufacturing behind a tariff wall. The term 'National Policy' is also used more widely to refer to the nation- building policies pursued by Macdonald's governments, including construction of the Canadian Pacific Railway and other transportation infrastructure and the promotion of immigration as a stimulus to western settlement and development.

Nationalism (1) An individual's internalization of the set of beliefs and values expressing love, pride and identification with a given nation state. Ritual and symbols are important tools in fostering nationalism among the citizenry. (2) The concept of nationalism like the concept of nation has two quite distinct meanings. Common to both definitions is the idea that it is the nation whic!l provides people with their primary form of belonging and that these nations should be self-governing. People of the world are thus located within nations, identify with these nation states and political activity is organized around these nation states. Michael Ignatieff distinguishes two forms of nationalism. First, 'civic nationalism', meaning that all citizens within a nation state are treated as equal and share political values. Within this sense of nationalism one would find pluralistic communities acting as one and treating citizens with equality. It is this sense of nationalism which many thought was . emerging after narrow religious and ethnic struggles of the 19th and early 20th century. The second sense of nationalism revolves around the equation of 'people' with the nation state. In this formulation the nation or the people exists prior to the state and in a sense creates the state. In these communities then the nation and sense of national identification flows from a common characteristic (usually ethnic heritage) and thus excludes others. This form of nationalism may be less tolerant of difference and can be found in the German nation state where citizenship continues to be defined in terms of ethnicity. The concern that nation states and thus nationalism are increasingly being organized around ethnic (or other) characteristics are frequently described as the tribalization of the modern world. Tension between the two meanings of nationalism can be found in discussions around Quebec's right to self-determination; is civic nationalism at work or is it 'people' nationalism? See: Tribalism / Identity Politics! Postmodern.

Nationalization The collective or public ownership or management of economic resources. In contrast to privatization. Canada has long relied on public (or state) ownership of economic resources. In 1962 the Liberal government of Jean Lesage nationalized the hydro-electric industry in Quebec anti this was an important component of the rapid economic growth and emerging sense of self-confidence that has come to be referred to as the 'quiet revolution' in the province. See: Crown Corporation / Privatization.

Nation-State The modern state in which a government has sovereign power within a defined territorial area, and the mass of the population are citizens.

Natural Attitude As used by Alfred Schutz (1899-1959) refers to characteristics of the world as it is encountered by people living in it. Some of the properties of this attitude are: the world is experienced as being historically organized prior to their arrival; it is intersubjective - experienced similarly by others; people accept the world as it is .given through experience; people address the world" pragmatically.

Nazism The political doctrine of the National Socialist Party of Germany led by Adolf Hitler who became Chancellor of Germany in 1933 and who assumed absolute dictatorial power until the defeat of Germany in 1945 at the end of World War 11. Nazism is chiefly remembered for its ideology of racial purity and of the superiority of the so-called Aryan race. This ideology resulted in the conquest and destruction of much of Europe and its peoples and the mass murder of political opponents and those judged inferior or deviant. The greatest Nazi crimes were committed against the Jews of Europe on whom the Nazis unleashed a Holocaust of systematic mass killing, claiming six million victims, in the name of 'racial purification' .

NDP New Democratic Party. Successor to the CCF, the New Democratic Party was formed in 1961 to widen the appeal and broaden the organization of Canadian social democracy. It combined the old CCF with Canada's labour union movement and various social democratic organizations. Like its predecessor, the new party has had limited success in federal politics, although it has exercised considerable influence especially over the policies of the Liberal Party. The party had its greatest impact on federal politics in the years 1972-1974 when the minority Liberal government was dependent on it for parliamentary support. In provincial politics, the party has been much more successful and has formed governments in Saskatchewan, Manitoba, British Columbia and Ontario.

Necessary Condition In thinking about or looking for a causal relationship researchers have to decide if they are dealing with a necessary condition. A necessary condition (or variable) is that which must be present for the effect to occur. To put it another way, if B appears then A must have been present. Social sciences seldom deal with necessary conditions (other than logical ones), rather they are happy to find sufficient conditions.

Negotiation of Criminal Status Refers to the fact that authorities and offenders against the law are involved in an interactive process of defining criminality. Police or judges may ask: Was the offence intentional? Is the person who committed it someone who requires control from the criminal justice system? Is it important to deter them from further potential crime or is repetition unlikely? The behavior of the offender in interaction with police and judges will shape what label, if any, will be applied to the situation. Thus defining criminal status is an interactive process involving participants in interpretation and negotiation.

Neo-CQlonialism The informal dominance of some nations over others by means of unequal conditions of economic exchange (as between industrial and Third World countries)

Neo-Conservatism A resurgence of economic and political beliefs associated with classical liberalism of the early 19th century. Should correctly be called neo-liberalism. Aspects of this philosophy include: acceptance of an unregulated market economy; a minimal role for government; suspicion toward the welfare state; a view of citizens as motivated only by self-interest; a commitment to the central value of individualism. *See: Classical Liberalism.*

Neolocal Residence The custom of a newly married couple setting up a new residence independent of the households of either partner's parents.

Neo-Locality A family residential pattern in which the married couple lives apart from the place of residence of both the bride's and the husband's parents (see also Matrilocality).

Net Widening Within critical criminology this term is used to describe the effects of providing alternatives to incarceration or diversion programs to direct offenders away from court. While all of these programs developed since the late 1960's were intended to reduce the numbers of offenders in prison or reduce the numbers going to court, it has been found that what has happened instead is that the total numbers of offenders under the control of the state have increased while the population targeted for reduction has not been reduced. In short, the net of social control has been thrown more widely (or some might say the mesh has been made smaller). See: Crime Net.

New Deal When Franklin D. Roosevelt was elected president ofthe United States in 1932 he said: 'I pledge you, I pledge myself, to a new deal for the American people.' The new deal refers to the unprecedented government initiatives to stimulate industrial recovery from 1933 to 1939. These new programs and reforms of programs were designed to assist victims of the depression, to guarantee minimal standards of living, to provide financial stability for citizens and to create employment and economic growth. For example, the Social Security Act of 1935 set up a system of old-age pensions and unemployment insurance. This period can be seen as the beginnings of the welfare state in the United States. *See: Welfare State.*

Nomothetic *See: Ideographic.*

Non-State Actors International agencies, such as the U.N. or the World Health Organization, which playa part in the world system.

Norm A culturally established rule prescribing appropriate social behaviour. Norms are relatively specific and precise and elaborate the detailed behavioural requirements that flow from more general and overarching social values. For example, it is a value in Western society that one should respect the dead, it is a norm that one should dress in dark colours for a funeral. See: Values.

Normal Curve *See: Bell Curve.*

Norms Rules and expectations of conduct which either prescribes a given type of behavior, or forbids it.

Northwest Rebellion of 1885 Like the Red River Rebellion of 1869-70, the Northwest Rebellion was led by Louis Riel and the grievance of the settlers and Metis (of what is now Saskatchewan) were much the same. Demands were for democratic control of the region and for the protection of land, religious and language rights. The decade between the two rebellions, however, saw the English of Ontario transform the image of Riel into that of a traitor and stiffened their resolve to ensure that the West not become an extension of the French-speaking province of Quebec. Military and police strength had also been established and the railroad provided transportation for this colonial enforcement arm. The Metis were quickly suppressed and Riel was hanged in Regina on November 15, 1885. The Metis people prefer to refer to this incident as an act of resistance rather than a rebellion. See: Metis / Red River Rebellion.

Nothing Works In 1974 authors D. Lipton, Robert Martinson and J. Wilks, using 'meta-analysis', assessed all the evaluations of criminal rehabilitation programs between 1945 and 1967. They reached the following conclusion: 'With few and isolated exceptions, the rehabilitative efforts that have been reported so far have had no appreciable effect on recidivism'. The results of this assessment convinced them that not much seems to work and one program did not seem more effective than another. Robert Martinson made this conclusion available much more widely when he published a short piece in the Public Interest, (a liberal magazine begun in New York in 1965) asserting that 'nothing works' and the phrase has been associated with his name since. In a 1978 publication he admitted that they had left out of their study some pieces of research which may have shown rehabilitation to be more effective than they had publicly stated. This phrase 'nothing works', however, became the mantra of those opposed to rehabilitation and had some influence in moving the public away from liberal programs of rehabilitation and towards retribution or deterrence as justifications for punishment.

Nuclear Family (1) A basic family group consisting of married female and male parents and dependent children, living away from other relatives. (2) See family, nuclear.

Null Hypothesis When testing a research hypothesis, which the researcher has good reason to believe is true, it is customary to use a null hypothesis. This is typically a hypothesis of no difference or of no association between variables. If the research hypothesis is that men have a higher rate of suicide than do women, the null hypothesis would be that there is no difference in suicide rates between men and women. Researcher then try to disprove the null hypothesis and if they fail to reject it, they accept the research hypothesis. See: Falsifiability (or Refutability).

Numbered Treaties Treaties had been signed with many Native groups in Eastern Canada prior to confederation. With Confederation in 1867 and the purchase of lands from the Hudson Bay Company, Canada asshmed responsibility for the Natives of Western Canada and beginning in the 1870s negotiations were begun with Native groups. These negotiations resulted in treaties which were numbered, and are still known by those numbers. The total number eventually reached 11.

Nuremberg Trials A tribunal established in the German city of Nuremberg by Great Britain, France, the Soviet Union and the United States, to bring to trial those war criminals whose actions during the Second World War were deemed to be international crimes against humanity. Many were brought to trial and some sentenced to death. Another tribunal was established in Japan to try Japanese war criminals. Other nations brought to trial those thought to be guilty of war crimes against citizens of one nation. Israel, for example, brought Adolf Eichmann, a major figure in the organization of the Holocaust, to trial in 1960, found him guilty and he was hanged. See: War Crimes.

Objectivity (1) Objectivity means striving as far as possible to reduce or eliminate bias in the conduct of research. (2) This term is used in two distinct but related ways. The first refers to the actions of a social scientist: assuming a position of disinterestedness or impartiality, or being open-minded in the assessment of evidence. Objectivity is thought to be central to the procedures of the scientific method. The second meaning refers to the nature of the statements people make: a statement can be objective as opposed to the scientist being objective. An objective statement is one which can be agreed upon by others regardless of their backgrounds or biases.

Occupational Crime White-collar crime committed by an individual or group of individuals exclusively for personal gain. The distinction between this crime and organizational crime is difficult to maintain.

Occupational Distance This is the distance between one occupation and another where occupations are ranked on a hierarchy of status. The concept is central to studies of social mobility because it permits some measurement of the extent of mobility. For example, to change one's occupation from unskilled labour to semi-skilled labour involves less occupational distance than to move from unskilled labour to professional accountant. Occupational distance is therefore an important measurement in determining the relevance of social mobility. See: Social Mobility / Demand Mobility.

October Crisis On October 5, 1970 the Front De Liberation Du

Quebec (FLQ) kidnapped James Cross, the British Trade Commission in Montreal and on October 10, Pierre Laporte Minister of Labour in the government of Quebec. The federal government, led by Pierre Trudeau, invoked the War Measures Act and armed soldiers entered the province of Quebec. Laporte was murdered the next day. Over 450 persons were detained in Quebec, few of whom were charged. Cross was released in exchange for safe passage to Cuba for the kidnappers. The government's handling of the kidnapping and subsequent events were extremely controversial

OECD Canada is a member of the Organization for Economic Cooperation and Development, formed in 1961, along with most other industrialized 'free market' nations.

Oka Crisis For 78 days in the summer of 1990 Mohawk warriors engaged in an armed standoff with the Quebec police and the Canadian army. This incident arose over land claims: a decision was made to expand the golf course at Oka and this involved land the Mohawk peoples of the Kanesatake band claimed rightfully belonged to them. The incident represented the most dramatic of many confrontations between Native peoples and the police over land rights and also represents one of the very few times that Canada has used its armed forces against its own citizens (another being the FLQ crisis of 1970).

Oligarchy (1) A society or social system ruled by a few people. As societies or organizations become large it is thought that political power becomes concentrated in the hand of a few individuals. In See: Iron Law of Oligarchy / Plutocracy. (2) Rule by a few within an organization or in the society as a whole.

Oligopoly (1) A situation in which a small number of firms dominate a given industry or market. When four or f2wer firms supply fifty percent or more of a given market the effects of oligopoly become apparent. These effects are reputed to be a rise in price and a lowering of quality because of the decline of competition (see also Monopoly). (2) The situation where a small number of companies own or control the production of a particular good or provision of services within a market economy. This situation typically arises from the concentration of ownership and provides a challenge to liberal theory which claims benefit from a plurality of producers operating in a very competitive market. *See: Monopoly.*

One Big Union Begun in 1919, the movement for One Big Union highlights the early conflicts within the trade union movement over how unions should be structured. There was disagreement over whether unions should be based on craft groups (see craft unions), the dominant model in 1919, or should be based on entire industries (industrial unions). The One Big Union movement supported the second of these models and was successful in getting thousands of workers to join. *See: Syndicalism.*

One-Percenter A term coined after a gathering of the American Motorcycle 'Gypsy Tour' on July 4, 1947. The 3000 riders descended on Hollister, California which was sponsoring a 'dirt hill climb'. When violence broke out the Motorcycle Association issued a statement saying that 99% of riders were respectable, pleasure riders and the other one-percent were troublemakers. Since that date groups like the Hells Angels have referred to themselves as the 'one- percenter'. This event was depicted in the Hollywood movie 'The Wild One'.

Open Class Ideology This is a component part of liberal ideology : the key claim is that an individual has meaningful opportunity to rise (or fall) in social class and status as a result of personal ability, hard work and individual merit. The concept therefore claims that society's status system is based on achievement and not on ascription. See: Social Mobility / Liberalism.

Open Lineage Family A family system found in preindustrial Europe in which family relationships are closely intertwined with the local community.

Operant Conditioning The basic process by which an individual's behaviour is shaped by reinforcement or by punishment.

Operationalization In quantitative research the act of specifying exactly how a concept will be measured. Before measuring the concept of 'violent crime' a researcher must decide what are indictors of violent crime and then specify how these indicators will be counted. One might, for example, decide to use official reports of crimes known to the police and count all instances of homicide, manslaughter, attempted murder, assault levels 1, 2 and 3 and sexual assault levels 1, 2 and 3. Examining how a researcher has operationalized a concept is the first place to look for weakness in the research design. In the above example, for instance, many would argue that assaults level 1 (the lowest level of assault) contain many acts which many would not really see as indicators of the concept of 'violence'. The United States government, for example, does not include this kind of assault in their measures of violent crime.

Operationally Defined To define some concept of study in such a way that it can be observed and measured For example, "well being" might be measured by asking people to rate their overall satisfaction with their life style, or "anti-social behaviour" might be measured by frequency of arrest or criminal prosecution.

Opportunity Structure A shortened phrase referring to the notion that opportunity, the chance to gain certain rewards or goals, is shaped by the way the society or an institution is organized (or structured). The opportunity for girls to succeed in mathematics may be structured by the fact that all of the mathematics teachers are men, all teachers tend to discourage such an endeavor or suggest that girls are not good at this subject. There may be a sexist structure in the school which shapes opportunity.

Order-in-Council In the British constitutional system, inherited by Canada, the Monarch is Head of State, must approve all laws for them to be valid, and is advised by a Privy

Council of Ministers. By constitutional convention, the Monarch accepts only the advice of members of the Privy Council who are also Cabinet ministers and who have the support of the House of Commons. Most legislation passed by the House of Commons outlines only the broad principles of law and legal regulation and the law usually provides for the bureaucracy to develop detailed provisions that are then given legal status by being approved by the Governor General (representing the Monarch) in Council.

Organic Solidarity A term used by Emile Durkheim (1858-1917) to refer to a state of interdependency created by the specialization of roles and in which individuals and institutions become acutely dependent on others in a complex division of labour. The basis of solidarity is abstract and may be weakened by anomie when people fail to comprehend the ties that bind them to others. See: Mechanical Solidarity / Ideal Type.

Organization A large group of individuals that is formally organized for the purpose of attaining a goal.

Organizational Crime White-collar crime committed with the support and encouragement of a formal organization and intended at least in part to advance the goals of that organization. The distinction between this crime and occupational crime is difficult to maintain.

Organized Crime (1) Criminal activities carried out by organizations established as businesses. (2) The operation of illegal business entities whose members are bound together because of their group interest and their desire to profit from illegal activity.

Overrepresentation A group that has a number of its members in some condition in greater numbers than their population would suggest. If a group makes up 20% of the population then a researcher might for example predict, other things being equal, that they would represent 20% of offenders, victims and those in prison. For example, men are overrepresented in prisons, as are Aboriginals. Women are overrepresented as victims in sexual assault offences.

Ozone Depletion Theory that societies production of chloroflourocarbons and other gasses is depleting the ozone layer that protects plant and animal life from harmful ultra-violet radiation (see also Pollution, and Environmen t).

P

Panel Study A form of longitudinal research in whi.ch a panel of respondents or subjects is selected and then followed or interviewed over time. If a panel of first year university students is selected the researcher would, for example, be able to learn what their routes are towards an undergraduate degree. Drawing a sample of undergraduates at year one, year two and year three would not provide the same degree of detail.

Pan-Indianism This term has been applied to social movements among both Asian India:1s and North American First Nations people3. In both contexts it refers to a social movement and a political philosophy that asserts a peoples' common identity and unity across political or state boundaries and tribal divisions.

Paradigm A framework used in thinking about and organizing an understanding of natural or social phenomena. All societies, and the individuals within them, tend to have relatively fixed assumptions about how to understand and interpret the world, but there is great variation in these assumptions from placc to place and from time to time. For many centuries, for example, natural phenomena like the eclipse of the sun, thunder, lightning or flood were explained within a paradigm of religious belief and myth, today they fall within the paradigm of science. As sets of assumptions change over time this process can be referred to as a paradigm shift: there emerges a new way of looking at the world.

The term came into social science vocabulary from the writings of Thomas Kuhn (1970), a historian of science. He challenged the conventional wisdom of history that claimed that science was a long, slow process of building on previous knowledge. Rejecting this view Kuhn argued that the history of science can be seen rather as a history of dominant paradigms and paradigm shifts. A paradigm in his presentation was a set of assumptions about the kinds of questions to ask in science and how to go about looking for answers. As a particular body of knowledge builds up there are a growing number of anomalies which can only be forced with difficulty into the dominant theory. At some point people begin to see things differently and to ask different questions in an attempt to explain their observations and they eventually arrive at a Hew theory which is a better way to account for the anomalies.

Parallel Cousins Offspring of siblings of the same sex. Paramount Chieftanship. A political. system similar to a kingdom that brings together a number of partly autonomous villages or communities under the hierarchical rule of a grand chief

Parti Quebecois Founded in 1968 under the leadership of Rene Levesque the party had the main aim of achieving political sovereignty for Quebec within the framework of a continued association with Canada. It first came to power in 1976 and began to prepare a political strategy leading to a referendum vote on 'sovereignty-association' in 1980. The referendum proposal was defeated by a majority of 60% to 40% but, under its immensely popular leader, the party was able to comfortably win the 1981 provincial election. After losing the subsequent election under new leadership, the party returned to power in 1994 and immediately prepared for a new referendum on sovereignty -association. The proposal was brought to a referendum in 1995, defeated once more, but by a very narrow margin, ensuring that the issue of Quebec's relationship with Canada will remain at the centre of Canadian political life into the next century.

Participatory Democracy A system of democracy in which all members of a group or community participate collectively in major decisions. Most nation states today are to large and complex for participatory democracy to be a feasible form of government.

Participatory Management *See: Industrial Relations.*

Participatory Research Distinguished from other research techniques in that the subjects, usually oppressed or exploited groups, are fully involved in the research, from the designing of topics to the analysis of data. While the findings of such research may be useful and indeed emancipatory, the process of community or neighborhood building during the carrying out of the research is of equal importance.

Pastoral Societies Societies whose subsistence is based on domesticated animals (see also Traditional States).

Patient Dumping The practice of only treating patients that can pay leaving the poor to government or charitable organizations.

Patriarchy (1) Literally 'rule by the father' but more generally it refers to a social situation where men are dominant over women in wealth, status and power. Patriarchy is associated with a set of ideas, a 'patriarchal ideology' that acts to explain and justify this dominance and attributes it to inherent natural differences between men and women. Sociologists tend . to see patriarchy as a social product and not as an outcome of innate differences between the sexes and they focus attention on the way that gender roles in a society affect power differentials between men and women. See: Ideology / Hegemony. (2) Social organization that structures the dominance of men over women.

Patriation of the Constitution The 'bringing home' of all legal authority over the laws and Constitution of Canada. The Constitution Act, 1867 (formerly the BNA Act) was British legislation and it could be changed only by Britain's parliament (although this was done only on the request of Canada's parliament). In the Constitution Act 1982, a new exclusively Canadian amending procedure was established and the parliament of Great Britain no longer holds any legal authority regarding Canada.

Patrilineal Descent (1) A system in which family descent is reckoned through the blood links of males. Typically names and property follow the male line of descent. A man's descendants are his own children, and women are little recognized as ancestors. See: matrilineal descent. (2) The practice of tracing kinship only through the male line (see also Matrilineal Descent)

Patrilocal Residence The custom of a newly married couple taking up residence in the groom's family household or village. See: Matrilocal Residence / Neo-Local Residence.

Patrimony A right, a status or tangible asset inherited from a father or other ancestor. In principle, a patrimony may be inherited by either sex although the term is generally associated with patrilineal transmission of status, property and wealth.

Pattern Variables Are five dichotomies, developed by Talcott Parsons (1902-1979), to draw out the contrasting values to which individuals orient themselves in social interaction.

Peasants People in agrarian societies who produce food from the land, using traditional farming methods of plow and animal power. Farm workers in agrarian societies.

Peer Group A friendship group with common interests and position composed of individuals of similar age.

Penitentiary Prisons built in the early part of the 19th century and embodying the principle of solitary confinement as punishment for a criminal offense. The first penitentiary in North America was at Auburn, New York, built in 1816-25, and came to be known as the silent system. Offenders were confined in solitary cells at night and worked in congregate (and silence) during the day. Eastern State Penitentiary, built at Cherry Hill, Pennsylvania in 1829, embodied the solitary system, as offenders were confined to solitary cells for the entire period of confinement. Canada's Kingston penitentiary was opened in 1835 modeled after the Auburn penitentiary. As suggested by the name, penitentiaries had a strong Christian influence. A penitent is one who repents of sins, or feels pain or sorrow for offenses. Also one who is admitted to penance, which is the sacrament consisting in repentance or contrition for sins. Early advocates of the penitentiary, such as John Howard, were influenced by their Christian faith and equated crime with sin. This model provided a philosophy of punishment and also shaped Anglo-European penology by assuming that criminal offenders would be reformed or rehabilitated.

Penology The study of the treatment and punishment of criminal offenders. Penology is now included within criminology.

Per Capita 'Capita' comes from a Latin term referring to head. Criminologists and sociologists refer to crimes (or divorce rates etc.) per capita. For example if there are only0.01 crimes per capita, this would mean meaning you have a risk of 1% of being victimized.

Plutocracy Literally 'rule by the rich', the term is used to denote a wide range of situations where a group of individuals are able to exert disproportionate power and influence in society and social institutions because of their wealth.

Polarization of Classes In Marxian analysis the inevitable historical process of the class structure becoming increasingly polarized. Over time, it is argued, the secondary classes of capitalism (the self-employed, the residual aristocracy, etc.) will disappear and be absorbed into either the bourgeoisie class or the pruletariat. The class structure will come to consist only of these two classes. *See: Class.*

Police Culture An example of an occupational culture to which new recruits become socialized. It is thought that police culture is one of several demand characteristics which shape routine decision-making by the police. See: Demand Characteristic.

Political Economy Theory A major tradition in Canadian history and the social sciences. This is not a specific theory but a general approach to social analysis that stresses the interconnection of social, political and economic processes in society. Classic writers within this tradition include Harold Innis (1894-1952) and C. B. Macpherson (1911-1987). It remains central to contemporary Canadian social analysis and academic discourse.

Political Party An organization of people with similar interests and attitudes established with the aim of achieving legitimate control of government and using that power to pursue a specific program.

Political Policing The way in which the process of policing the community acts to maintain and reinforce deference to authority. By living within a system of social order people are socialized to accept that order and the way this it is justified by legitimating ideas, like tradition, inspired leadership or representative democracy. It can also mean more narrowly the way in which police activity, while superficially about maintenance of the criminal law, can be about the control or surveillance of particular groups and communities.

Political Socialization The component of the process of individuals coming to learn and internalize the culture of their society or group that is directly related to the transmission of political values and behaviours.

Politics (1) Attempts to influence governmental activities. (2) This can be narrowly defined as all that relates to the way a society is governed. Politics is the process by which the community makes decisions and establishes values that are binding upon its members. This definition comes from the original Greek meaning of 'politics', the government of the city state. In general speech, politics refers much more widely to processes that involve the exercise of power, status or influence in making decisions or establishing social relationships. This latter meaning is implied by the idea of 'office politics' or 'sexual politics' (as used by Kate Millett) or the claim that 'the personal is political'.

Polity An 'umbrella' term used to refer to the roles and institutions of a society that directly shape the way the society is governed. There is debate about what institutions should be included in a description of the polity. It involves state institutions of government, the political parties, interest and advocacy groups. It will also include the media and other institutions directly affecting political values, opinions and behaviour.

Pollution One of the principal constraints of the environment. Refers to the contamination of soil, water, or air by noxious substances (see also Depletion, Environment, and Intensification).

Polyandry (1) A form of marriage in which a woman may have more than one husband. (2) A marriage structure where a woman has more than one husband at one time. It is rare, but when it is found there is often fraternal polyandry, in which the husbands are brothers.

Polygamy (1) A form of marriage in which a person may have more than one spouse. (2) A marriage structure in which there is more than one spouse at a time: the term covers both polygyny and polyandry.

Polygyny (1) A form of marriage in which a man may have more than one wife. (2) A marriage structure where men have more than one wife at a time. Widely spread in world societies, but practiced by only by a minority of those communities because population sex-ratios and a lack of economic resources make it inaccessible for the majority.

Polytheism A form of belief in which a person has two or more gods.

Popular Culture Intellectual opinions of popular culture, the culture of the masses, have been deeply shaped by critical theory. Since the Frankfurt School, which identified with the 'high culture' of the intellectual classes, popular culture has been seen as trivial, demeaning and commercialized, serving the interests of the capitalist system. Post-modernist theorists, however, no longer accept the belief that there is some objectively superior high culture setting a standard from which to make evaluations of others.

Post-Industrial Thesis The theory that modern economies" in the Western world have moved from a focus on goods production (an industrial base) to a new foundation of knowledge and sophisticated services. This new economy is assumed to demand different kinds of workers, to allow for more job satisfaction and to foster less labour conflict.

Postmodern A difficult term to grasp and having somewhat different significance in architecture, literary criticism and art than in the social sciences. In social theory it is best seen as a rejection of central assumptions of the modern world or of what has been described as the 'enlightenment project'. This project has had at least two core beliefs. First is the assumption that modern society will become more democratic and just because of our growing ability to rationally and objectively understand the community's best interests. Second is the assumption that scientists and social theorists hold a privileged viewpoint since they are taken to operate outside of local interests or bias. Each of these assumptions suggests the possibility of disinterested knowledge, universal truths and social progress. The late twentieth century writings of Michel Foucault (1929-1984) and Jean Francois Lyotard called these assumption into question. Foucault's work has argued that knowledge and power are always intertwined and that the social sciences, rather than empowering human actors, have made humans into objects of inquiry and have subjected them to knowledge legitimated by the claims of science. Similarly Lyotard has argued that social theory has always imposed meaning on historical events (think of the writing of Marx) rather than providing for the understanding of the empirical significance of events. This rejection of the idea of social and intellectual progress implies that people must accept the possibility of history having no meaning or purpose, abandon the idea that we can know what is or is not true and accept that science can never create and test theories according to universal scientific principles because there is no unitary reality from which such principles can be established. We are left living in a fragmented world with multiple realities, a suspicion of science or authoritative claims and many groups involved in identity politics in order to impose their reality on others. The clearest Signs of a postmodern approach to sociology can be found in social constructionism, ethnomethodology and labeling theory.

Potlatch A custom of the First Nations peoples of the Pacific north-west coast, where a ceremonial period of feasting was accompanied by lavish giving away, and sometimes destruction, of goods and property. Those who gave away or destroyed the most property earned the greatest social prestige. Anthropologists have described the ceremonies as a form of 'war with property'. The Potlatch also had important elements of economic distribution, social bonding and political processes, all central to the maintenance of a society. The Canadian government considered the practice to be destructive of the stability and established hierarchy of native communities and it was outlawed (from 1884 until 1951) and rigorously suppressed. *See: Cultural Genocide.*

Poverty Line That division, arbitrarily arrived at and usually based on income, which divides the poor from the non-poor. There is considerable controversy about how this line should be determined and Statistics Canada uses the term low incomes rather than poverty and calculates low-income cutoffs. This line or cutoff ~an be determined in a variety of ways. One method is to determine the minimum income required to purchase a basket of goods and services thought to be

Prestige Social respect accorded to an individual or group because of the status of their position.

Prevalence This term tell us about the number of particular events in the community. AIDS for example may be very prevalent (the total number with this syndrome) but the incidence (new cases) is going down each year.

Primary Deviance The deviant act itself, the violation of a norm.

Primary Group Structure A term used in sociocultural materialism to refer to structural groups in which members tend to interact on an intimate basis. They perform many functions such as regulating production, reproduction, socialization, education, and enforcing social discipline. Examples include family, community, voluntary organizations, and friendship networks *(see also Structure, and Secondary Group Structure).*

Primary Group (1) A typically small group of individuals standing in an enduring personal relationship to one another-examples would include parents, spouse, or close friends (see also Secondary Group). (2) See group, primary.

Primary Labor Market The term refers to the economic position of individuals engaged in occupations that provide secure jobs, and good benefits and working conditions (see also Secondary Labor Market).

Primary Labour Market All research on labour markets has shown them to be divided or fragmented. The term used today is 'segmented labour market' suggesting there are many components to the market. Earlier it was thought the market was divided into a primary labour market and a secondary labour market. This was interesting because men dominated the primary market and women and minorities dominated the secondary market. Primary labour markets tend to offer high salaries or wages, better working conditions, and more job stability. This market tends to be found in those sectors of business that are capital intensive. Labour that is required tends to be more skilled and the high costs of labour can often be covered by the profit generated from an efficient plant. Workers are more apt to be unionized and to be able to make greater wage demands than workers in a secondary labour market. See: Secondary Labour Market.

Primary Sector That part of a modern economy based on the extraction of natural resources directly from the natural environment-includes such areas as mining and agricultural production.

Primitive Communism An imagined first society in which all resources were owned in common. Has a close correspondence with some actual hunting and gathering societies.

Primitive Society A term to denote simple human societies that are assumed to represent how human beings lived in communities in the earliest times of history. The dictionary defines the word as 'belonging to the beginning or to the first times'. The term is now out of favour in both sociology and anthropology because it appears to denigrate these simple societies by suggesting they are less civilized than . modern societies. While 'primitive' can be used in its formal sense to describe simple societies, the favoured term today is 'hunter-gatherer society'. See: Hunter gatherer society

Prison Subculture The culture of prison society and thought by some to arise from the 'pains of imprisonment', while others believe it is imported to the prison. Also known as the 'convict code', some of the features of prison subculture are: do not inform on your fellow prisoners, do not trust staff, help other residents, show your loyalty to other residents, share what you have.

Prisonization The process of being socialized into the culture and social life of prison society to the extent that adjusting to the outside society becomes difficult.

Private Domain (Sphere) The distinction between the public domain (or sphere) and the private domain became an important tool of early feminist analysis as it helped in describing and understanding women's location in society. The parts of society consisting of politics and paid work are seen as the public domain and family life as the private domain.

Private Health Care Fee-for-service health care available only to those who pay the full cost of them.

Private Sector That part of the economy which is controlled or owned by private individuals, either directly or through stock ownership. See: Public Sector.

Privatization (1) The process of moving economic resources from the public sector to- the private sector. Publicly owned transportation resources, natural resources, hospitals, etc., may be sold to private individuals or to privately owned corporations. Canada has been unusual in having a large public sector. Classical liberal theory, however, is opposed to government involvement and interference in economic activity and the recent resurgence of interest in

Psychological Reductionism The process of reducing all social activity and behaviour to the psychological characteristics of the human actors involved. Such reduction eliminates the possibility of sociology since it denies that there is anything greater than the individual. Society is simply an aggregation of individuals. Emile Durkheim (1858-1917) argued against this in his study of suicide by arguing, and demonstrating, that even after providing a psychological explanation for individual acts of suicide there was something still to account for: the difference in suicide rates between societies. This he showed was derived from characteristics of the society and could be not explained as dependent on individual psychological characteristics.

Psychologism *See: Methodological Individualism / Psychological Reductionism.*

Psychopath A personality type that denotes a lack of moral sense and concern for others.

Psychopaths Although there is considerable debate about whether 'psychopath' is an authentic psychiatric disorder it is typically classified under 'personality disorder'. Psychopaths tend to be lacking in what is considered conscience, are unable to form emotional attachments (even to friends or family), are quite impulsive, and are only self-interested. There is also considerable debate about whether this group can be changed.

Psychosis A serious mental disorder that involves a failure to distinguish between internal and external reality, the affected person cannot function effectively in social life.

Public Health Care Government funded health-care sprvices available to all members of the population.

Public Health Model Unlike a 'crime control model' which focuses on punishment or moralizing with the offender, a public health model looks at particular kinds of crime (often drug abuse, prostitution, youth violence) as public health issues. A public health officer takes a very different view of crime than does a police constable. The public health model encourages us to think of ways to stop the spread of drug abuse or violence, for example, or how to prevent drug abusers from harming themselves or spreading infection to the community, or on initiating education programs in schools to teach young people how to recognize the possible onset of violence, how to prevent it, who to call if violence is experienced, etc.

Public Images of Crime The perception of crime and the threat of crime generally held by members of the community. Their perceptions may be manipulated by authorities and the media to focus on some types of crime and criminal behaviour and divert attention from others.

Q

Qualitative Research Research using methods such as participant observation or case studies which result in a narrative, descriptive account of a setting or practice. Sociologists using these methods typically reject positivism and adopt a form of interpretive sociology. See: Quantitative Research / Ethnographic Research.

Quality Control Circles See: Industrial Relations. **Quantitative Research.** Research using methods allowing for the measurement of variables within a collection of people or groups and resulting in numerical data subjected to statistical analysis. By its very nature this is a form of positivism. See: Qualitative Research / Variables.

Quasi-Experiment A research design having some but not all of the characteristics of a true experiment. The element most frequently missing is random assignment of subjects to the control and experimental conditions. Examples of this research design are the natural experiment (where nature has assigned subjects to the two conditions) or trend analysis.

Queer Culture The word 'queer' was a derogatory term for many years but has now been appropriated by a radical section (the 'in your face' section) of the gay and lesbian community to identify gay and lesbian culture or studies. Gay and lesbian studies is becoming as legitimate in the academic community as are women's studies or black studies. Cultural studies is interested in examining gay and lesbian culture as depicted in the writings, films, or art work of the community and in analyzing the public identity of this cultural community. See: Cultural Studies / Identity Politics.

Quiet Revolution A period of rapid social change in Quebec symbolised by the 1960 election defeat of the conservative rural-dominated Union National by Jean Lesage and the Liberals on a policy of modernization and nationalism. This resulted in the unleashing of modern liberal ideas and the transformation of social institutions such as schooling the family, politics and government to reflect those values. These changes led to a decline in influence for the church, an increased divorce rate and a decreased birth rate, the creation of modern universities and schools and expansion of the role of government in society. The dynamic new role of government became a focus for the nationalist aspirations of the Quebec people. In 1976 the Parti Quebecois was elected and this led to a 1980 referendum on the issue of changing Quebec's position within Canada from that of a province like others to some form of sovereignty-association. This referendum was defeated and a second, conducted in 1995 on a question of separation with some form of continued economic association, was defeated by a margin of less that 1%.

R

Race (1) A classification of humans beings into different categories on the basis of their biological characteristics. There have been a variety of schemes for race classification based on physical characteristics such as skin colour, head shape, eye colour and shape, nose size and shape etc. A common classification system uses four major groups: Caucasoid, Mongoloid, Negroid and Australoid. The term was once popular in anthropology, but has now fallen into disrepute, because the idea of racial classification has become associated with racism - the claim that there is hierarchy of races. The idea of race categories also appears to be unscientific, since humans are able to mate across all 'races' and have done so throughout history, creating an enormous variety of human genetic inheritance. In addition the defining characteristics of 'race' do not appear in all members of each so--called race, but merely occur with some degree of statistical frequency. If the defining characteristic of each 'race' does not appear in all members of each 'race' then the whole definition is clearly inadequate. (2) A socially defined category of people who share genetically transmitted physical characteristics.

Racism (1) An ideology based on the idea that humans can be separated into distinct racial groups and that these groups can be ranked on a hierarchy of intelligence, ability, morality etc. See: Ethnocentrism! Race. (2) The attributing of characteristics of inferiority to a particular racial category.

Racism is a specific form of prejudice focused on race.

Radical Feminism This form of feminism is relatively recent and differs from traditional Marxism in arguing that women's oppression is historically primary, harder to transform, causes more harm and is more widespread than class oppression. Similarly it is argued that women's oppression provides a model for understanding other forms of oppression such as racism and class domination. Some radical feminists claim that women's oppression is rooted in biology and its elimination will require a biological revolution transforming women's relation to reproduction. Within criminology, they focus on documenting and analyzing ways in which the content of law and practices of law enforcement have Served to entrench and strengthen male dominance in society. See: **Feminism / Liberal Feminism.**

Rand Formula A method of ensuring union security which resulted from a Supreme Court ruling (handed down by Justice Ivan Rand) resolving a 1945 strike by the Canadian Autoworkers against Ford Motors in Windsor, Ontario. The ruling declared that unions must bargain on behalf of all workers in the plant and thus allowed for the automatic deduction of union dues from all workers whether members of the union or not.

Rape Shield Laws Legal prohibitions which restrict the ability of the defence to explore the sexual past of the victim (usually a woman) during a rape or sexual assault trial. This provision entered Canadian law as section 276 of the Criminal Code of Canada in 1983. The provision was struck down by a 1991 Supreme Court decision ruling that the prohibition could deny an accused a fair trial.

Rape (1) The use of force to compel one individual to engage in a sexual act with another. (2) Until 1982, rape was a criminal offense in Canada and was defined as the offence of forcible sexual intercourse, involving penetration, with someone who has withheld their consent, or, in the case of consent, with someone whose consent has been obtained by threat, impersonation or misrepresentation of the nature of the act. Feminist critiques of this law and the coming of the Charter of Rights and Freedoms produced changes and the offense of rape was replaced with three offenses of sexual assault.

Rate When studying crime, if a researcher wishes to compare the amount of crime over time or between communities of different sizes, it is not adequate to do a gross count of the amount of crime because the population basses may be different. To get around the problems involved with this, criminologists calculate crime rates (or incarceration rates, conviction rates, recidivism rates). This is done by dividing the amount of crime by the population size and multiplying by 100,000. This produces a rate per 100,000, but occasionally it is useful to calculate a rate per million or some other figure.

Ratio Measures *See levels of measurement.*

Rationalization This term has two specific meanings in sociology. 0) The concept was developed by German sociologist Max Weber (1864-1920) who used it in two ways. First, it was the process through which magical, supernatural and religious ideas lose cultural importance in a society and ideas based on science and practical calculation become dominant. For example, in modern societies science has rationalized our understanding of weather patterns. Science explains weather patterns as a result of interaction between physical elements like wind-speed and direction, air and water temperatures, humidity, etc. In some other cultures, weather is thought to express the pleasure or displeasure of gods, or spirits of ancestors. One explanation is rationalized and scientific, the other mysterious and magical. Rationalization also involves the development of forms of social organization devoted to the achievement of precise goals by efficient means. It is this type of rationalization that we see in the development of modern business corporations and of bureaucracy. These are organizations dedicated to the pursuit of defined goals by calculated, systematically administered means. (2) Within symbolic interactionism, rationalization is used more in the everyday sense of the word to refer to providing justifications or excuses for one's actions. *See: Accounts.* (3) Weber's concept to refer to the process by which modes of precise calculation based on observation and reason increasingly dominate the social world. Rationalization is a habit of thought that replaces tradition, emotion, and values as motivators of human conduct. Bureaucracy is a particular case of rationalization applied to human social organization (see also Bureaucratization).

Reaction Formation A psychological mechanism which emerges when failure is imminent. Albert Cohen, for example, found that lower-class boys often turned middle-class values, the very values causing them to fail, on their head. There was a certain degree of nihilism; rather than taking money to purchase things they needed, they may throw the money away, give it to others, or purchase useless articles. Or, rather than valuing the middle-class sofa, they might defecate on it.

Rebellion (of 1837-38) in Lower Canada Rebellions occurred in both Upper and Lower Canada (and in many other parts of the world) in 1837-38 with the main issue being the rejection of colonial rule and demand for local, responsible government. In Lower Canada an additional objective of rebellion was the desire to establish primacy for the Quebecois nation within Canada. British troops put down the rebellion, often rather brutally, and this event is seen by many as the reconquest of the Quebecois (a repeat of the battle of the Plains of Abraham, 1759) which stimulated growth of Quebec nationalism.

Rebellion Rebellions are aimed at removing particular rulers or regimes rather than bringing about significant structural changes in a society (See also Coup D'etat and Revolution).

Recidivism (Criminal) Repetition of criminal behaviour by an offender previously convicted and punished for an offence.

Recidivism is a measure of the effectiveness of rehabilitation programs or the deterrent effect of punishment. While an important concept in evaluation research, criminologists have great difficulty in determining just how to measure recidivism. For example, is it recidivism to commit a less serious offence than the previous offence? Is it recidivism to : BCh;rl;turned to prison for a violation of the terms of parole (i.e.: a criminal offence has not been committed)?

Recidivism Rate The percentage of ex-convicts who are convicted of new offenses after being released from prison.

Reciprocity A system of the exchange of goods based on social ties.

Red River Rebellion A revolt during 1869-70 of the settlers and Metis of what is now Manitoba. In 1867-68 the government of Canada negotiated the purchase of the lands owned by the Hudson Bay Company without consulting with the residents of the territories involved (the largest group were French speaking Metis). This annexation led to fears, particularly among the French-speaking and Catholic Metis, that language, religious and education rights would be lost. The residents declared a provisional government in direct opposition to the federal government's wishes and this led to negotiations resulting in the creation of the province of Manitoba and established French language rights, acknowledgment of the tenure of existing farms and the promise of millions of acres of land to settle Metis land claims. Metis peoples prefer to refer to these events as acts of resistance rather than a rebellion. See: Metis / Northwest Rebellion of 1885.

Reference Group A term from social psychology identifying that group to which people refer or make reference in evaluating themselves. One may make reference to 'social science students' when contemplating what political party to vote for or one might refer to 'feminists' when deciding to change or not to change one's name after marriage.

Referendum To refer a political question to an electorate for direct decision. Referendums do not fit well with a parliamentary system of government and Canada has used them infrequently. The first was in 1898 on a question of prohibition and the next in 1942 on the matter of conscription. English speaking Canada voted in support of allowing the government to use conscription, while French speaking Canada voted against it, thus creating a crisis for government. A federal referendum was also held in 1992 to seek support for a constitutional change (the Charlottetown Accord); this was soundly defeated. Provincial governments have relied on referendums somewhat more often. Newfoundland, for example, held a referendum in 1948 on the question ot entry to Canada (it took two votes to ".vin agreement, and then by only 52.3%); in 1988 the province of Prince Edward Island held a referendum on the question of whether a fixed link with mainland Canada should be established; in 1980 Quebec held a referendum on permission to negotiate-sovereignty-association with the rest of Canada (this was defeated by 60% of voters), and a second referendum was held in Quebec in 1995 on a more direct question of separating from Canada (this was rejected by 51% of the voters).

Reflexivity As used by ethnomethodologists the term means that an object or behaviour and the description of this can not be separated one from the other, rather they have a mirror-like relationship. Reflexivity and indexicality are properties of behaviour, settings and talk which make the ongoing construction of social reality necessary. Both of these properties question the objectivity of accounts, descriptions, explanations, etc. An ethnographic description of a setting is reflexive in that the description seeks to explain features of a particular setting (e.g.: village life) but the setting itself is what is employed to make sense of the description. *See: Indexicality.*

Reform Movement A social movement concerned to implement a limited program of social change, say changing the health care system to provide universal access to care.

Regina Manifesto The founding party political program of the Co-operative Commonwealth Federation adopted at a convention in Regina in 1933. The Manifesto was strongly socialist and called for extensive nationalization and radical measures to promote equalization of wealth and incomes. In subsequent years, the party retreated from the radical goals of the Manifesto and, in 1956, this change of policy was made explicit. embodied in the policies followed by the New Democratic Party which succeeded the C.C.F. in 1961.

Regression (Analysis or Line) A measure of association between two quantitative variables. This form of statistical test is only possible with interval or ratio data. If an independent variable and a dependent variable are placed on the two axis of a graph with the actual data then scattered on the graph, it is possible to draw a line through the resulting points in a way that minimizes the distance between the points. The resulting line (which may be straight or curved) is a regression line. Any particular value for the dependent variable can then be predicted by multiplying the value of independent variable by the regression coefficient (a number which determines the slope of the line).

Regressive Taxation A tax structure which requires the more well-off to pay a lower percentage of their income (or wealth) in tax than a less well-off citizen. Sales tax and the federal goods and services tax (GST) are of this type as these taxes remain constant regardless of one's income. The consequence is that the more well-off citizen pays a smaller percentage of their income to cover the tax on a new refrigerator than does a less well-off person. See: Progressive Taxation! Flat Tax.

Rehabilitative Ideal As defined by F. Allen (1981) refers to the belief that a primary purpose of punishment is to effect a change in the character, attitudes and behaviour of convicted offenders so as to strengthen the communities social defence but also to contribute to the welfare of the individual. This belief can be traced back to the 18th century work of John Howard and its influence is seen again in an American Congress of corrections held in 1870 and put into place in the Elmira Reformatory (opening in 1877) In Canada these ideas shape the discussions the "new penology' through the 1920's and 1930's but they were not firmly implemented until the early 1950's and are perhaps best demonstrated by the 1957 Haney Correctional Institution located in British Columbia. See: Nothing Works.

Reification To treat as though real that which is just an abstraction or a conceptualization. Sociologists since Durkheim have been accused of reifying society which critics say is just an abstract concept and does not exist. To act as though society exists and thus can act or make decisions or coerce people is to reify society.

Reinforcement A process in which a behaviour is strengthened; increasing the probability that a response will occur by either presenting a contingent positive event or removing a negative event.

Relations of Production *See social relations of production.*

Relative Autonomy A theory of state power based on Marxist ideas. This perspective assumes that the state can and does play a limited independent role in the maintenance and stabilization of capitalist society. Differs from pluralism in viewing state power as strongly constrained by the ideological and structural characteristics of capitalist society. See: Structuralist Approach.

Relative Deprivation (1) A perceived disadvantage in social or economic standing based on a comparison to others in a society. (2) Relative deprivation and absolute deprivation are often contrasted. Absolute deprivation refers to the inability to sustain oneself physically and materially. Some right wing groups suggest that this is how Canada should define and measure poverty. Rather, Canada uses a form of relative deprivation; deprivation is not judged against some absolute standard of sustain ability but of deprivation in relation to others around you. You may have sufficient money to meet your needs and even meet them adequately but feel relatively deprived.

Relative Poverty Poverty defined by reference to the living standards of the majority in any given society.

Reliability Identifies one of the standards (another being validity) against which the tools used to measure concepts are judged. Reliability refers to consistency of results over time. If a bathroom scale is used to measure the concept of weight, one must ask: Is this tool (the bathroom scale) reliable? Does it provide consistent results? To check this get back on the scale a second time to see if it produces the same results. Notice that the bathroom scale may be reliable and yet be inaccurate. Are I.Q. tests a reliable measure of 'intelligence'? Are official suicide statistics reliable measures of the 'suicide' rate? Are questions about which political party a person would vote for a reliable measure of 'political preference'? Since in many of these examples it is difficult to assume, like weight, that the results would remain the same over time, it may be more correct to think of reliability as indicating consistency of results among users of the tool or measurement. *See: Validity.*

Religion A set of beliefs involving symbols regarded as sacred, together with ritual practices in which members of the community engage.

Religiosity The degree to which one believes in and is involved in religion. For example, attending church, volunteering for the church, giving donations to the church, believing in the values, morals and mythology of their religion.

Religious Right Found more frequently in the United States than in Canada (where its influence is chiefly located in the Reform Party), refers to groups or individuals who combine the economic conservatism of classical liberalism (beliefs in free market economies, small government autonomy of the individual) with the socially conservative views of many fundamentalist religions (e.g.: against abortion, intolerant of homosexuality, non-supportive of single parent mothers, propose censorship of children's reading material, recommend reducing rights of criminal offenders, etc.). Since these groups support an economic doctrine which is gaining wide acceptance they are able to move into positions of power and influence and their social views are giving shape to many aspects of life. See: Neo-Liberalism.

Renewable Resource A resource that can be exploited without depletion because it is constantly replenished. This includes forest resources, the fisheries, naturally occurring food crops and the fertility of agricultural land. There is heated debate in Canada about where to set the appropriate levels of resource use compatible with long term renewal. See: Sustainable Development.

Rep Street language for reputation.

Representative Democracy Based on the existence of two or more political parties, in which voters democratically elect politicians to represent their interests.

Republic This has come to mean a society where there is no hereditary or appointed monarch or emperor as head of state. Originally it referred to a system of political rule where citizens, through representative institutions participated in government and exercised political power. This meaning derives from the original Latin res publica which means 'things public', those things that are connected to ruling the public realm. In its narrower meaning the term distinguishes Canada, Britain, Norway, Sweden, Denmark, the Netherlands, Thailand and other countries formally headed by monarchs, from France, Italy, Germany, the United States and many others where the head of state is a president either directly elected or appointed by an elected assembly.

Research Methods The diverse strategies used to gather empirical (factual) material in a systematic way.

Reserve Army of Labour In Marxian analysis, that segment of the labour force which is held in reserve, to be called into the work force when need arises. If there were no reserve labour it might be difficult for new businesses to open or for temporary or emergency projects to be undertaken in the economy. In addition labour shortage would create upward pressure on wages and increase union power. This reserve labour of course needs to be doing something during the period it is held in reserve, so it may be on welfare or working in the household. The term has been useful for understanding women's relationship to the work force. Women were pulled into the workforce during World War II and then pushed out when the men returned. During the economic boom of the 1960-70's women entered the work force in large numbers and there is fear that they will be the first fired during recession. (Although this appears not to have happened in the 1990's recession.) Women, young people and the elderly may all be thought of as reserve labour since they have traditionally stayed out of the labour force.

Reserves Land set aside, or reserved, for a designated group. In Canada as the Anglo-Europeans colonized the land and occupied territories previously inhabited by Natives, they designated lands for Native groups. Although reserved for Native bands the lands remained the property of the crown. In Canada there are 576 Native bands recognized by the government and 2,281 reserves (often called reservations) as well as some crown land settlements set aside for these peoples. These figures reveal a distinct Canadian pattern of creating reserves - many small reserves were created and typically distributed among the larger non-Native population. All of the reserve lands

Restructuring Usually refers to the re-organization and rationalization of administration and production in both public and private sectors. In the public sector it has been encouraged by growing deficits, in the private sector cost cutting and reorganization has been encouraged by high interest rates, recession and lower corporate profit margins.

Retirement Center A city or town to which many people move when they retire.

Retribution Deriving from the notions of retribute (to give back or return) or to receive in recompense and the Christian sense of deserved, adequate or fit, the term is now used exclusively to refer to punishment. Retribution is punishment deserved because of an offence and which fits the severity of the offence. Punishment is justified because it makes the offender give up money, personal freedom or comfort that is equivalent to the harm or loss done to others. Retribution must be distinguished from revenge and retaliation.

Retributive Justice *See distributive justice.*

Reverse Discrimination Discrimination against a privileged group in order to correct previous discrimination against a disadvantaged group. The accusation of 'reverse discrimination' is often directed against those favoring equity programs or affirmative action programs. See: Affirmative Action.

Reverse Onus There are some offences in Canadian criminal law where the prosecution does not have to test criminal intent. For example, if one is robbing a bank witn frienu.s, one of wnom pulls out a gun and kills the teller, you may well be convicted of murder and not just robbery. Even if you did not know this was going to happen nor that the friend even had a gun, you will be charged and perhaps convicted of murder without the crown having to prove you intended to kill the teller.

Revolution A process of change involving the mobilizing of a mass social movement in order to radically transform the society (see also Cuup D'etat and Rebellion).

Riots An outbreak of collective violence directed against persons, property or both.

Rites of Passage (1) Communal rituals that !!lark the transition from one status to another (such as a confirmation or a wedding ceremony). (2) The ritual or ceremonial acknowledgment of a person's passage from one stage of life to the next. For example, the graduation ceremony or the retirement party. Many cultures provide a ritualized acknowledgment of the passage to adulthood but sociologists note that this has all but disappeared from modern societies.

Ritual (1) An action performed because of its symbolic significance and its ability to evoke the emotions of those engaged in the performance. These actions are usually clearly specified by the group and there are additional rules about who can perform the ritual, and when the ritual should be performed. Ritual may be important in maintaining the values of a group or in strengthening group ties. Examples of ritual include communion, aspects of the marriage ceremony, or singing the national anthem before sports events. (2) Formalized ceremonial behavior in which' the members of a group or community regularly engage.

Role Convergence An aspect of one explanation for the rising crime rate among women: their roles have converged with (become similar to) those of men.

Role Distancing The act of presenting your 'self as being removed or at a distance from the role you are being required to play. For example, by keeping your eyes open when asked to pray or say grace, you communicate to the group that you are making no commitment to the role. A concept from dramaturgical sociology. See: Presentation of Self.

Role Playing Where an individual plays at or pretends to occupy the role of another This concept is useful for understanding the socialization of children a,nd in particular that stage during which they play at being mothers, fathers, doctors, nurses, or truck drivers. It is during this playing that they master the ability to engage in reflexive role-taking and thus to develop their own sense of self. See: Role-Taking, Reflexive.

Role Strain Captures the stress or tension that may arise from the performance of a role.

Role Theory, Gender The theory that women's lesser involvement in crime can be attributed to their socialization into traditional roles within the family and in society.

Role A position, or status, within a social structure that is shaped by relatively precise behavioural expectations (norms). A role has been described as the active component of status. The individual, placed within a status in a social structure, performs their role in a way shaped by normative expectations. Individuals have varying ideas about normative standards and their own unique values, so role behaviour is not standardized, however' radical departure from expected role behaviour will usually result in social sanctions.

Role-Taking, Reflexive Where an individual looks at their own role performance from the perspective of another person. In taking the view point of another, they are able to see themselves as an object, as if from the outside. When we ask: 'Am I talking too much?', or, 'Am I being responsible?' we are engaging in reflexive role-taking: we are using outside standards -the point of view of another - to look at ourselves.

Routine-Activity Theory A theory developed in the 1970's to explain variations in victimization rates among categories of persons, areas or over time. Dependent on the notions of life style and opportunity, this theory argues that it is the life styles (Le.: their routine activities) of young males which explains their high rate of victimization compared to seniors, or that it is the changes in routine-activities accompanying the increase in small households and two-income families which has increased the opportunity for property crimes.

Royal Commission on Aboriginal Peoples A Commission of inquiry established by the Conservative government in 1991 as a strategy to obtain First Nations' support for constitutional change after the Meech Lake Accord was defeated in 1990 by Elijah Harper, an Aboriginal member of the Manitoba legislature. The Commission reported in 1996 having examined a wide range of matters affecting Aboriginal peoples. The report has the potential to help Canadians redefine the relationship between First Nations peoples and government. Royal Commission on Canada's Economic Prospects.

Chaired by Walter Gordon, the 1956 Report displays a new period of concern for Canadian nationalism. Gordon warned of the dangers of economic subordination to the United States and recommended some measures to reduce this danger. The Liberal government of Pierre Trudeau returned to this concern in the early 1970's and brought in legislation protective of national interests. Many argue, however, that the Free Trade Agreement of 1989, implemented by a Conservative government, was a victory for continentalism and accelerated the process of integrating the Canadian and American economies. See: Continentalism.

Royal Proclamation of 1763 This proclamation, signed by King George, provides the basis of Native land rights in North. America. Signed at the conclusion of the Seven Years' War at which time the French signed over much of North America to the British, the document proclaims British rule over the territory. The contents of this Proclamation are significant. It acknowledges pre-existing ownership of land by Native peoples; it stated that Indian land could only be bought or treated for by the British government; it established a procedure for obtaining land; and it used the term 'Nations or Tribes of Indians'. These provisions provide a powerful legal foundation for current disputes over land rights. The Royal Proclamation has an entirely different significance for the Quebecois since it was intended to make the colony of Canada with a British mold: British civil and criminal law was imposed on the Quebecois and Catholics were virtually prohibited from holding public office.

Rule of Law One of the cornerstones of democratic society, meaning that everyone is subject to the law. It is not just the rule that everyone is covered by the Criminal Code and must be charged and convicted if ·appropriate. It also means that no one in the society, the Prime Minister, cabinet, senior civil servants, judges or police has power except as it is derived from law. Authority can only come from law, namely the Constitution, a statute, legal regulations, Common Law, municipal by -law. There is a rule of law rather than rule by individuals.

S

Sacred Something set apart from the everyday world which inspires attitudes of awe or reverence among believers (see also Profane).

Sacred-Profane Emile Durkheim (1858-1917) claimed that all religions divide objects or phenomena into the sacred and the profane. Sacred objects are those which are extraordinary and are treated as if set apart from the routine course of events in daily life. The profane are those objects or phenomena seen as ordinary and constituting the reality of everyday living. Durkheim believed that the celebration of religious beliefs and sacred ritual united the community and integrated individuals and that it enhanced the sharing of collective sentiments and solidarity in profane areas of social life. The secularization and rationalization of Western societies has reduced the realm of the sacred.

Sample When it is difficult to conduct a census of an entire population, a researcher will work with a portion of that population, a sample, which is thought to be representative of the population in question. Researchers typically try to ensure that a sample has been drawn in a random fashion. This ensures that the distribution of population characteristics corresponds to the assumptions of probability theory. This allows inferences to be drawn about the population. Many times non-random samples are used, however.

Sampling Error Any sample is only one of many samples which could have beep- drawn from a population. Consequently, a researcher may not get the same results with each sample (e.g.: the mean or average might vary). As the sample gets larger this variation is less drastic, and the sampling error is smaller. Social scientists have ways .of calculating the sampling error and you can see this in the news many times when a reporter says: 'a survey of this size is accurate within 3.5% 19 times out of 20'. For example, the 3.5% is the sampling error. 95 times of 100 times the mean would fall within +/- the mean or average reported.

Sampling Frame The actual physical representation of a population, a voters list or a student class lists, for example, from which a sample is actual drawn. A population is a somewhat abstract concept while the sampling frame is the real listing of members of that population such that you can imagine them being placed into a hat for purposes of random sampling.

Sampling (1) Refers to the process or method of drawing a sample from a population. This process can be based on random selection such that each member of the population has an equal probability of being selected (e.g.: putting all the names into a hat). Many statistical tests assume a process of random selection. However, the method may net be based on random selection. One might, for example, select for convenience the first 100 people you meet or all the students in an introductory sociology class. (2) Taking a small representative part of a population for purposes of drawing inferences from the analysis of the sample characteristics to the population as a whole.

Sanction (1) A positive or negative response by an individual or group to behaviour and designed to encourage or discourage that behaviour. Positive sanction would include rewards, compliments, applause, or smiles, while negative sanctions would include punishments, frowns, avoidance, or gossip. Sanctions can be informal (coming from friends and neighbors) or formal (coming from authorized institutions like the police, the government, the school, and must be seen as forms of social control. (2) A reward for conformity or a punishment for nonconformity that reinforces socially approved forms of behavior.

Sapir-Whorf Hypothesis The conjecture that people perceive their world through the framework of language.

Schizophrenia A serious mental disturbance in which an individual typically has delusions or hallucinations and a distorted sense of reality.

Science The application of systematic methods of observation and careful logical analysis; the term also refers to the body of knowledge produced by the use of the scientific method.

Scientific Management A method of work organization where management implements a specialised division of labour and sets out detailed instructions for the performance of work. Associated with the innovative methods introduced by Frederick Taylor (1856-1915) to separate workers from their knowledge of the work process, to divide labour so as to pay only for the specific skill required to perform a narrow function and to establish management as the controller of work and the work process. See: Industrial Relations / Taylorism.

Secondary Deviance The deviant role behavior that a person adopts as a result of being labeled as deviant.

Secondary Group Structure A term used in sociocultural materialism to refer to structural groups in which members tend to interact without any emotional commitment to one another. These organizations are coordinated through bureaucracies. They perform many functions such as regulating production, reproduction, socialization, education, and enforcing social discipline. Examples include governments, parties, military, corporations, educational institutions, media, service and welfare organizations, and professional and labor organizations (see also Structure, and Primary Group Structure).

Secondary Group A group of individuals who do not know each other on a personal level interacting in pursuit of a goal (see also Primary Group).

Secondary Labor Market (1) Refers to the economic position of individuals engaged in occupations that provide insecure jobs, poor benefits and conditions of work (see also Primary Labor Market). (2) Refers to those occupations which tend to be located in the most competitive areas of the economy and are more labour intensive. These occupations tend to pay lower wages, have insecure employment, be less unionized, and provide less opportunity for advancement. Typical industries are restaurant and hotel services, cashiers and retail sales. This labour market has been dominated by women and minorities, while the other market (the primary labour market) has been dominated by white males. This term was originally part of what was referred to as dual labour market theory. The term segmented labour market is now used but studies continue to find a significant dualism to the labour market and this continues to be useful for understanding women's occupational location and their low wages relative to men. See: Primary Labour Market.

Secondary Sexual Characteristics Characteristics that are sex related but are not directly connected with the physiology of reproduction (the sex organs). For example, statistically, men tend to be heavier with more muscle mass and physical strength than women although there are some women heavier, more muscular and stronger than some men. See: Sexual Dimorphism.

Sect Usually contrasted with churches or denominations, sects are thought to be small and inward-looking religious or spiritual groups which reject the values of the wider society. Examples would be the Jehovah's Witnesses, Salvation Army, Christian Science. These groups typically begin with a charismatic leader who articulates a strong rejection of the compromises made with the secular world by other religions.

Over time, as leadership is routinized and members experience some upward mobility, there tends to be more acceptance of worldly matters and secular values.

Secularization (1) A process of decline in the social influence of religion (see alsu Rationalization). (2) The process of organizing society or aspects of social life around non-religious values or principles. The term is linked closely to Max Weber's concept of a growing 'disenchantment of the world' as the sphere of the magical, sacred and religious retreats in cultural significance before the driving force of rationalization of culture and social institutions powered by emergent capitalism. See: Rationalization.

Self (or Self-Consciousness) The individual's awareness of being a distinct social identity, a person separate from others. Human beings are not born with self-consciousness, but acquire an awareness of self as a result of early socialization.

Self-Control One of the aims of all socialization is to place a 'police person' inside each of us, rather than relying on external controls. Many experience 'self-control' when a voice inside says: What will mother think? Will this harm my chances of being accepted as a police recruit? This is effective self-control.

Self-Government In the Canadian context this term has clearest reference to the aspirations of First Nations peoples. While the term is as yet without a clear definition, as used by the federal government it means something like self-determination. The Indian Act replaced traditional Indian governments with band councils that acted as agents of the federal government. These councils only exercise those powers granted by the Indian Act. Whatever form self-government takes it would involve legislative changes to give First Nations peoples the tools to be much more self-determining. For some First Nations peoples the idea of self-government is an acknowledgment of nationhood. For these groups their status as self-determining nations was never given up through colonization or treaties, so to have self-government recognized is seen as an acknowledgment of this earlier, and continuing, nationhood. As currently envisaged by federal and provincial governments, self government is not equivalent to territorial sovereignty, although it implies extensive legal autonomy within the general framework of the federal government's overriding power to make provision for 'peace, order and good government'.

Self-Report Studies A method for measuring crime involving the distribution of a detailed questionnaire to a sample of people, asking them whether they have committed a crime in a particular period of time. This has been a good method for criminologists to determine the social characteristics of 'offenders'.

Self-Reported Delinquency A count of delinquency based on the method of asking young people if they have committed an illegal act in a specified time period. See: Self-Report Studies.

Semi-Periphery Countries Countries that are in the initial stages of industrialism which provide labor and raw materials to the core countries (see also Core Countries, and Periphery Countries).

Separation of Powers A constitutional structure of government where legal authority is divided between various institutions. In the United States, the Constitution divides federal authority between the President, Congress and the Supreme Court, all of which have delimited powers and responsibilities. This concept of government differs from the idea of parliamentary supremacy which confers complete authority to Parliament and grants it unconstrained legal powers. Canada exhibits a blend of the idea of parliamentary supremacy and the idea of separation of powers, since the written part of the Canadian constitution explicitly divides federal and provincial powers and establishes a framework of constitutional law by which Parliament is restrained in its actions.

Sequential Analysis As used by ethnomethodologists this is the same as conversation analysis. See: Conversational Analysis.

Serf An unfree status associated with agrarian economies dominated by feudal social relationships. Serfs were labourers bound to the land and to service to a landlord but differing from slaves in that they possessed security of the person, the right to personal property and customary rights to use land and other resources. Serfdom has occurred in many world societies including England, France, Russia, China and Japan. While serfdom was first extinguished in England in the 16th century it persisted in Russia until the general emancipation ordered by Tsar Alexander 11 in 1861. A modified form of serfdom, based on indentured or bonded labour, is still widespread in world societies. See: Feudalism.

Serial Monogamy The process of contracting several marriages in succession-marriage, divorce, and remarriage.

Seriousness Rule The national governments of Canada and the United States use this rule in deciding how to count occurrences in a multiple crime situation: only the most serious crime is counted.

Service Economy Usually contrasted with a goods-producing economy and refers to an economy based largely on the provision of service rather than manufactured goods. These services may include medical service, accounting, social work, teaching, design, consultancy, short order cook, waiting tables, driving taxi. The shift to a service economy is sociologically interesting because it appears to be associated with different labour market demands, differing educational requirements, and differing wage structures. See: Goods Producing Economy.

Sex Role The gender specific role behavior that a person learns as a member of a particular society.

Sex Stratification The ranking and differential reward system of the sexes.

Sex Typing Refers to stereotypes of the sexes and the consequent actions of characterizing men and women on the basis these stereotypes. For example, women are mediators and men are competitive; boys prefer trucks while girls prefer dolls. See: Stereotype.

Sex (1) The biological categories of females and males. (2) The biological classification of individuals as males and females. Sociologists would note, however, that even though this is a classification based on biological differences it is a socially constructed classification. See: Gender Roles.

Sexism (1) Actions or attitudes that discriminate against people based solely on their gender. Sexism is linked to power in that those with power are typically treated with favour and those without power are typically discriminated against. Sexism is also related to stereotypes since the discriminatory actions or attitudes are frequently based on false beliefs or over generalizations about gender and on seeing gender as relevant when it is not. See: Stereotype. (2) Beliefs which hold one sex superior to the other thereby justifying sexual inequalities.

Sexual Assault A broader classification of sexual offence than 'rape'. Rape occured only when sexual penetration was involved, but this new definition of a sexual assault is broader. It is an assault that has as its consequence a violation of the sexual integrity of the victim. This is now the defined criminal code offence.

Sexual Dimorphism Differences between males and females in size and appearance. Sexual dimorphism in humans is greater than in some animals and less than in many. Evolutionary psychologists and biologists are intrigued to understand the function of sexual dimorphism.

Sexual Division of Labour The allocation of work task, either in the private household or in the public economy, on the basis of the sex of the person. Women may cook the meals and men wash the dishes, or women may perform caring roles such as nursing or social work in the public economy, while men perform the tasks of driving trucks, fighting fires, or manufacturing goods. Most societies have had some division of labour by sex. The sexual division of labour is related to stereotyping. Although this expression seems to have survived criticism from social scientists it is actually incorrect: the division of labour between the sexes is chiefly gendered: it is based on cultural practices rather than any inherent suitability of either sex to perform specific roles.

Sexual Harassment The making of persistent unwanted sexual advances by one individual towards another.

Shifting Agriculture A system in which land is cleared and then cultivated until it is exhausted, at which point new land is cleared and the process restarted.

Sick Role Patterns of behavior expected of one who is sick-this role often exempts the person from their normal role obligations.

Signifier A term from semiology - the study of signs. For example the expression ' a pig is coming' is the signifier (or the signifier could be a gesture, clothing style, form of architecture, consumer good), while the content of this expression is the signified. The signifier and the signified always exist in some relationship (called signification) and the hearer is always decoding this relationship. For example in one instance the hearer may 'hear' the signifier 'pig' and assume that an animal pig is in the area suitable for hunting. Another time the hearer may 'hear' that a policeman is in the area, while at another time the hearer may 'hear' that the speaker's supervisor is arriving.

Silent Spring Published in 1962, and written by Rachel Carso]}, this book was an early call to arms for the environmental movement. Carson portrays the forces that modern society has brought into being which assault nature and human life itself. The title comes from an imaginary community in which 'There was a strange silence. The birds, for example where had they gone? Many people spoke of them, puzzled and disturbed. The feeding stations in the backyards were deserted. The few birds seen anywhere were moribund; they trembled violently and could not fly. It was a spring without voices. On the morning that had once throbbed with the dawn chorus of robins, catbirds, doves, jays, wrens, and scores of other bird voices there was now no sound; only silence over the fields and woods and marsh.'

Situational Crime Prevention Premised on the belief that most crime is opportunistic rather than being the outcome of those driven to commit a crime no matter what. This form of prevention attempts to reduce the opportunities for crime rather than just relying on the police after the crime has occurred. This approach is also called 'effective guardianship'.

Slavery Describes a relationship between people in which one person is not legally free but is treated as the legally owned property of the other. As such the slave can be sold or exchanged. Slave relationships have been found in many parts of the world and have sometimes been the central economic relationships of the society. As legal property of their owners, slaves can be forced to produce goods or services whose value remains with the owner.

Social Bond The degree to which an individual is integrated into 'the social'. Do they have binding ties to the family, to the school, to the workplace, to the community ? While Durkheim first focused on the importance of the social bond it has gained wide acceptance in the theory and research of Travis Hirschi. Hirschi argues that as the social bond is weakened the degree of deviant involvement goes up.

Social Change Alteration in social structures or culture over time.

Social Construction of Reality An aspect of many

micro-interpretive perspectives in sociology and must be understood as a contrast to positivistic and structural sociology. Rejecting the notion that events or social phenomena have an independent and objective existence, they examine the methods that members of societv use to create or construct reality. Durkheim, for example was a positivist and a structuralist and argued that suicide had an objective existence, independent of himself and others. That is, there was something about the way of death that constituted something as a suicide. An adv6ca~e of the social construction of reality perspective would argue that suicide is just a label for a death and is constituted, or created, by the accounts that people like police, family, or coroners give of the death. Our accounting methods then construct reality rather than there being some independent reality which we can describe or explain. This phrase was used in 1966 by Peter Berger and T. Luckmann *See: Symbolic InteractionismI Labeling Theory/ Phenomenological Sociology / Ethnomethodology.*

Social Contract Theory Used metaphorically to suggest that a group of self-interested and rational individuals came together and formed a contract which created society. Each was willing to .give up a little bit of freedom to create social rules that would protect their self-interest. This theory suggests that individuals were historically prior to societies. It was this view which sociologist Emile. Durkheim argued against in the late nineteenth century with his claim that society must come before the individual since human culture and communication can only arise in society.

Social Control Theory Attempts to explain why it is that all of us do not commit crime. Or to put this another way: why are most people law-abiding? The answer lies in dimensions of social control. The many ways in which people are controlled by family, schools, work situations, conscience, etc. Most ccnventional theories, by contrast try to explain why individuals commit crime.

Social Credit Party Members of the Social Credit party were first elected in Canada under the leadership of evangelical Christian preacher and radio broadcaster William Aberhart. In the Alberta general election f)f 1935, Aberhart led the party to a decisive victory when they won 56 of the 63 seats. Later that same year, 17 members were elected to the House of Commons. In subsequent years, Social Credit members were elected in Saskatchewan, Manitoba, British Columbia and Quebec. The party's political program was founded on the theories outlined by Major C. Hugh Douglas in his 1920 book, Economic Democracy. Douglas argued that the economic problems of capitalist societies resulted from a failure to balance production with sufficient mass purchasing power to absorb the goods produced. According to Douglas this was because industrialists had to hire labour and also purchase raw resources, but when the object was proliuced the worker would only be paid for labour and thus receive less than the market value of the goods produced and be unable to purchase the objects produced. These rather strange economic notions led to the belief that the government should correct this imbalance by giving each citizen a portion of a 'national dividend' to support economic stability. The Social Credit government of Alberta attempted to introduce policies based on these ideas, some of which were disallowed by the federal government. With the world-wide recovery from the depression in the late 1930's, the party moved away from Douglas's economic theories and adopted more main -stream free-enterprise policies. Social Credit remained somewhat distinct, however, in its strong identification with regional issues and its evangelical and fundamentalist Christian roots. The last Social Credit government anywhere in Canada was defeated in 1991 in the British Columbia election. The party ceased to have representation in the British Columbia legislature after the 1996 provincial election and appears to have collapsed.

Social Darwinism (1) A late nineteenth century social philosophy which unites an interest in social problems (e.g.: inequality) with an interpretation of Darwin's work on the origin of species. Advocates argue that the central Darwinian principle of evolution, development and progress, is the survival of the fittest and extinction of the weakest. Applied to social affairs this implies that those who get ahead in society are the most fit and deserve their position. More importantly, perhaps, this perspective suggests that supporting those who fall behind (by providing welfare, for example) interferes with the principles of evolution and obstructs social progress. Sociologists of course believe that social problems like inequality must be understood within a social and cultural context, rather than a context of biological competition. (2) An early and now largely discredited view of social evolution emphasizing the importance of "survival of the fittest" or struggle between individuals, groups, or societies as the motor of development. Social Darwinism became widely popular and was often used to justify existing inequali ties.

Social Democracy. A general term for political doctrines that claim an important role for the state and the community in the shaping and directing a society's economic and social life. Social democracy differs from socialism because it is committed to preservation of a largely capitalist and free market economy, but shares with it an emphasis on the importance of redistribution of wealth and income so that citizens may have social and economic conditions that effectively provide for reasonable equality of opportunity. Modern welfare-state liberalism is closely allied to social democratic ideas. *See: Socialism.*

Social Disorganization Theory The theory that crime and other deviant behaviour is most likely to occur where social institutions are not able to direct and control groups of individuals. It is argued that gangs will arise spontaneously in social contexts that are weakly controlled. Some criminologists think that the concept of social disorganization just reflects middle-class failure to comprehend organization different from their own.

Social Disorganization A structural condition of society caused by rapid change in social institutions, norms, and values.

Social Evolution Theories of social change which generally hold that human societies move from simple to complex forms of organization.

Social Formation A term used by critical sociologists with a meaning similar to that of 'society'. When we talk of Canadian society, however, we tend to think only of one society and imagine it being static. Critical sociologists wish to talk about Canadian society being formed in different ways over time. Each would be a different social formation although all would be called Canada. Each formation would be characterized by a particular organization of economic and political relationships.

Social Gospel Movement An attempt to use the Gospel, the teachings of Christ, to deal with social problems arising in an expanding industrial nation like Canada. This movement appeared in Canada in the 1880's and was a major force in social and political life through the 1930's. Its central belief was that God was at work in the creation of social change, social justice and moral reform. This core value can be found in the Social Service Council of Canada (1912), United Church (1925), and the CCF (1932) and played an important part in shaping the nature of sociology in Canada. The movement is particularly associated with the work of J.S. Woodsworth, T.C. Douglas, Grace McInnis, and others. These ideas would now be part of what is referred to as 'liberation theology'.

Social Groups Two or more individuals who interact in systematic ways with one another and share a high degree of common identity. Groups may range in size from dyads to large-scale societies.

Social Institutions Major structural entitities in sociocultural systems that address a basic need of the system. Institutions involve fIxed modes of behavior backed by strong norms and sanctions that tend to be followed by most members of a society.

Social Intervention Programs Activities by government, social agencies and volunteers designed to change and improve the social situation of individuals, groups and communities, strengthen social bonds and encourage internalization of social control.

Social Maps The term map is used primarily as a metaphor (though one could actually place **data or**

statistics on a geographic map). Mapping in the first sense means identifying the social characteristics of victims, offenders or inmates or other groups.

Social Mobility Upward or downward movement within a stratification system. Liberal theory claims that capitalist societies are open-class and therefore one can expect a high degree of social mobility. According to liberal theory this movement within a stratification system should result from a person's achievements and should not be based on ascribed characteristics such as sex, race, region of birth, and parent's class position. Social mobility is typically measured by comparing the status positions of adult children to that of their parents (intergenerational mobility), but it can be measured by comparing a person's status position over their own lifetime (intragenerational mobility). Sociologists see social mobility as a useful way to measure equality of opportunity. See: Demand Mobility / Equality Of Opportunity.

Social Movement (1) A group of people organized, outside of institutions established for this purpose, so as to bring about political and social change which will satisfy their shared interest or goal Political parties therefore would not be social movements although the New Democratic Party often describes itself as part of a social movement. It is more correct to talk about the environmental movement, the gay rights movement, the women's movement, the labour movement, victim's rights movements, prisoner's rights movements, movements for drug decriminalization. Sociologists are interested in studying the dynamics of such movements and the conditions or forces which make some successful and others less successful. (2) A large grouping of people who are organized to bring about, or to block, a change in the sociocultural system.

Social Relations of Production Another way of referring to the class structure. The social relations of production refers to the social relationships that people enter into in the production or delivery of goods and services. From a Marxist perspective these relationships are inevitably those of owners and non-owners or those who control the work and those who do not control the work. In this way of thinking, social class is founded on the economy of any society and it is the pattern of class relations that give a society its central character.

Social Reproduction The processes which perpetuate characteristics of social structure over periods of time (see also Agencies of Socialization).

Social Role The expected patterned behavior of an individual occupying a particular status position.

Social Structure The patterned and relatively stable arrangement of roles and statuses found within societies and social institutions. The idea of social structure points out the way in which societies, and institutions within them, exhibit predictable patterns of organization, activity and social interaction. This relative stability of organization and behaviour provides the quality of predictability that people rely on in every day social interaction. Social structures are inseparable from cultural norms and values that also shape status and social interaction.

Social Forces The term refers to the fact that society and social organizations exert an influence on individual human behavior.

Social Mobility Movement between different social positions within a stratification system

Socialism (1) A political doctrine that upholds the principle of collectivity, rather than individualism, as the foundation for economic and social life. Socialists favour state and co-operative ownership of economic resources, equality of economic condition and democratic rule and management of economic and social institutions. See: Social Democracy. (2) An economic system in which the means of production and distribution of goods and services are public ally owned.

Socialist Feminism A perspective that examines women's social situation as shaped by both patriarchal gender relations and by the class structure of capitalism. It sees gender and class oppression as inseparable and rather than working for the equality of women within a liberal, democratic capitalist society, it argues for the equality of women within a society that is not dependent upon the exploitation of one group by another i.e.: a classless society. See: Feminism / Liberal Feminism.

Socialization (1) A process of social interaction and communication in which an individual comes to learn and internalize the culture of their society or group. Socialization begins immediately at birth, with the conditioning influences of infant handling, and continues throughout an individual's lifetime. Sociologists recognize the limitless variety of individual experiences of socialization, but have given much attention to general patterns of socialization found in individual societies and groups within them. The sociological use of the term refers to the learning and absorption of culture and not simply to the process of interacting with others. (2) The term is also sometimes used to refer to the collective ownership and management of economic resources e.g.: a nationalized industry or resource, or to publicly provided and financed services e.g.: 'socialized medicine' (medicare). (3) The lifelong processes through which humans develop an awareness of social norms and values, and, achieve a distinct sense of self.

Society (1) A human community, usually with a relatively fixed territorial location, sharing a common culture and common activities. There is cultural and institutional interdependence between members of the society. and they are, to some extent, differentiated from other communities and groups. Societies are generally identified as existing at the level of nation states, but there can be regional and cultural communities within nation states that possess much of the cultural distinctiveness and relative self-sufficiency of societies. (2) A society is a group of people who live in a particular territory, are subject to a common system of political authority, and share a common culture.

Sociobiology (1) A perspective on human social behaviour made accessible by the publication in 1975 of E.O. Wilson's Sociobiology and Richard Dawkins's 1976 publication of The Selfish Gene. This perspective begins with the assumption "that humans are above all else animals and therefore the roots of human social behaviour can be found in our evolutionary heritage. Since this way of understanding relies on—genetics and biological adaptation it is not a sociological perspective. The term sociobiology has been replaced to a great" extent by the term evolutionary psychology. (2) An approach which attempts to explain the social behavior of humans in terms of biological principles.

Sociocultural Materialism An ecological-evolutionary world view. A variant of cultural materialism, it is the world view developed and taught by your instructor, F. Elwell (see also Cultural Materialism).

Socioeconomic Status A term which is often contrasted with that of social class. Socioeconomic status, largely an American usage, has developed as a way to operationalize or measure social class on the assumptions that class groupings are not real groups. It is a rather arbitrary category and is developed by combining the position or score of persons on criteria such as income, amount of education, type of occupation held, or neighborhood of residence. The scores can then be arbitrarily divided so as to create divisions such as upper class, middle .class, lower class. Soci010gists are interested in socioeconomic status, as they are in class, since it is assumed that this status affects life. chances in numerous ways. See: Class.

Sociological Imagination (1) A term used by C. Wright Mills that refers to the application of imaginative thought to the asking and answering of sociological questions. (2) As used by C.W. Mills (1916-1962) this term refers to the ability to imagine and understand the intersection between personal biography and historical social structures. This is indeed the essence of sociology: imagining that every individual's life is given meaning, form and significance within historically specific cultures and ways of organizing social life. Having a sociological imagination then is identical with being a good sociologist: it isa standard against which to judge sociology.

Sociology of Knowledge The study of the social bases of what is known, believed or valued bo~h by individuals and society. The essential idea is that knowledge itself, how it is defined and constituted, is a cultural product shaped by soCia1 ~ontext and history. In this view knowledge cannot be treated as a thing in itself, as an objective, universally true body of facts and theory, but must be understood in the social context in which it originated. The principal ideas of postmodernism are closely linked to this long tradition in philosophy and the social sciences. See: Postmodern.

Sociology The study of human behavior and societies, giving particular emphasis to the industrialized world.

Solid Waste Refers to the accumulation of noxious substances (see also Depletion, Environment, and Intensification) .

Somatotypes Refers to body types and behind this idea lies the belief of early criminologists that there were distinctive body types and these types were associated with personality and temperament. It was believed that the mesomorph with a well-built, muscular body (note the sexist connotation of this) was associated with aggressive personality, insensitive to pain and tended to act impulsively.

Soul As used by Michel Foucault (1926-1884) refers to what psychologists mean by the psyche, the self, subjectivity or human consciousness. Foucault argues, for example, that the development of the penitentiary in the early 19th century resulted in a shift from punishing the body to punishing the soul.

Sovereignty The authority possessed by the governing individual or institution of a society. Sovereign authority is distinct in that it is unrestricted by legal regulation since the sovereign authority is itself the source of all law . The idea of state sovereignty appears to have developed first in Europe, in the late middle ages, where it emerged once a division was made between the sacred authority of the church and the secular authority of the state. So long as state power was subject to religious institutions -like the Catholic church - state sovereignty could not emerge. In Britain, state sovereignty is possessed by the Crown in Parliament: law passed by Parliament and consented to by the Crown has unchallengeable legal authority. In Canada, the locus of sovereignty is more ambiguous since the written parts of Canada's constitution, the Constitution Act of 1867 and the Constitution Act 1982, prescribe a federal-provincial division of powers and special procedures for constitutional amendment that limit the authority of the Crown and Parliament. Major changes to Canada's constitution require the unanimous consent of parliament and the ten provincial legislatures thus suggesting that political sovereignty in Canada is shared by the Crown in Parliament and the Crown and legislatures of Canada's ten provinces.

Sparrow Case A legal case advancing the aboriginal rights of natives in Canada. Ronald Sparrow, a Musqueam, was charged with violating federal regulations while fishing in an area not covered by existing treaties. A 1986 Court of Appeal ruled that section 35(1) of the Canadian Constitution meant that an aboriginal right to fish for food c'ontinued to exist in non-treaty areas of the province.

Speciesism The attitude that it is naturally right and appropriate to give priority to human interests and demands over those of all other living creatures. It has led to endangerment and extinction of many animal species and to extensive environmental damage and depletion.

Specific Deterrence As used in criminal justice, refers to crime prevention achieved through instilling fear in the specific individual being punished such that they refrain from future violation of the law. Also referred to as individual deterrence. *See: General Deterrence*

Specific Land Claims Claims to land made by Native groups covered by treaties but where the terms of treaties have not been met or land has been removed over the years without consent. *See: Calder Case / Comprehensive Land Claims.*

Spirit of Capitalism According to Max Weber (1864-1920) the spirit of capitalism is rationalization -being

Statistical School Associated with early social scientists like Adolphe Quetelet (1795-1874) and Andre-Michel Guerry (1802-1866), who began to explore the structure of emerging European societies with the assistance of statistical methods. While their early use of statistics is important they also developed a structural explanation of crime and other social problems. Although this work was to become important later, it was overshadowed by the importance given to the more individualistic theories of Lombroso.

Statistically Significant When researchers study within groups or between group differences, they need a technique to determine if this difference would have occurred by chance. Various statistical techniques can determine this and if it is unlikely the differences could have occurred by chance it is called a statistically significant difference. Usually a .05 level of significance is used (there are 5 chances of one hundred trials that this difference would occur by chance) but other levels can be used.

Statistics Refers to a collection of tests or techniques that are applied to the data, or observations, which social scientists have gathered. There are two categories of statistics: descriptive and inferential. Descriptive statistics are used to describe characteristics of the sample or population the researcher is working with, for example one can calculate a mean, standard deviation, etc. Inferential statistics are used for drawing inferences about a population based on the observations of a sample.

Status Ascribed A status that is automatically transmitted to an individual at birth or at a particular time in the life cycle. An individual is accorded this status through inheritance or as a result of such characteristics as sex, ethnicity or physical features.

Status Indian A Native person who is registered under the Indian Act as an Indian, and a non-status Indian is one whose ancestors were never registered or who lost status for various reasons. Women and their children lost status, for example, when they married a non-Native man or a Native man who did not have status. Under Bill C-31 (1985) these people have been able to regain their status. Court decision are beginning to make the distinction between status and non-status Indians less significant.

Status of Women Report A Royal Commission Report tabled in the Canadian House of Commons in 1970. The Commission of Inquiry had been created in 1967 and, chaired by Florence Bird, held public hearings into the status of women in society and made numerous recommendations to government. The report is built on the premises of liberal theory and measures women's status against the values of equality, individualism, and freedom.

Status Offence A delinquency or crime that can only be committed by people occupying a particular status. The Juvenile Delinquents Act (replaced in 1984) for example, created criminal offences of school truancy, incorrigibility, sexual immorality and violations of liquor laws. Only young people could be charged with or found to be in a state of delinquency because of these behaviours. It was found that approximately 20% of young girls coming to youth court did so because of their sexual behaviour while few boys were brought to court on these grounds. See: Double Standard.

Status, Achieved A position in a social structure that has been attained by the individual as a result of their individual abilities, work and personal involvements. While occupational statuses are generally achieved, often in a competitive process, one can also achieve more personal statuses, for example 'married' is an achieved status. See: Status, Ascribed.

Status, Ascribed A status that is automatically transmitted to an individual at birth or at a particular time in the life cycle. An individual is accorded this status through inheritance or as a result of such characteristics as sex, ethnicity or physical features.

Status (1) A position in a social structure regulated by norms and usually ranked according to power and prestige. Status differs from class in that it is a measure of a person's social standing or social honour in a community. Individuals who share the same social class may have very divergent status. For example, people's status is affected by ethnic origin, gender and age as well as their level of recognition in the community. While status is statistically related to class it is common for individuals to have inconsistent class and status locations. Most sociologists use both the concepts of class and status to describe the systems of social stratification (the way individuals are ranked in various hierarchies of income, wealth, authority and power) found in societies. (2) A social position within a society. The term can also refer to the social honor or prestige which a particular individual or group is accorded by other members of a society.

Statutes Laws enacted by a sovereign law-making body such as a provincial legislature or the House of Commons.

Structural Explanation An explanation for crime (such as homicide) that focuses on social structure (usually this refers to inequality, poverty, or power differentials). For example the patriarchal structure of the family might help explain the abuse of women and children within the family. Sociologist Rhonda Lenton argues that the racial structure of the USA and the depth of its poverty (and the weakness of its welfare state) compared to Canada, might help explain the difference in homicide rates.

Structural Functionalism A perspective used to analyze societies and their component features that focuses on their mutual integration and interconnection. Functionalism analyses the way that social processes and institutional arrangements contribute to the effective maintenance and stability of society. The fundamental perspective is opposition to major social change. See: Macro-Perspective.

Structural Unemployment Unemployed workers whose skills and training have become "obsolete" and who have little chance of ever finding employment at comparable paying jobs.

Structuralism (French) Refers to French social theorists such as Claude Levi-Strauss and Jean Piaget who claim that in the most ordinary of events there is a hidden structure or pattern (often called deep structure, a term taken from linguistics) which is not immediately apparent but can be discerned by careful analysis. For example, what can be learned from the names given to pets; from food categories; from the way a child compares volume in two containers? For the early structuralists the hidden structures in these practices reveal the structure of the human mind. This being so there should be some uniformity in the pattern found in these practices around the world.

Structuralist Approach An approach to understanding the role of the state within a conflict or Marxist perspective. The state is seen as captured by the structure of capitalism and while having a degree of autonomy or freedom from the dominant class of society finds it must act so as to reproduce the economic and social structures of capitalism. This approach typically sees the state doing this through attending to three functions: capital accumulation, legitimation and coercion. See: *Capital Accumulation / Coercion / Instrumentalist Approach / Legitimation Crises / Relative Autonomy.*

Structuration A term used by British sociologist Anthony Giddens in order to capture elements of macro and micro-sociology, structure and agency, determinism and free will. By structuration Giddens means that human actors recreate through their interactions (and this makes social change possible) the very social structures which constrain their actions. It involves the reproduction on a daily basis of the structures and institutions of society.

Structure Sociological term to refer to all human institutions, groups and organizations.

Subcultural Transmission Part of a wider theory which argues that behaviour is learned through socialization into the norms and values ofthe society. This is taken further to argue that some groups have values which are supportive of illegal behaviour. Those exposed to this subculture are more likely to exhibit deviant or criminal behaviour.

Subculture (1) A culture-within-a-culture; the somewhat distinct norms, values and behaviour of particular groups located within society. The concept of subculture implies some degree of group self-sufficiency such that individuals may interact, find employment, recreation, friends and mates within the group. (2) A group within the broader society that has values, norms and lifestyle distinct from those of the majority.

Subjectivism In traditional positivistic and macro-structural sociology, the subjectivity of the researcher and of the subjects is seen as something to be avoided. The preferred stance for the researcher is objectivity, making the assumption that the observation of the world can occur in a neutral fashion without being influenced by theory or cultural or personal assumptions. The subjectivity of the subjects being studied is to be avoided since it is assumed that peoples lives are shaped by structural and cultural forces of which the subject may be unaware. More recent sociology (e.g. Interpretive Theory, Ethnomethodology) is open to acknowledging the subjectivity of both researcher and subjects. One might study, for example, the ways in which the coroner interprets notes, slash marks, family environments, or medical histories, in an effort to arrive at an interpretation of a death. The coroner's subjectivity then is a valid area for investigation. Similarly one might be interested in how the scientist too is also involved in arriving at an interpretation and examining how this is shaped by the subjective assumptions made. Subjectivism then is an approach to doing science which acknowledges and makes room for subjectivity. *See: Macroperspective / Objectivity.*

Suburbanization The development of areas of housing outside the political boundaries of cities.

Sufficient Condition In a causal relationship a sufficient condition (or variable) is any variable which is sufficient to bring about the effect in question. For example, a growing unemployment rate might be sufficient to cause an increase in the crime rate. Obviously many other factors (variables) could also cause the increase. Typically there are many conditions sufficient to cause an increase, or a decrease, in crime. See: Necessary Condition.

Suffrage The right to vote in political matters; the franchise. Suffragists were early members of the women's movement who protested in order to win women the vote. The beginnings of the suffrage movement in Canada can be dated to the founding of the Toronto Women's Literary Society in 1877. The Canadian Woman Suffrage Association grew from this organization under the leadership of Dr. Emily Stowe. Women achieved the federal vote in 1918. Provincial voting rights for women were achieved between 1918 and 1940, first in Manitoba and last in Quebec.

Summary Offense Less serious criminal offenses with a maximum punishment of six months imprisonment, a $2,000 fine or both. These crimes are tried by lower courts. Some offenses, however, are hybrids and can thus be defined as summary or indictable.

Superego A concept developed by psychoanalyst Sigmund Freud (1856-1939) that describes one of three components of the individual personality or self. The personality consists of the id, the innate impulses and drives, the ego, the unique and individual self; and the superego, the internalized social norms or conscience. Much Freudian analytical theory is based on articulating the development of these aspects' of self and their relationship.

Superstructure (1) A general term used in sociocultural relaterialism to refer to the symbolic universe-the shared meanings, ideas, beliefs, values, and ideologies that people give to the physical and social world. The

Surveillance Monitoring the activities of others in order to ensure compliant behavior. Modern techniques of surveillance include not only video cameras and microphones but also a whole range of computer surveillance as well.

Survey A questionnaire or interview.

Sustainable Development Economic activity or growth which does not reduce or deplete the resources available to future generations.

Symbol One item used to meaningfully represent another-as in the case of a flag which symbolizes a nation.

Symbolic Analyst Those who engage in what Robert Reich calls symbolic-analytic services. This is Reich third occupational category and refers to tasks such as problem-solving, problem-identification, and strategic brokerage services. In short it is all those jobs which involve the manipulation of symbols (data, words, oral and visual representations). This is a way to talk about a particular form of service worker, which others might call 'knowledge work', and is seen as the area of substantial growth in the developed capitalist nations of the world. Reich also believes that symbolic-analysts, due to the nature of their work, develop distinctive life styles and social attitudes and political beliefs.

Symbolic Communications All communication with others is symbolic and involves the use of language, sound, bodily gesture and expression.

Symbolic Interactionism A sociological perspective that stresses the way societies are created through the interactions of individuals. Unlike both the consensus (structural functionalist) and conflict perspectives, it does not stress the idea of a social system possessing structure and regularity, but focuses on the way that individuals, through their interpretations of social situations and behavioural negotiation with others, give meaning to social interaction. George H. Mead (1863-1931), a founder of symbolic interactionism, saw interaction as creating and recreating the patterns and structures that bring society to life, but more recently there has been a tendency to argue that society has no objective reality aside from individual interaction. This latter view has been criticized for ignoring the role of culture and social structure in giving shape, direction and meaning to social interaction. See: Micro-Perspective.

Symbolic Interactionism A theoretical approach in sociology which focuses on social reality as constructed through the daily interaction of individuals and places strong emphasis on the role of symbols (gestures, signs, and language) as core elements of this interaction.

Syndicalism A political doctrine advocating worker's ownership and control of the productive resources of a society. Syndicalism emerges in France in the late 19th century and was influential in much of Europe. Syndicalism ('syndicat' is a Latin-French term for 'union') was founded on the idea that organizations of workers within any particular industry or service provided the organizational basis for the direction and administration of the means of production on collective and co-operative principles. Syndicalists envisaged a revolutionary, but largely non-violent, overthrow of private property and the workers seizing ownership and control. The resulting power structure would be highly decentralized with each industry and service being owned and directed by the workers involved within it.

T

Taboo The term taboo refers to prohibitions conconduct which if enacted would endanger some or all of the relationships constituting the universe in which men live. In many socieites the universe of relationships commonly includes physical forces as well as social relations.

The word *tabu* entered English through the narratives of Captain Cook who first encountered the word, in its Tongan form, in 1777, Cognate forms of the word occur in various languages of Polynesis, Micronesia and Melanesia.

Taboos may be regarded as symbolizing the structure of relationships peculiar to a group. Their observance by an individual serves to mark membership of the group, commitment to one's roles and recognition of other roles and forces interdependent with one's own. A sociocultural prohibition on some act, person, place, animal, or plant.

Target Suitablity A target refers to a person or a property which an offender may approach to commit a crime. Some targets are more suitable than others. If a home is unlit, shrubs block a view of the front door, there are no neighborhood watch sticker, the door has an old fashioned and ineffective lock, this may be a target that an offender would view as suitable.

Taylorism The work management principles followed by Frederick Taylor (1856-1915) designed to transfer control of the work process to management and to achieve the greatest rate of productivity from workers through dividing labour and having work performed in a manner detailed by management. *See: Industrial Relations I Scientific Management.*

Technology The application of logic, reason and knowledge to the problems of exploiting raw materials from the environment. Social technologies employ the same thought processes in addressing problems of human organization. Technology involves the creation of material instruments (such as machines) used in human interaction with nature as well as social instruments (such as bureaucracy) used in human organization (see also Rationalization)

Terrorism The use of violence to achieve political ends. Many would restrict the definition to include only those acts committed by non-government groups, but state terrorism is also a major factor in the social world.

Tertiary Sector That part of an economy that provides services (nursing homes, psychological counseling, and so forth)-engaged in by both private and government entitities.

Textual Analysis An analysis of written or spoken texts as a way to understand social life. While this form of analysis has become more common with postmodern sociology, it is derived largely from French structuralist such as Claude Levi-Strauss, Michel Foucault and Jean Piaget who studied human thought, myths, story telling, and texts. Foucault, for example, argues that the way we see and understand the· world, which is represented in written or spoken texts, is central to understanding a particular time period or society and the way power is organized.

Theory All sciences use theory as a tool to explain. It is useful to think of theory as a conceptual model of some aspect of life. We may have a theory of mate selection, or the emergence of capitalist societies, or of criminal behaviour, or of the content of dreams. In each case the theory consists of a set of concepts and their nominal definition, assertions about the relationships between these concepts, assumptions and knowledge claims. Carl Jung's theory of the self, for examples, begins by asserting the key concepts -introversion and extroversion, and the relationship between these two components - one is dominant and the other subordinate. It assumes that the dominant characteristic will be displayed in behaviour and the subordinate one in our dreams or unconscious. The content of dreams can be explained by bringing Jung's model to the inquiry. In the classic model of how science is conducted, the scientist begins with a theory, deduces a hypothesis about the real world from the theory and then engages in the necessary research to determine if the hypothesis is true or false. In this way science is always about theory testing.

Third World This way of categorizing societies has lost much of its meaning with the breakup of the Soviet Union and the decline of communism as an economic system. First world countries once referred to the developed, capitalist societies, while the second world identified the developed socialist societies. Third world countries were those large political communities in the initial stages of development while fourth world societies are those that are traditional communities marginalized from economic development and political power. The concept of 'fourth world' has been applied to the aboriginal communities of north America.

Token Economy A behaviour therapy procedure based on operant learning principles; individuals are rewarded (reinforced) for positive or appropriate behaviour and are disciplined (punished) for negative or inappropriate behaviour.

Tort An area of law concerned with intentional violations of the private rights of individuals or neglect of legally recognized duties of care to others. In these cases the public interest is not directly harmed. This is an aspect of civil law and is usually contrasted with criminal law (where the pubic or society is considered to be the injured party), although sociologists note that the distinction between the two is somewhat arbitrary and shifting.

Tory A member of the Tory political party. A term originating in 17th century Britain and referring to that party, supported largely by aristocratic interests, which defended royal prerogatives and divine inheritance of the throne and was resistant to democratic ideals and the growing political and economic power of the middle class. In modern Canada the term is used to refer to the Conservative party. See: Conservatism.

Totemism A system of religious belief studied by Durkheim which attributes sacred qualities to a particular type of animal or plant.

Totems Symbol associated with a descent group as an identifying insignia.

Traditional States Societies in which the production base is agriculture or pastoralism (see also Agrarian Societies and Pastoral Societies)

Transitional Classes Marx's term to refer to social classes based on previous relations of production which linger on in the beginning stages a new one-such as peasants or landowners of a feudal system which has become capitalist.

Transnational Companies *See Multinational Companies.*

Transnational Corporations Corporations whose sales and production are carried out in many different nations. As a result of their multinational r~ach these corporations are often thought to be beyond the political control of any individual nation states.

Transsexual An individual who has physically crossed the boundary between the sexes and thus becomes the other sex. While movement may be in either direction, more transsexuals are men who have become women. Western cultures have been criticized frequently for being extremely dualistic in gender or sexual identities, making little room, or no room, for a third or fourth sex. Hinduism by contrast has an elaborate repertoire of sexual transformations, bisexuality and sexual expression. The term transgender is now preferred since it clearly suggests that sexual categories are themselves social constructions.

Treaty Indian A Native person or descendant of a Native person who signed a treaty. The registration list under the Indian Act was drawn up to include those band members who signed treaties, so all treaty Indians are also status Indians (unless they have lost their status). Treaties were signed with bands in parts of British Columbia, Ontario and the Northeast Territories and most of Alberta, Saskatchewan and Manitoba. See: Numbered Treaties / Status Indian.

Triads These Chinese groups came into existence in the seventeenth century as resistance fighters against the Manchu invaders. They eventually developed into crime groups.

Tribalism The use of this term must be understood against the assumption that citizens of the modern world would develop significant identification only with large groupings which included a plurality of social categories. For example, the identity of Canadian would include many ethnic groups, sexual preferences, social interests and religious groupings. Tribalism is used to describe those situations where broad social identification has broken down so that people identify themselves exclusively with a narrower category. For example, people may organize their lives around ethnic identification or sexual preference or religious belief. This retribalization of the society is thought to lead to fragmentation and divisiveness as people identify with an in-group, making a shared sense of citizenship among larger groupings more and more fragile. *See: Identity Politics.*

Tudor Refers to the period of English history from 1485 to 1603 when the nation's monarchs were descended from Owen Tudor and Queen Catherine (1401-1437) widow of King Henry V. This line of English monarchs included Henry VllI (1491-1547) famous for his six marriages and the establishment of Protestantism in England and for strengthening the central power of the state. The greatest of the tudor monarchs, and the last, was Elizabeth 1 (1533-1603) Henry's daughter who ascended the throne in 1558 and during her 45 year reign modernized the English state administration, rationalized public finance and further strengthened central government. These achievements established conditions where trade and commerce could rapidly expand and created some of the early foundations for the age of exploration and the industrial revolution.

Type A type or class is an abstract category having empirical reference. Thus there is a type of stratified society known as a caste society, where members are also members of a social category known as a caste and such membership is related *inter alia* to both occupation and ritual pollution. Such a stratified society may be distinguished from another known as a class society. Or again, there is a type of social group known as a dyadic group, consisting of two and only two members. Individual examples may be found for such types which wholly fit. An ideal type is a concept of a special kind and examples may only approximate to the type.

Typology A set of two or more ideal types used for categorizing behaviours, events, societies, groups, etc. For example, Emile Durkheim (1858-1917) developed four types of suicide: anomie, egoistic, altruistic and fatalistic. Ferdinand Tonnies (1855-1936) identified two types of society: Gemeinschaft and Gesellschaft.

U

Ultra Vires From the Latin meaning to act beyond the scope of powers. Government powers in Canada are distributed between the federal and provincial governments; each government then must act within its own power. If provinces pass criminal law, ror example, this would be ruled ultra vires since criminal law is an exclusive federal power.

Unconscious Freudian concept referring to motives and ideas unavailable to the conscious mind of the individual.

Underclass (1) A class of individuals in mature industrial societies situated at the bottom of the class system who have been systematically excluded from participation in economic life. The underclass is normally composed of people from ethnic or minority groups. (2) A term similar in use to Marx's concept of Lumpenproletariat. A group that is not in a regular economic or social relationship with the rest of the community. Refers to the chronically unemployed, those who live on the proceeds of petty crime, panhandlers, or bag ladies. American sociologists use this term since a large underclass is thought to pose a threat to the stability of society because they are not adequately connected to the institutional and cultural regulation that is experienced by most social members.

Uniform Crime Reporting Since 1961 Canada has had a Uniform Crime Reporting System developed by Statistics Canada and the Canadian Association of Chiefs of Police. This system is designed to provide a measure of reliability for crime statistics through providing police agencies with a standardized set of procedures for collecting and reporting crime information.

Unilinear Evolution A largely discredited view of social evolution according to which all societies pass through the same stages of development.

Union A social organization set up to represent the worker's interests in both the workplace and in the broader society as well.

Unit of Analysis Most social research looks for patterns when comparing 'things' one to another. The things that researchers are comparing or examining are referred to as the units of analysis, or the units to be analyzed. The most frequent unit of analysis is the individual, suggesting that researchers look for patterns among a collection (perhaps a sample) of individuals~ Research can also be conducted in which a pattern is sought among a collection of groups; the group would be the unit of analysis. For example, like Durkheim, one might try to determine what social factors are linked to the variation in suicide rates among nations or regions. One can also look for patterns among things like newspaper stories, advertisements, a category of social interaction, social events, or speech utterances. In this case the unit of analysis would be what Earl Babbie has called social artifacts.

United Empire Loyalists. Those residents of the United States who remained loyal to the British Crown during the American war of independence and fled to Canada. Approximately 40, 000 emigres arrived in Canada and most settled in Nova Scotia, although some 7000 relocated in Quebec to provide the first substantial British population in the province. The attitudes and political philosophy of these new settlers are seen as significant for understanding the subsequent development of Canada. See: Constitutional Act (1791).

United Nations See: Universal Declaration of Human Rights Universal Declaration of Human Rights. Following the Second World War and the horrific experiences ofthat struggle, many nations set to creating the United Nations. The original Charter of the United Nations contained a general statement on human rights. The need for a more detailed and substantial statement on human rights was seen and a Commission was established to create such a document. This commission wrote the Universal Declaration on Human Rights (drafted largely by a Canadian}which was adopted by General Assembly of the United Nation on December 10, 1948. This document was described as humanity's response to the death camps of the Nazis, the countless refugees and the tortured prisoners-of-war. In 1966 the United Nations adopted two further documents on human rights: the Covenant on Civil and Political Rights and the Covenant on Economic, Social and Cultural Rights. These covenants contain many of the rights asserted in the Universal Declaration but they differ in that they are legally binding on those nations signing the covenants. The first of these covenants declares that everyone has the right to: life; freedom of thought; equal treatment in the courts; freedom of assembly; and no one shall be subject to torture, slavery or forced labour. The second declares that everyone has the right to: the enjoyment of just and favorable work conditions; to form trade unions; an adequate standard of living; education; and to take part in cultural life and enjoy the progress of science. In 1989 a third covenant was added, the Convention of the Rights of the Child. These four documents together comprise what is call the International Bill of Rights.

Universality A philosophy concerning the provision of the benefits of the welfare state which declares that all citizens have access regardless of their need. For example, all citizens receive the same access to health care in Canada, regardless of their income. The underlying principle is that less powerful citizens can be more easily deprived of benefits, or benefits can be more easily reduced, if they are not received by most people in th€:" population. In recent years the principle of universality has been seriously eroded in Canada. The baby bonus, once given to mothers of all children, has been replaced with a child tax credit which gives income to mothers on the basis of their household income. See: Means Test.

Upper Class A social class roughly composed of the more affluent members of society, especially those who have great wealth, control over businesses or hold large numbers of stocks and shares.

Urban Ecology An analysis of urban life that examines the relationship between the city and its physical surroundings-based on an analogy with the adjustment of plants and organisms to the physical environment.

Urban Renewal Governmental programs of encouraging the renovation of deteriorating city neighborhoods through the renovation or destruction of old buildings and the construction of new ones.

Urbanism Similar to the notion of modernity, this term refers to the form of social organization and values typically found in large urban settings. The central values are those of individualism and impersonality and the major characteristics of social organization are a developed division of labour, high rates of geographic and social mobility and predominance of impersonality in social interactions despite the acute social interdependence. See: Mass Society.

Urbanization The increasing concentration of the human population into cities.

Utilitarianism As a justification for punishment utilitarianism asserts the utility of the act of punishment or the punishment of a particular offender. The utility of punishment refers to any future benefit for the society (or the greatest number) which can be derived from the act. Justifications in terms of deterrence (individual or general), rehabilitation, incapacitation, and crime prevention are an aspects of utilitarianism. Utilitarian justifications are contrasted with retribution.

V

Validity One of two criteria (the other being reliability) by which researchers judge their results or measurement tools. A valid result is one that accurately measures what it claims to be measuring. Using shoe size as a measurement of intelligence is not a valid measure of intelligence. It lacks face validity since it is not obvious that it is measuring what it claims to measure. One test of validity might be the extent to which your measurements allow you to make predictions about future behaviour. If your measurement of intelligence does not predict how people perform on exams then perhaps it is not a valid measurement of intelligence. See: External Validity / Internal Validity / Reliability.

Values The term value is of importance to economics, sociology and philosophy. In economics the theory of value is usually co-terminous with the theory of price, but in Marxist economics this is not completely the case for value there is implicated in a theory of the distribution of the goods and services produced in a given economic order and in an assessment of the justice of this distribution. To the sociologist, value are constituent facts of social structure. The sociologist does not try to assess their intrinsic worth, but he treats them as scarce objects of socially conditioned desires, unevenly distributed and differentially ranked.

Relatively general cultural prescriptions of what is right, moral and desirable. Values provide the broad foundations for specific normative regulation of social interaction. See: Norm.

Van Der Peet Decision A 1996 decision by the Supreme Court of Canada clarifying Aboriginal rights. The case came to the court because a lower court had convicted Van der Peet, of the Stolo peoples of British Columbia, of violating a section of the B.C. Fishery Regulations for selling fish caught under a food fish license. Van der Peet was arguing that Aboriginal rights (section 35 of the Charter of Rights and Freedoms) gave Natives the right to sell their fish food since this was an aspect of traditional life. The Supreme Court did not overturn the Van der Peet conviction but did clarify the test that must be met to establish Aboriginal right. Briefly, the Aboriginal defendant must demonstrate that the practice in question was an aspect of Native life prior to European contact.

Variable A characteristic that varies in value or magnitude along which an object, individual or group may be categorized, such as income or age.

Variables A term central to quantitative sociology and to macro-structural sociology. The term refers to that which varies, rather than being constant. In particular its reference is to structural features that vary (things like gender, age, race, social class) and have an influence on behaviour or attitudinal variables (discrimination or attitudes about abortion). Researchers work out ways to measure these variables (often by asking questions) and determine their importance in understanding human behaviour. Those variables thought to be causal variables are called independent variables and those thought to be effects are called dependent variables. A variable has two or more values; the variable of sex, for example, has the values of female and male. See: Dependent Variable! Independent Variable.

Vertical Mobility Movement up or down a social stratification system (see also Stratification).

Vertical Mosaic A term introduced by John Porter (1921-1979) to describe Canadian society. The term 'mosaic' is used to capture the multiethnic and multiracial character of the society and the term 'vertical' implies that these ethnic and racial groups are arranged into a hierarchy. A similar term would be ethnic stratification.

Vested Interest An expectation of private gain that often underlies the expressed interest in a public issue.

Victimization Survey A survey of a random sample of the population in which people are asked to recall and describe their own experience of being a victim of crime.

Victimless Crime The conventional conception of crime implies that there is a victim of the criminal behaviour who experiences harm. There are, however, criminal behaviours like illegal gambling, drug use, and selling sex, where the victim does not experience harm and is indeed a willing participant. Many argue that crimes of this nature are victimless and should not be regulated by criminal law.

Victimless Crime Violation of law in which there is no other person (aside from the offender) victimized, such as drug-taking or illegal gambling.

Violent Predators This group of offenders is particularly found among sexual offenders, a group who appear to be hunters or predators and violently sexually assault citizens. This group tends to be thought of as 'psychopaths' but not all psychopaths are violent offenders.

W

War Crimes During the Second World War Allied nations determined to prosecute German war criminals and defined 'war crimes' as plotting aggressive warfare and committing atrocities against any civilian population. This definition was used in the trials of war criminals which began in 1945. In recent years there have been suggestions that Canada (for its involvement in the fire bombing of German civilians) and the United States (for the dropping of atomic bombs on largely civilian inhabited cities) as well as other nations were also guilty of committing atrocities against civilians, but these nations were never brought to trial. In the 1990s the United Nations again initiated tribunals to prosecute war criminals in the former Yugoslavia and in Rwanda.

Ward American palaeobotanist and sociologist, his systematic sociology hardly influenced American thought on the subject, although subsequently he has been venerated as one of its founding fathers. He was more interested in studyign the functioning of society than its structure. Borrowing his ideas both from Comte and Spencer, he asserted that the four stages of evolution were consmogeny, biogeny, anthrougpogeny and sociogeny. Like Comte, he distinguished between social statics and social dynamics; the former deals with the formation of structures and with equilibration, the latter with social processes. besides pure sociology, he described applied sociology which is concerned with what he called social telesis, or purposive action byman designed to influence his condition.

War Measures Act A 1914 statute giving emergency powers to cabinet, allowing it to govern by decree (without the usual approvals of democratic institutions) in times of war, invasion or real or apprehended insurrection. It was this power the federal government invoked in 1970 to deal with the FLQ crisis which the government called a state of 'apprehended insurrection.' The Act had been used in early years to intern members of the communist party, Japanese-Canadians, Jehovah's Witnesses and Italian-Canadians. In 1988 this statute was replaced with the Emergency Act.

Wealth Accumulated money and material possessions controlled by an individual, group or organization.

Wealthfare Government aid to the upper and middle classes. Often times this aid is disguised in the form of tax breaks (a deduction for interest on home mortgages) or subsidised services (higher education).

Welfare State A government system which provides a range of human services for its citizens.

Welfare Government aid (in the form of services and money) to the poor.

Whig A member of the Whig political party. A term originating in the 17th century in Britain and referring to that party, supported largely by the new commercial interests, which defended the power of Parliament against royal prerogatives and thus encouraged the democratic revolution in Britain. The term was transplanted to the American colonies and referred to the supporters of independence from Britain. An American Whig political party was formed and it remained a major party until the 1850's when it was succeeded by the Republic party. The term has had little currency in Canada, although the Whig ideal of popular parliamentary government was a strong force in 19th century Canadian politics. See: Liberalism.

White Collar Originally used as a contrast to blue-collar workers and captured the distinction between non-manual and manual labour or workers. With the rise of the service economy and the shrinkage of manual labour,· the term has become less useful.

White-Collar Crime As originally used by Edwin Sutherland in 1945, referred to the illegal activities of businesses and corporations committed to further the goals of the business. These acts were not regulated by criminal law but by regulatory laws of various kinds. These acts included false advertising, anti-trust violations, environmental pollution or dumping product on the market below cost. Criminologists now call this corporate crime or organizational crime and reserve the term white-collar crime for those illegal acts committed by people in positions of trust (usually in white-collar jobs) for personal gain. For example, making personal long-distan~'e calls on an employer's account.

Whorf-Sapir Hypothesis The assertion that the concepts and structure of languages profoundly shape the perception and world view of speakers. Rather than just being a means of expressing thought, language is claimed to form thought. Thus, people of different language communities will see and understand in different ways. Developed by Benjamin Whorf and Edward Sapir in the 1930 and grew out of contact with the Native languages of North America. Most sociologists regard the theory as too deterministic and stress the dynamic way in which language responds to social and technical transformation of society.

Wolfenden Report A 1959 British report of the Departmental Committee on Homosexual Offenses and

Prostitution (Chaired by Sir John Wolfenden) Its major recommendation was that sexual activity between consenting adults should no longer be a criminal offense. This report had influence in many western nations and in 1969, after Pierre Trudeau became Minister of Justice, Canada repealed sections of the criminal code that had made homosexual activity a criminal offense.

Women's Liberation Thesis The theory, within criminology, that women's involvement in crime will come to more closely resemble men's as gendered differences between women and men are diminished by women's greater social participation and equality. Although sounding plausible, there is little empirical evidence to support this theory.

Women's Movement A broad term for a range of social and political organizations and activitie&" lilt.e research, writing and criticism that have the main goal of advancing the status of women in soCiety and overcoming cultural marginalization of women's perspectives and experience in society.

Working Class A social class of industrial societies broadly composed of people involved in manual occupation. The bulk ofthese jobs are unskilled, poorly paid and provide few benefits or job security.

X

Xenophobia An individual's irrational and obsessive hatred of people perceived as different and foreign. Related to the concepts of racism and ethnocentrism. All of these can be overcome by the study of the social sciences and coming to appreciate the ideas of culture and social structure as tools for understanding ourselves and others.

Z

Znaniecki, Florian (1882-1958) Polish sociologist who was resident in U.S.A.; his important contributions lie in his work on systems and in his studies of social groups and specific social roles. *The Social Role of the Man of Knowledge,* 1940, discusses this role in the belief that therein lies a useful approach to the sociology of knowledge. Znaniecki's ideas about the closed system are elaborated and developed in *Laws of Social Psychology, 1925; The Methodology of Sociology,* 1934; and *Cultural Sciences: Their Origin and Development,* 1952. He argued that the task of the sociologist is to determine the limit and elements of the system under investigation.

Zone A *zone* is an area of a city characterized by some par-ticular physical or social feature or features. Thus a city may be divided into one or more business, commercial, manufacturing and residential zones according to the use to which buildings are put. Sociologically, the zones distinguished may reflect differential degrees of wealth or poverty, crime or social amenities. The practice of *zoning,* however, is a matter of official policy regarding the treatment of city areas so that differing treat-ment is related to planned development. Thus certain building restrictions may operate to guide the development of, say for example, a commercial and shopping zone so that it does not spread in an undesirable direction.

Zoning Zoning was first practised in Germany but introduced into Britain through the Town Planning Act of 1909, and was shortly afterwards practised in many large American cities.